TAFF'S

THE TRUE STORY

MICHAEL J HENNESSY'S ROYAL NAVY CAREER 1972 – 1997

AUTOBIOGRAPHY

MICHAEL J HENNESSY

©MJHennessy2024

ALL RIGHTS RESERVED. No part of this publication may be reproduced, distributed, or transmitted in any form or by any means, including photocopying, recording, or other electronic or mechanical methods, without the prior written permission of the publisher, except in the case of brief quotations embodied in critical reviews and certain other noncommercial uses permitted by copyright law.

TOAD
PUBLISHING

Toadpublishing@mail.com

DEDICATION

To my lovely wife Donia,

who never stopped encouraging me to get off my arse and do something with it, and the wonderful people I wrote it for.

My amazing family.

My children and grandchildren:

Daniel, and Nikki Deanne, and Wes Emily and Craig

Ellis, and Poppy. Chloe, Deryn, Elsie, and Tobie. Freya, and Willow.

Donia's daughters, their partners, and her lovely Granddaughter

Kara, Roger, and Niamh

Anne-Marie, and Gwynn

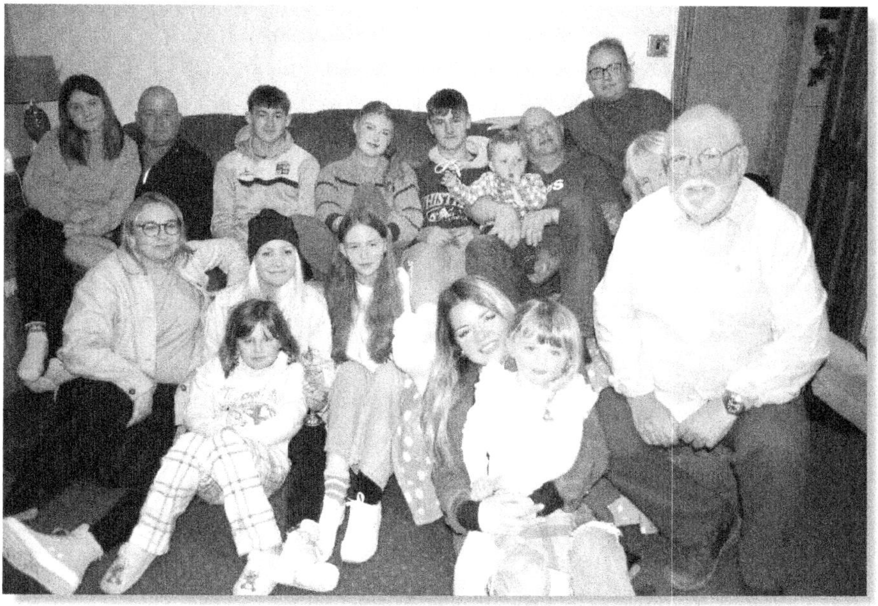

ACKNOWLEDGEMENTS

I started making notes about my Royal Navy career because I realised that my three kids had no idea what I did in the RN, just as I have no idea what my dad got up to in the mob.

He served during the war, and I wish he'd recorded his time.

I kept adding to my notes until I found myself with over eighty thousand words.

My wife kept encouraging me to do something with them and, half-heartedly I did. I Googled a few things, a couple of times.

I knew if I started doing something, I would have given up somewhere along the line, and all those notes, those eighty thousand plus words, would still be on my hard drive gathering digital dust.

Then, while on Facebook, I asked an author and fellow Royal Navy veteran, Knocker White, if he had some advice.

That was it. His advice and guidance couldn't have been more encouraging and generous. It is he who has turned my 'notes' into this book, and for that, I will be eternally grateful.

***

I mention the source of many of these stories, my friends and messmates from my favourite ship, HMS Tiger. (Fifty years ago.) Members of the 3L2 mess group formed a few years back. I can't wait for the next bi-annual get-together in Pompey. Thanks, lads and stay well.

Mick Gritt, John (Smudge) Smith, Paul Chambers, Mick Galvin, Dave (Johno) Johnson, Malcom's (Dinger) Bell, Laurie Parry, Peter Scott, Peter (Snaz) Synnott, Kev Goode, Aggie Weston.

IN MEMORY OF

John and Mona. (Mam and Dad)

Jeff Taylor my dearest and oldest friend

Frank Fleming. Great friend and shipmate

Nick Edmunds local drinking partner and good friend

Dale and Michael Eynon Donia's beloved brothers

MICHAEL J HENNESSY

CONTENTS

Introduction	Page 1
Home	Page 3
HMS Raleigh	Page 19
HMS Pembroke	Page 45
HMS Osprey	Page 53
HMS Leander	Pages 61
HMS Royal Arthur	Pages 109
HMS Tiger	Page 123
HMS Excellent - Part1	Page 199
RNPHQ HMS Nelson	Page 205
HMS Sultan	Page 211
HMS Hermes	Page 215

The Falklands Campaign	Page 259
Gibraltar	Page 315
RNSIB - Part1	Page 343
RAF Newton	Page345
Deago Darcia	Page 353
RNSIB - Part2	Page 367
HMS Excellent	Page 383
HMS Daedalus - Part1	Page 385
HMS Argyll	Page 393
HMS Daedalus – Part2	Page 419
HMS Sultan – Part2	Page 431
HMS Nelson – Part2	Page 433
Home – Part2	Page 435
Photographs	Page 439

MICHAEL J HENNESSY

INTRODUCTION

The following is a simplified, or abbreviated, account of my time serving in the Royal Navy.

I noticed, over the years since I left the RN (1997), that the kids, grandkids, and many other members of my family do not have a clue about what I did during those years.

I thought it would be a good idea to recall many of the incidents, activities, and events which happened, recording them for all to read.

It may seem, as you read on, that I spent most of my naval life having fun and drinking, but these are the times when most of the interesting incidents, activities, and events happened.

So, bear in mind, that there was a lot of serious stuff, hard work, study, and training, which would be quite boring to detail, so I have 'cherry-picked' the best, and most interesting periods of my career.

I cannot remember the names of all the people involved in all these happenings, but they are real people, they may not necessarily be in the right incident, on the right ship, or at the right time.

But I assure you, if they were not the guilty party in one story, they are the culprits in another.

MICHAEL J HENNESSY

HOME

AGE: 12 TO 15 YEARS OLD

I grew up in 2, Lower Taff View, Coedpenmaen Road, Pontypridd. It was a great childhood; lots of playing outdoors, making dens, and playing sports. The local park had everything Rugby, Football, Tennis, Bowls, Golf, Swimming, and much more.

I watched Pontypridd RFC every week and travelled to their away games with the player's coach. This was because my mate's father was the Trainer and a family friend. Tommy David was our star player and Welsh International. Ponty didn't get many in those days, so to be in the same company as Tommy was a huge deal. I got the autographs of most of the great 70's Welsh team, Gareth Edwards, JPR, JJ, Phil Bennet etc. and my biggest claim to fame was getting Tom Jones's autograph when he visited his mother-in-law, who lived next door to my junior school, St Michael's RC School, which was next door to the synagogue (where else!) in Treforrest.

I loved rugby at this time, and I wasn't a bad player. I played full back and never minded throwing myself around tackling the opposition, and to a certain extent, I had no fear, but this changed when I had an accident at the local swimming baths.

We were often at the baths when the weather was good, and we were always there when it was bad. We didn't realise at the time that having such a good pool in our area was a great privilege, but we took full advantage of it.

One sunny Saturday afternoon we were diving for stones off the highest of three diving boards. I threw my stone into the pool, but it was too close to the side for me to dive in and get it without surfacing, so I went down to the next board, but it was the same problem there.

On my way down the ladder to the lowest board, I slipped. The handrails on the ladder came to a 'V' where they joined with the steps, about halfway down. My hands were on the handrails of course, and when I landed on my arse at the bottom of the flight, the little finger of my left hand remained in the 'V' on the ladder.

I knew I had lost my finger but otherwise, I was OK.

At this point, I was holding my left hand with my right, and I must have been whimpering a little because Shamus, one of my friends asked, "What's wrong with you?"

I said I had lost my finger. "Shut up," he said, "gimme a look."

As I took my right hand away to show him, my blood spurted onto his chest.

All I can remember from then is everyone panicking or staying out of my way. Shamus took me to the first aid people who went looking for my finger, they must have looked everywhere except for hat 'V' on the ladder. From then on, my confidence on the rugby pitch went out of the window until years later.

The diving boards at the pool were only erected scaffolding and temporary. If that were to happen today, I am sure I would be in line for a tidy sum. But in those days, it was expensive to sue. My parents did try but were given very little help, and they didn't have the sort of money needed to see it through.

So, that little accident took the guts out of my game for fear of damaging my hand.

Or so I thought.

I was never a lover of school and was always happy to find an excuse not to go.

When I did go to school the emphasis was more on having a laugh and fooling around. Most of the teachers did not inspire me to learn, nor did it make going to school anything to look forward to. If you didn't show potential, you were left to just get on with it and not encouraged to improve. Not that I think I was capable of much improvement, but we will never know now, will we?

I always planned to leave school at fifteen. I simply had no idea what I was going to do after that.

The most apparent option was to go down the mines and dig coal like the old man. He didn't want that for me, but it looked like the only option.

Until I was introduced to the Royal Navy.

There was always talk between my friends about wanting to join the army, mainly because we did a lot of 'playing soldiers' from an early age. Of course, we had no idea what being a real soldier was like, and 'playing soldiers' was easy. Thus, they were the only thoughts I held about joining the military.

That changed.

My love for the Royal Navy, and my blinkered intention to join up, started in 1969 when my sister, Marlene, was going out with a sailor, a local boy from Maesycoed, which is a couple of miles from our home in Trallwn, Pontypridd.

I was a bit disappointed with her choice of boyfriend at first because shortly before meeting him she was going out with a drummer in a band. I only met him once, but he gave me a pair of drumsticks which sealed our friendship, and he probably thought sealed his friendship with Marlene, but this wasn't to be.

Terry, (the sailor), was a Leading Radio Operator on HMS Juno, a Leander class frigate based in Portsmouth. There was a 'Family's Day' coming up in the summer. Marlene, Terry's mother, father, and brother were going, and they invited me along.

I wasn't looking forward to it. Going away with strangers, and staying in a B&B with them, wasn't my idea of an adventure. Terry's mum and dad seemed a bit 'posh' and above everyone else, and they turned out to be exactly that. But they were happy to leave me, and Terry's brother, Gary, to do our own thing.

Gary was a nice lad, a few years older than me but he was fun to be with.

Sometime in the summer of 1969, we travelled to Gosport, a place I later lived for over twenty years, and after a night in, what I remember to be an old Victorian bedroom, one with a funny smell, and a jug and bowl, in which I had to wash myself in the morning, we took a short ferry ride over to Portsmouth, and into the dockyard.

I started to feel an excitement course through me once inside the dockyard.

Sailors were wandering around looking as smart as guardsmen, I thought. There were ships tied up alongside the wharves, with more sailors going about their work. The ships looked 'the business', guns, rocket launchers, and helicopter pads.

This was some seriously good shit.

Then we climbed up the gangway onto the flight deck of HMS Juno. From that point, until we went ashore again, I was in awe of everyone working on that ship.

I loved every minute of it. I took it all in.

We went to sea for a couple of hours, saw the helicopter fly, weapons being fired, and anything else they could do to keep us amused and interested.

I remember eating my lunch in the Junior Rates dining room, standing up looking out of the port hole and gently swaying with the ship. No one else could feel the ships move and laughed at me swaying. I must have been one with the ship at that time.

Crap!

The ship hadn't gone to sea yet. I was just swaying to the music played throughout the ship. But I was 'at one with the ship' sounds better.

I went everywhere I could on the ship and wished I could work on one like it. As it happens, HMS Juno was a Leander Class Frigate and the first ship I served on was to be HMS Leander, the first of the class.

That was my introduction to the Royal Navy; from that point on it was all I wanted to do, which is why my education took a back seat to me collecting anything I could regarding the Royal Navy.

This is something I regret, my lack of education I mean. I believe that whatever anyone decides to do, they can do it better with an education. You'll see why, later.

I was twelve years old when my future was decided, so I had to mark time for three years until I was old enough to apply to join.

I couldn't wait for my fifteenth birthday, so around November time in 1971, when I was fourteen years old, and six months from leaving school with a 'diddly squat' of an education, I sent for an information pack.

It arrived a week later.

Most of the stuff included things I had seen many times before, but this time there was a little card inside which I could send off to request an interview.

Send it off I did, and promptly so.

Soon, after I received a date for the interview, and a Rail Warrant (a free train ticket) to Cardiff. This is where I needed to report to the RN Careers Office. It was a place I visited many times while collecting information and booklets on RN careers.

I had set my sights on becoming a Chef, I loved cooking, or trying to cook anyway, and I couldn't think of anything else that interested me as much.

So, I had my interview.

It went very well, and I took the test, which was an hour of varied questions. One I'll always remember was a picture of a screwdriver and four smaller pictures of a nail, screw, bolt, and a tack. The question was... "'What would you use the screwdriver on?"

Now, I could just about manage that sort of question, but they were not all like that. Unfortunately, there were questions on grammar, fractions, and other subjects I knew very little about.

This is why, boys and girls, whatever you decide to do, try and learn something at school because everyone needs a good education.

Not only did I find out I was as thick as two short planks, (like I thought I was Einstein anyway), but I found out after my medical that I was red and green colour blind.

The medical was an adventure, having to get to Bristol alone, and then going through the embarrassment of having your nuts cupped by a middle-aged man, who I thought was a doctor, but could have been a postman for all I know. Go through all sorts of tests and examinations, and then not knowing, until weeks later, whether I was fit enough to join up.

I was apprehensive that my missing 'Pinkey' was going to spoil it for me, but there was no need to worry, the only thing it was any good for anyway was picking my nose. That was the first time I ventured outside of Wales alone.

Throughout my childhood, we used to laugh at my dad being colour-blind, not knowing he passed his rogue genes onto me. It must be karma, poetic justice. Happens to me again later.

Being colour blind is not as obvious as everything being grey, or black and white. I can see all colours, but my eyes perceive different shades.

To me some greens look blue, and some blues look green.

When the Doctor shows you the book of coloured dots, the ones where you are supposed to see a number hidden in amongst them, well, that is where I am knackered. I cannot see anything but coloured dots. That makes me red and green colour blind.

This turned out to be quite a scary thing in years to come, when one of my jobs at sea was as the Flight Deck Officer, which means one needs to stand on the flight deck waving a couple of wands, or their hands, when covered in bright orange gloves, at a helicopter, directing it to land or take off.

These helicopters are often armed with torpedoes or other weapons, and when they take off or land at night all you can see are the red and green navigation lights.

But I never lost a chopper.

Mainly because they could see more of me and the ship than I could see of them.

Anyway, I digress.

The other thing my navy medical highlighted was what was to become a lifelong fight, my weight. I was a bit on the fat side for my height. My argument was I was not too fat, I was too short for my weight. They wouldn't have it though.

Before I could be offered a job, I needed to lose weight. It was something like a half-stone. I was determined a few pounds of blubber was not going to stop me from joining up.

I went home and became one of my brother Ray's football team, never expecting or wanting to play, I just wanted to attend their training evenings. As it happened, their trainer was an ex-Royal Marine who kept me focused, and he kept the training interesting. I tried dieting, but I was a growing lad for god's sake, I needed those carbs.

It took about six weeks, but I did it, I lost the weight required and was congratulated by the Chief Petty Officer on my next visit to the career's office. He sat me down and went through my options.

This did not take too long.

Because of my low colour perception and that I was as thick as shit, my choices were extremely limited. I was offered options for my career, one as a Naval Airman, which is a labourer on a flight deck or airfield. The other was as a steward, a sea-going waiter.

My first thought was to be an airman, sounds pretty good, better than a steward, out in the fresh air playing with aircraft. But the CPO had other ideas. If I joined as a Steward, it would be easy work and rapid promotion, a cushy number, and a chance of becoming a Cook later if I still wanted. But the main reason was, that the navy was short of Stewards at the time. So, this gullible fifteen-year-old was an easy catch for the steward's branch.

As it happened, there was a year's waiting list to become a chef and a horrendous wait for promotion once you were in. The fact is what the CPO told me was all true.

I just hated the steward's job from day one.

I was ready now. I had been accepted.

I had a job and a career waiting for me. As soon as my mother and father signed the consent form, I could join. Dad could not wait. So long as I did not end up down the coal mines, he would have signed me up as a lion tamer in the Serengeti.

Mam, on the other hand, was not having any of it. This was surprising because I had given her enough hassle and grief over the years. I thought she would have had my bags packed. I am not sure why she wouldn't sign, but I remember once, Marlene and her friends using a Ouija board in our kitchen. It was not a true board, but a deck of cards face down in a circle, with the alphabet written on them in lipstick (to attract the male spirits I suppose) and the words 'yes' and 'no'. It did the same thing as a real Ouija board. It was the working-class version.

Anyway, I watched the glass go around the table telling everyone it was my Nan (mum's mum) on the 'other side'. She was asked numerous questions, and the girls seemed impressed.

Then Marlene asked if she knew if I was to join the Navy.

"Yes."

What did she think about it?

"No." came the reply. Mmmm, interesting.

"Why?" asks Marlene.

"Billy,' came the reply.

Billy was my uncle. Nan's son and my mother's brother. He was onboard HMS Repulse in the Far East during the war when it was bombed and sank by Japanese aircraft. He died in the action and went down with the ship. He was a Stoker 1st Class.

I think maybe this was a reason for Mam not wanting to sign the consent form, but I never got a reason from her.

Ten years later, when I was onboard HMS Hermes during the Falklands Conflict, I thought of that Séance and cursed my mother for signing that bloody form.

It took some serious nagging, lots of tears, and a visit from the Careers Office CPO before she relented.

Now, I was ready.

It was around April time, and I was about to leave school. I had no idea when I would be called forward, so I needed to get a job. In those days it was so easy, you just turned up and asked if there were any jobs and started the next day. I got a job as a shelf stacker at Lipton's Supermarket in town.

I lasted for five days.

The next week I got a job as a van boy with Mothers Pride Bakery, delivering bread up and down the Mountain Ash Valley. I was thrown about in the back of the van while sorting the bread and cakes into delivery boxes during the journeys to the next shop. It did my sense of balance the world of good. I was up at four am and finished by one pm. I was in bed by nine every night, so no social life, not that I had one anyway.

I took home six quid, and I think I gave Mam three for my keep. That, and the odd loaf of bread and cream cake, made up my wages.

In September, I received the long-awaited letter. It included a one-way Rail Warrant to Plymouth.

I was to join the Royal Navy on 28th November 1972, at HMS Raleigh, Torpoint, Cornwall.

There was a chance I may have been sent to HMS Ganges in Ipswich, which is where fifteen-year-olds go for twelve months before going on their trade courses.

I think I was lucky, I must have been a month or two older, so I was to become a Raleigh 'Six Week Wonder Boy' instead of a trainee for a whole year. I knew lads who went the Ganges route, they all said they had second thoughts about staying in the mob whilst at Ganges. So, I was more than happy with HMS Raleigh.

I wanted to build my strength and psych myself up for it. So, to my dad's utter annoyance, I packed in work two weeks before the big day in preparation.

What a stupid thing to do.

I had no money and lots of time to waste. It was only for two weeks, and then it was into the great big unknown, broke.

Mam and Dad saw me off at Ponty Station, where Mam uttered those words of wisdom, ones which she uttered on more than one occasion, and not only to me, "Don't volunteer for anything."

Mam, Mona Elizabeth, was a local 'Ponty' girl. She married my father in about 1948. I didn't know until the 90s, but she was pregnant with my sister at the time, a situation which would have been a nightmare in those days.

She was a great mother, and she spoilt me, or so my siblings would have you believe. She was a typical wife of that era, one where her job in life was to look after the man of the house, keep everyone fed, and the house clean. There was never a day when my dad's dinner was not on the table as soon as he came home from work.

That is what the women did for their hard-working miner husbands in those days. She became a little more independent in the 1970s, when she insisted, against my dad's wishes, that she be 'allowed' to go to work and earn some money for herself. She did, getting herself a small pension at the same time. She died in June 2013 at the age of 88. She is missed by everyone.

My dad, John Joseph, was born in Waterford, Ireland in 1925. He came to Pontypridd, with his mother and father, when he was about six months old. His mother and father were British citizens, but because my father was born after Ireland's independence, he was classified as Irish; something he did not know about, or never considered, until he applied for a passport in the early 70s and encountered all sorts of problems.

He was never sent back to Ireland, some would say 'unfortunately'; but Dad considered himself Welsh through and through. He ended up being the only boy of seven children, (a brother was killed as a child, going home from school in the 30s), living in a three-bedroomed house in Sycamore Street, Rhydifelin. A house I would visit almost every Saturday while my Nan was alive.

A memorable time, as all the cousins, aunties, and uncles would be there. The chip pan was never off the stove. Dad was a respected member of the community; by the community I mean the 'Trallwn Workmen's Club'. He was consistently on the committee. Dad was very strict. He took no nonsense, but his bark was far worse than his bite. I remember him kissing me as a small boy, but not so often as I got older, but that did not seem to matter to me, he was my hero.

He left the Royal Navy after the War. He was lucky enough to see little or no action, thank God. After the war, he worked in the local coal mines. There was always something wrong with him when he worked in the mines, being laid up with his back, bronchitis (as with all miners), or cuts and scratches, which turned blue with the coal dust. He told me once that there were lads in the pits who would get to pay their bills by cutting themselves with coal because they would be compensated for the injury. If it was a big bill, then the cut would be on the face. The more visible the scar the more money.

Dad retired in 1984, after being ill with a cancerous kidney which was removed. From then his health rapidly declined, and worse with the industrial diseases which go arm in arm with the job of mining.

By the end, he could not walk more than a couple of steps without stopping or needing oxygen. He died in April 1997 aged 72. My Mam once let slip that he was proud of what I had achieved in the Royal Navy. He wouldn't, or couldn't, say things like that to you personally, but I know he was as proud of his three of his kids, as I am of mine.

In 2012, I took a couple of the grandkids to the Ty Mawr Colliery, which is just outside Pontypridd It is now a museum.

I got talking to one of the guides, mentioning that my father worked in the mine. When I told him his name, he picked up his radio and said: "Dai, we've got John Hennessy's 'boy' with us today."

Dai replied, "Keep him away from the sledges, we don't want another incident."

Years ago, my father oversaw the shoring of the roof and walls, this was done by hammering a wooden framework into position. This one time they were having a problem jamming one sleeper-sized post into position, so one man held the post as my father swung his sledgehammer to force it into place. I don't know if the lights went out, or his helmet slipped over his eyes, but Dad missed the post, hitting the bloke on the side of his head, and knocking a few of his teeth out.

The strange thing was, today, the men at the mine were talking about this as if it had happened last week, but it happened over thirty years ago. The camaraderie of the miners is only equalled by the same kind of friendship you find in the Forces.

This is just a summary of the more interesting or amusing events that happened to me.

I wasn't always childish and immature... but most of the time I was. I make no apology for enjoying myself or making the best of a bad situation.

I recommend it to anyone.

HMS RALEIGH

1972- Aged 15

It was three months before my sixteenth birthday. I was off to join the Navy.

I would spend six weeks of basic seamanship training, and then on to Chatham, Kent, for another six weeks of trade training at HMS Pembroke.

Who knows what, or where I would go after that?

It was dark and cold when I arrived at Plymouth station. It was hectic, trains were arriving from just about everywhere, all of them seemingly full of recruits. You just gave someone holding a clipboard your name and went wherever they sent you, eventually ending up on a dark blue RN bus (Tilly), which took us to HMS Fisguard, situated alongside HMS Raleigh, in Torpoint, Cornwall. Fisguard was an

Artificers training establishment, but a few dorms were set aside for 'new entries' for induction before they were moved across the road to Raleigh.

I found the first night terrifying. Many long dorms, all connected by corridors. A bunch of us, about twenty, were put into one dorm, told to shower and get turned in. We were all young lads, between fifteen and twenty-two years old. We were to do everything together for the next six weeks.

The younger ones, me included, were a bit intimidated by the older lads, we were nervous and shy about introducing ourselves. But everyone slowly got around to meeting and exchanging names, discussing the towns and cities we came from. I was christened 'Taff' straight away, for obvious reasons, which is a name I would be called for the next twenty-five years.

The others came from all parts of the country. They spoke in accents to match. It took me some time to get used to understanding a Geordie, Jock, or Yorkie when they got talking. Whatever age we were, we were all in the same boat, one which was absolutely another world from the ones we were familiar with. It did not take long for us to start relying on each other to get us through this tense start to our new careers.

I only met three of those lads again during my career.

One was Graham Parker. I bumped into him at HMS Sultan while he was waiting to be discharged. He had a knackered knee which was the end of his naval career.

Lofty Eaton, a Naval Airman, was on the Hermes, and Kev Goode was on the Tiger, a nice quiet lad and good friend. He was changing branches to Regulator, but injured his back and left the RN after about seventeen years. He told me it was because he had simply had enough.

I still see him occasionally, on my visits to Pompey.

We were ordered to go outside and 'fall in'.

This was our first experience of forming a platoon and marching as a group. Well, I would not call the first time we got together in this form 'marching', but it was the way we were to go everywhere from that time on.

This first time we marched to the dining hall for supper. At home I was fed well, mam cooked a roast beef meal three or four times a week. Beef was the cheapest of meats in those days, chicken was a real treat. My first meal in this cafeteria-style dining hall was amazing. There must have been eight choices of main course, chips, boiled spuds, loads of veg, and salad, AND a choice of puddings with tea, coffee, and soft drinks available. And… you helped yourself.

This was a good start.

The next few days were inductions.

Uniform issued, polishing boots and shoes, filling in forms for passports, medical etc. The main form was to have us commit to the Royal Navy for the next twenty-two years. Some of the lads left it to the very last minute before signing, if they signed at all. Some could not cope with being told what to do, or have the piss taken out of them by the instructors and the lads who had been in for some time. So, they decided not to sign.

They were given a rail warrant home.

I had no problem signing, it was still the only thing I wanted to do.

I said I was as thick as shit, didn't I?

The instructors went through just about everything in the first few days, even how to brush your teeth, along with how to keep certain parts of your body clean, where to put soap, and where not to put soap.

Nothing was left out.

Two days later, we were considered ready to move into the mainstream training establishment.

We needed to visit the NAAFI shop to buy all the cleaning materials we would need, soap powder, starch, polish, and polishing cloths. If we didn't have the money, we were loaned it until payday.

Every ship and Establishment has a NAAFI (Navy Army and Air Force Institute) run by civilians. On ships, the staff are civilians but are subject to the Naval Discipline Act, so they can be punished by the captain, or handed over to local authorities if abroad and breaking local laws.

All our uniforms had to have badges attached, we were shown how to sew them on. Only a certain stitch was allowed. We had instructions on how to press our uniforms to Navy standards.

Now, that might sound simple to some people, but to press a naval uniform in those days took some doing. There was the White Front with its square collar that needed to have a razor-sharp crease down the exact centre. This was worn under the 'sailors' jumper, which was a blue serge jacket, or in the summer it was just worn with uniform trousers, no jacket required. This form of dress is called 'half blues'.

However, the trousers were not pressed with a single straight crease down the centre of the legs as most trousers are, oh no, these needed five or seven, (depending on the length of your legs/how tall you were), razor-sharp horizontal creases across the legs. The distance between each crease was four inches, or the width of your RN Pay Book, which funnily enough, has nothing to do with your pay.

These creases, it was said, represented the five oceans, or the seven seas. The jacket was simple but needed a 'blue collar', which was a separate item, and not part of the jacket itself. This was the most difficult and bizarre part of the uniform, too difficult for me even to explain here. It involved a weird folding, and three more razor-sharp creases, two creases facing outwards, while the third, the centre one, faced inwards.

When you wore it, you knew it looked bloody good because you spent so much time making it that way. The three white lines around the edge of the collar are said to represent victories over the French in various wars.

But this is arguable.

I noticed, that in later years, the French also had three white lines around their collar, surely not to represent the defeats.

Then there was the silk, which was about half a square yard of silk that needed to be folded in a certain way, before pressing until it looked like an inch-and-a-half width ribbon. This silk was worn around the neck, underneath the blue collar, and fastened at the front of the jacket with short tape just below the chest. Finally, a lanyard, which was a small length of thin white rope, the type of rope an army officer uses to attach a pistol to their belts, but it was simply a traditional part of the Naval uniform. It was worn much in the same way as the Silk, under the collar, and around the silk, fastening in a loop at the same point on the front of the jacket.

That uniform was called 'Full Blues', and we had the best uniform, called No1's. These were the same but made from a better grade of serge, and the badges were made from gold thread, not red cotton, as on the No2 uniforms.

No1 uniforms are used for ceremonial occasions, or when going ashore in uniform. The second-best uniform with the red badges, No2s, are worn for anything else when a full dress is required.

The general day-to-day working uniform, or 'Rig' were No8s. This was a light blue colour, heavy cotton shirt, with a branch badge sewn onto the right sleeve, and a nametape above the left-hand breast pocket. The shirt is worn with dark blue trousers.

As it was winter, we were to wear a dark blue woolly seaman's jumper instead of the white front. You would swear it was full of ants because it made you itch like having a dose of crabs, not that I ever had crabs.

We also were instructed on how to fold our kit for 'Kit Musters', which was, for me and quite a few of the lads, the worst part of training. Our kit had to be immaculate, folded to the right size and placed (laid out) in the correct position on our bunks, which also had to be made to a certain 'design'.

If anything was dirty, creased, or in the wrong position it would end up being thrown across the mess, or out of the window, depending on how bad it was, and the mood of whoever was doing the inspection. This was done in front of the whole class, who were standing to attention next to their bunks waiting their turn to be inspected.

Our kit was inspected by the Divisional CPO or Divisional Officer.

The Divisional Officer seemed to be the nicer one of the two, and this turns out to be because of the very good divisional system the RN has. Everyone has a divisional officer who is responsible for helping you with your career, promotion, appraisals, morale, and any personal problems you may have, so he must be approachable. Hence the Mr Nice Guy.

The Divisional CPO was, in this case, a Chief Marine Engineering Mechanic, or Chief Stoker as they were known from the old days when ships ran on steam and the fires needed 'Stoking'.

We learned that if you were to get an afternoon off, this was called a 'make and mend', used these days for sport, or a reward for a job well done. In the old days, the time off was specifically for making and mending clothing, hence 'make and mend'. In training, if our kit needed fixing it was done in our own time, which was during that very evening, because if it was picked up at a kit muster you would be having another inspection the next day.

All Officers and Warrant Officers (Fleet Chief Petty Officers at the time) were called 'Sir'.

Chief Petty Officers were 'Chief', Petty Officers were 'PO', and Leading Hands were 'Leading Hands' whilst in training but were just one of the boys after that.

But respect for rank and position was always a factor, you learn the right time to call someone by their first name. Leading hands, most of the time, POs when working with them, above that it was always by Rank or Rate. There were a couple of exceptions, one being the Regulators or Naval Police, which I will explain later.

Induction was over, and we became Drake 48 class.

Drake is one of six divisions in training, a bit like the 'Houses' at school. We moved to another dorm, in another part of HMS Raleigh. We learned to call the dorm the correct naval term, a mess.

Our mess was one of several old wooden huts, which were connected by a corridor with bathrooms and toilets (Heads). The same metal bunk beds and a floor... sorry deck, which needed polishing every day with a polisher, a heavy block with a polishing pad on the underside attached to a long broom handle, this contraption was pushed back and forth over the deck, after rubbing in the polish with a cloth by hand first. There were none of those fandangled buffing machines here mate.

Cleaning was a huge issue, everyone had to do their share. There was a class leader and deputy class leader, both selected to ensure things like this were done to the standards required. All we seemed to do was clean the mess, and then clean and press our uniforms. There were no washing machines, all washing was done by hand and dried in a dedicated 'Drying Room'. Our civilian clothes (civvies) by the way, were packed away in a storeroom. They were not to be seen again until training was complete.

As the junior class in the division, we were told we could expect a visit from the most senior class in the division that night, who was to perform an initiation ceremony.

We had no idea what to expect, but had to be in sports clothes, sorry 'rig'. At 9.30 pm, I mean 21:30hrs. At that time the doors burst open, and in ran the whole of the senior class armed with shaving foam, shoe whitener, and a lot of other stuff that would make a mess of us and our clean and polished dorm, sorry 'mess'.

We had to stand still and take whatever initiation they wanted to do to us. We were covered in all sorts of crap, and it took most of the night to clean ourselves and the mess, which we had become very protective of. The initiation was a bit of an anti-climax, after days of crapping ourselves and wondering what would happen, we ended up with just a lot of mess everywhere.

Now it was down to the nitty-gritty stuff.

How to tie knots, learn naval slang, (which is a whole new language), and how to fire an SLR, (Self Loading Rifle), which was the only time I fired a weapon until nearly twenty years later and, of course, how to march, and march with a rifle, and a rifle with a bayonet attached.

The people who taught us the parade ground drills were the Drill Instructors, or GIs (Gunnery Instructors) as they were known. They were a breed of their own.

They were there to abuse you.

They had gravelly voices and smoked forty Woodbines a day to keep it that way.

Everyone feared them, so you needed to learn quickly to keep them off your back. I met a few of these strange animals in different circumstances over the years, and they seemed quite normal, but the Parade Ground was their jungle, and they were the kings of it.

In six short weeks, they needed to train us to march as a unit and stop us 'tick-tocking', which is when your arms and legs move in the same direction at the same time, instead of in the opposing direction. Once we were able to set off, marching, and stopping as a single unit, and on the correct foot, they gave us SLRs to make things complicated. This brought another whole new set of orders and manoeuvres to learn.

But, if I could make up bread orders in the back of a moving van while travelling up and down the valleys, without a net, or losing a loaf, I could walk around with a rifle, even one with a bayonet attached without impaling myself.

How hard can it be?

Well, it was hard. It took a lot of practice, and we suffered a lot of abuse. The good thing is, it was never taken personally because we all got it. It became a bit of a joke when someone didn't get shit off the GIs.

Without knowing it, this discipline, abuse, and instruction were making us 'team players' and we all, without exception, were willing to help each other out. Whether it be helping someone to stop 'tick-tocking', climbing ropes in the gym, or studying for tests with general seamanship instruction. Everyone helped everyone else.

There was also the Navy's obsession with cleanliness to get used to. It did not take long.

When you are living in a mess with thirty other lads or, as it was in the future, a mess with thirty-plus grown men, the last thing you want is to live in a small area with someone who did not wash his clothes regularly or take pride in his personal hygiene. The ones who did not care how they looked, or smelled, (crabby) were educated radically by their messmates, who would shower them with washing powder and a scrubbing brush if necessary.

This would happen, thankfully rarely, but on more than occasion. Traditionally, the mornings on ships and in shore establishments are spent cleaning, then, before an officer carried out rounds (inspections) of accommodation in the evening, we would clean again.

The pain in the arse was the brightwork. Anything that could shine had Brasso applied until it shined better and brighter. Even the fire extinguisher handles and nozzles were brass, so were polished with Brasso.

This was all still the case when I left the mob twenty-four years later. I'd say one thing for all the cleaning, it is a great incentive to get promoted as quickly as you can, as it is much easier to supervise the cleaning than to do it yourself.

The Navy even helps you with your education. (So, there was still hope for me). They have something called the NAMET test. That is 'Naval Maths and English Tests'. It is graded from 0 to 9 on each of the tests, with 0 being the best score. If you intend to stay in the RN and make it a career, you need a NAMET score of at least 5-5 before you can be promoted. Unexpectedly, my English grade was a 4. As expected, my Maths grade was a 9, so 4-9 was not going to get me anywhere. But I did not leave school to join the navy and worry about Maths grades, so, at least for now, that went way down on my list of priorities.

Right now, it was six weeks of parade training, Sport, Gym, Fire Fighting, Damage Control, Nuclear Biological and Chemical Defence (NBCD), First Aid, and Assault Courses.

Ahhh, the Assault Course.

Everyone thought they were fit until we had the assault course.

It was a cold, rainy, muddy December day, and no one was ready for it. Up and down walls, over, under, and through obstacles, through a water tunnel, and finally the rope over the pond.

We would start well on the rope, with one foot hooked on the rope behind us, and one dangling for balance, while pulling ourselves across on our stomach and chest.

Once we were about a quarter of the way across the rope, the next lad in line was told to start their crossing. As they got onto the rope, the lad in front was usually catapulted off. You needed to swim to the side of the pond, where you could see the instructors giggling as they told each lad to start and burst into laughter as the lad who was already on the rope went flying into the cold muddy pond.

No one made it across dry.

Firefighting was a bit hairy.

There were metal structures to simulate the compartments and decks of a ship. There are no windows or doorways, just hatches as you would find on a warship.

Oil fires are lit inside one or more of the compartments, and a team of trainees enter to find and fight the fires. The compartments quickly fill with thick black smoke, so visibility is zero. Often you could not see any fire or flames until the guy with the thermal imager pointed you in the right direction.

We dragged pressurised hoses from compartment to compartment, and deck to deck. When you are wearing a breathing apparatus, I can assure you it is not an easy task. This course was completed every time I joined a ship. Fire at sea is an extremely serious business, and training on board is continuous.

The Damage Control course was also terrifying.

Again, there are simulators constructed like the compartments on a ship, but this time there were holes in every bulkhead, where water gushed in, just as it would do on a battle-damaged ship.

A team of us were sent inside to block the holes and save the ship. This needed to be done before the compartment was fully flooded with water. We were up to our chins before they turned the water off.

We did this during a winter's day in January. You cannot imagine how cold we were.

The NBCD training was intense and an eye-opener.

You do not realise you must prepare for gas, chemical, and nuclear attacks. Everyone is issued with a gas mask and is trained in wearing the suits that protect you from chemicals and gasses. Of course, you must test the gas mask, and experience a gas attack. We did this every year in various gas chambers throughout the fleet. They used tear gas.

It is not a nice experience.

All navy personnel are issued with 'Anti-flash gear when they join a ship. It comprises a pair of white cotton, elbow-length gloves, and a matching hood, which covers your head and neck, just leaving a slit for your eyes so you can see. These are very effective garments which help prevent burning from fire, explosion, chemical, or gas, and they are compulsorily worn during 'Action Stations'.

The fire fighting and damage control exercises were always hard work but a lot of fun, and you do not realise the seriousness, or importance, of what you are doing until you are in a position where it may happen for real, as was the case during the Falklands conflict.

No one was having fun on the bombed ships, or when we were waiting to be hit during Action Stations.

For those unlucky enough to have their ship hit, it was not a case of firefighting or damage control.

It was a case of survival.

When the shit hits the fan big time everything happens at once. So, fun it may be in a controlled environment, but it always needs to be taken extremely seriously.

I never experienced a major fire at sea until thirty-five years later, after I left the RN and joined the Princess Cruise Line as the Officer in charge of security. One of my duties was as second in charge of the fire party.

Onboard the Star Princess, whilst at sea in the Caribbean, a fire started on one of the balconies and spread to destroy over one hundred and twenty cabins.

I can confirm that a fire at sea, in whatever navy you are in, is a horrific experience. You can never have too much training to prepare for such an event. Fortunately, there was only one fatality, and that was a passenger having a heart attack. The ship limped into Jamaica after fighting the fire for over eight hours.

Another compulsory course was First Aid. The medics acted as injured people. They had incredibly realistic injuries, compound fractures, burns and such. We needed to address the various traumas, (after being instructed on what to do, of course.) So realistic looking were the injuries, one of our lads went white, throwing up over the medic, who then had to give him first aid for real.

After a week of training, we were allowed to go to the NAAFI club on a Wednesday. It was a disco night, wow.

We spent ages pressing our No2s, looking each other up and down, and getting any visible white lint off the blue fabric before we went to take those NAAFI girls by storm.

We stopped at the entrance of the NAAFI in stunned silence, looking for anything that resembled a female in the huge bar. But no, even the barmen were, well, men.

As there were five other divisions in HMS Raleigh, it was just wall-to-wall baby sailors. So, the older lads went to the bar and bought us sprogs (youngsters) a beer.

This is where I first saw men dancing with men, because there were no girls, and it was always the same dance which they danced to, a Status Quo song. With their hands on hips, twisting from side to side, and bending at the waist, the opposite side to where your 'partner' was bending. I will admit to taking part in this just once, after three or four beers, but never again. Which is why I hate dancing so much now.

We were given a night off one Saturday.

We all, on mass, went into Plymouth and a Disco called 'Roof Tops', which was probably established for the underage sailors at Raleigh, but there were girls and booze, and there didn't seem to be an age limit to buy alcohol. Within two hours quite a few of us were throwing up against a wall outside. Some lads did not make it outside. They were escorted/carried from the premises.

What was amazing was the ardent dancers from the NAFFI still danced with their mates as the girls looked on. I honestly think they thought they were cool.

We learnt how to get help if a fight started with the few 'civilians' who dared come in and laugh at the sad-os dancing with themselves and each other.

It was aid you were to throw your cap in the air and scream 'Matelots' (a new name we learnt for sailor). We saw it happen once, no one turned up, and the poor lad did not get his cap back after throwing it in the air. So, from then on, we just ran if there was any sign of trouble.

The following morning was my first hangover, but it was nothing to what was to come when we were allowed home for Christmas and New Year.

Our training was interrupted by Christmas, so everyone, in uniform and carrying our full kit bag and suitcase, went home for two weeks, using one of four travel warrants we were issued each year.

Walking through Ponty on the way home was a bit of an experience.

You never saw many sailors walking through the streets of Ponty in uniform as I did. On a few occasions, women would come up to me with their hand outstretched saying "Touch your dickey", (WOW, you would think), and they would put their hand on my shoulder.

I later learnt it was good luck to touch a sailor's collar. I have no idea why they referred to it as a dickey. It wasn't fair getting a young lad's hopes up like that, and then getting tapped on the shoulder.

Anyway, it was nice doing the rounds of all the aunties, uncles, and cousins, and being considered a bit of a celebrity, albeit a temporary one. But on New Year's Eve, I went, in full regalia, to the Trallwn Workmen's Club where my old man was on the committee and was the bingo caller.

I remember being handed my fourth or fifth pint of lager, making a false call at bingo, and being allowed to keep my card, (you are normally disqualified from the rest of the house if it is a false call), so I was given a bit of leeway.

Then I threw up in the toilet. I was carried home by my father and brother-in-law, dropped a few times going up the stairs, and woke up with a pool of vomit next to the bed.

I was told it was a very good night.

The morning was not too good though, I had to clean my cold, congealed vomit from the floor, and listen to my mother give my father a hard time for letting me get in such a state.

Plenty of time was spent with mates in the local pubs, but the twenty-five quid I was given for leave did not last very long.

So, back to Raleigh for the final couple of weeks of basic training.

As I was to be a Steward, I and a few others in the same branch were told we would be working at the next Officer's Mess Dinner.

Let's see what we have let ourselves in for.

It was a grand occasion. The Wardroom (Officers Mess) was like a five-star hotel, with works of art, silver tableware, and sculptures everywhere. The Officers and their wives dressed to the nines and seated, waiting for us to serve the meal.

My job was to serve about ten of them their vegetables. It was well organised, and everyone had specific jobs. The veg came in two serving dishes, which were balanced on heat-resistant placemats in the palm of each hand, I would present one dish to an Officer to help himself, whilst the other dish was tucked away, ready to be presented, after he had taken his fill from the first one.

Not as easy as it sounds, and I soon found it takes a bit of practice to become proficient. I proved this by watching one of the dishes slide from the heat-resistant pad on my hand onto the lap of a Sub Lieutenant.

Again, everyone was well organised, one Steward quickly guided me away before the other dish, which was about to go the same way, also fell into his lap. Another steward began pacifying the Lieutenant and cleaning up the mess.

I was 'disappeared' into the kitchen (Galley), sharpish.

The steward said, "Thank God it was only a 'Subby'," (Junior Officer), and said, "Well done. We've all wanted to do that to some Officers at one time or another." This was my first experience being a Steward, no wonder I hated it.

We also had regular physical training, not to the extent the Army does, it was just enough to keep our fitness ticking over. It was a lot of fun and a welcome break from the Parade Ground and classrooms.

Our passing out parade was a grand occasion.

Mam and Dad came to watch my class, and many others, do our march past, with the local Admiral taking the salute. Tea and bickies after; then we were allowed to do anything, and go anywhere, with our parents.

My parents took me for a meal, and later to the cinema, there was not much else we could do as I was only fifteen, and a good piss-up was out of the question.

So, after the cinema, they went to the B&B, and I went back to my mess where the other underage lads were already packing their bags.

That, in a nutshell, was HMS Raleigh.

My first eight weeks (including leave) in the RN. It was hard work but a lot of fun, which was only made possible because of the friends we made, and the help we gave each other. Some of us, those in the same branch, would move on together to the next training Establishment. Others went elsewhere, and I only met one or two of them during my service. The rest disappeared without a trace. Most left the RN, with only one or two, including me, staying in for the full twenty-two years.

I wouldn't have believed you could make such good friends in such a short period.

This wasn't unique to Raleigh. It happened time and time again. Although it is with great sadness that you must leave a group of friends like those at Raleigh, it would not be long before more good friends are made in the next establishment or ship you are sent to, where the same form of camaraderie develops.

MICHAEL J HENNESSY

RALEIGH

HMS PEMBROKE

1973 – Aged 16

So, I was off to HMS Pembroke in Kent. The home of the Supply and Secretariat (S&S) Branch of the RN. Pembroke is the training Establishment for the Stewards, Stores Accountants, Cooks, and Writers. This is where they were going to teach me how to be a waiter and cabin steward, whoooo.

It was soon obvious that things here were going to be a lot easier than basic training at Raleigh. There was still a lot of marching, training, and kit musters but life was a lot more comfortable and a hell of a lot easier.

We were still segregated from the permanent staff or 'Ships Company' as they are known. We, the trainees, were housed in an area known as East Camp, but we could use the NAFFI and shops in the main area, which to me was more like a town, it seemed huge, and it was.

Every day we fell in (formed a marching platoon) outside our mess at 0700hrs and marched, as we did everywhere, to the Steward's school.

As in Raleigh, we had time to play sports, and every Wednesday afternoon was set aside for just that, we could try anything on offer. But, as I was Welsh, I was expected to play Rugby, mainly because the Rugby PTI (Physical Training Instructor) was also Welsh. Unfortunately, I was not to be an asset to his team.

The training started, and we covered many subjects we would come across when we joined the Fleet. Silver service, cabin cleaning, bookkeeping, bar tendering, and preparing foods like salads and breakfast, but nothing too difficult. I could not begin to like the job, but I was enjoying life and the friends I made. I was not thinking about my future.

We did not use the bar often, simply because we did not get paid a lot. I, as a Junior Assistant Steward, was earning around seven pounds per fortnight. This was not much, even back then, but I knew I would get a pay rise as I progressed due to age, or promotion, pay never seemed a big deal at this stage.

When we did get paid it did not last long, something I proved when I went to the bar for the first time with a Scottish mate, Jock Ireland. I will never forget his name.

It was the wrong day to go to the bar, not that we intended to get drunk, but we had an 'Exped' the following morning. An 'Exped' is the navy's adventure training, exped, meaning expedition. On this occasion, we were going for a twenty-mile hike and to spend a night in a field.

Anyway, Jock and I began to experiment with drinks we had not sampled before, which meant everything. We tried Lager, Guinness, Cider, and I remember drinking two bottles of Newcastle Brown Ale.

To say we were drunk was an understatement. The following is what we were told we had done.

We walked halfway to East Camp. Up a small hill, perched at the top and overlooking a large goldfish pond and fountain, was a row of four ceremonial canons used for twenty-one-gun salutes and other ceremonial things. We decided to sit on one and have a jolly good singsong. That is until I decided to run down the grass bank to the pond and have a look for the goldfish. I was in the pond; Jock was still having a singsong when the Royal Navy Patrol found us. They kindly gave us a room each for the night, in the establishment's cell block.

I woke up naked, covered by an itchy blanket, snuggled up to a hot water pipe which was running through my cell.

The routine is, that you are kicked out of bed, or in this case a wooden slab, at six o'clock in the morning, then made to mop out the whole cell block. After which we were sent to our mess.

The word had already gone around to where we spent last night. We still had the Exped to deal with, and after we were 'discussed' by our superiors it was decided, I think because I looked so bloody rough, that I would be part of the base camp party and would not take part in the twenty-mile walk.

How relieved was I? But I would still pay.

There was a long drive in an uncomfortable van. A lot of carrying equipment, food, erecting tents, and preparing and cooking for those doing the walk. It was a long day and night.

Probably, the most uncomfortable night ever, but worse was to come because when we got back to HMS Pembroke, Jock and I was charged with being drunk on board (ship or establishment it is always drunk onboard or ashore) and for me drinking underage.

I seem to remember having a Section thirty-nine charge, which covers anything they want, and in this case, it was for swimming in the goldfish pond.

The process was called 'being trooped', and the formality was called 'the table'. It would be the Executive officer's table, to investigate the offences. The XO would then pass the case on to The Captain's Table for the Commanding Officer to deal with us.

In other ships and establishments, there would be an Officer of the Days (OOD) table, who would pass it to the Executive Officer (XO, and second in command), who would pass it on to the captain, if it was too serious for him to handle at that level. If it was a really serious offence, then a punishment warrant would be written up and approved by the local or nearest Flag Officer. A Flag Officer is a rank between Commodore and Admiral of the Fleet. The ultimate procedure would be the Court Martial.

The facts of our case were read out by the Master at Arms, the Senior Police Chief. (Ironically, I would be doing the same job when I left the RN twenty-four years later), to the Executive Officer who was investigating the case.

Let's be fair, I was shitting myself, but I think everyone at that table had a giggle when they were hearing what we had to drink and what we did.

Anyway, it was passed on, and the captain awarded (sentenced) us to fourteen days number nine punishment, which is extra work in our own time, often at unsociable hours, fourteen days number fourteen punishment, which is mustering at unsociable hours, the forfeit of seven days' pay, and a five-pound fine.

We needed to muster with the Duty Petty Officer at certain times of the day, where he would send us wherever we were needed. We were gobsmacked when we were sent to the Provost Headquarters, where the patrolmen, or Leading Regulators (Navy term for Policemen) worked and played.

But after they made the point that they were the boss, and we did a good job for them, they would ask for us, and it became a good number, but it seemed to last forever.

After fourteen days, we were free of these punishments, I was also absolutely skinters, so it was early nights and an immaculate kit, as we found the time to work on it instead of going out.

After that, we used to get a toot from the RN Patrol vehicles as they passed, which caused us to be playfully called snitches because of our 'relationship' with the provost guys. So, the punishment was not as bad as we first expected.

The training continued.

HMS Bristol, a one-off Destroyer, was in Bristol for her Commissioning ceremony, and all the dignitaries, VIPs and such were attending. It was going to be a very busy time for them. To help with the labour, they asked for a bunch of trainees from the school to help. My class was volunteered (sent).

We were barracked in an old army camp out in the wilds. I thought we had it bad. There was no heating, and you had to wait for half an hour for hot water to appear out of the shower, and then it was a dribble. But we managed.

We went on board the ship the day before the 'Do' and met the ship's company, the stewards we would be working with. While having a coffee with a couple of them, one asked us if anyone had had a "Dose yet?"

Well, I had fourteen days of No 9s, so thought I was experienced in this kind of thing, so I said I had.

He said, "WHAT! You have had a dose of VD?"

Ah... I wish I had a dose of VD rather than need to tell everyone I thought a 'Dose' meant a 'Dose' of punishment... A simple mistake.

The lads never let me live it down.

The rest of the time at HMS Pembroke was uneventful, but it was a joy to watch the Royal Marine Band practising before a public event. They have always been considered the best military band in the world; you can tell why.

Whenever they were out practising there would be a large crowd watching them, and to watch the drummers doing their thing is something very special. The hairs still stand up on the back of my neck when I see and hear them play now.

We had an obstacle course to complete, which was not as sadistic as the one at Raleigh, but it was still knackering. I also spent a week in sick bay with Tonsillitis. I was lucky not to be backclassed.

All in all, a relatively easy eight weeks.

Our training at HMS Pembroke ended, and our class was split again. We were sent to different establishments around the country, where we learnt our new 'trade', by doing it for real.

Class photograph
HMS Pembroke 1973

HMS OSPREY

1973 - Aged 16

Eight weeks later, after we proved we could serve vegetables without spilling them on someone's lap, and we could clean cabins to an acceptable standard, we were classed as fully trained Stewards and sent to our first shore establishment as ships compliment.

I was sent to HMS Osprey in Portland, Dorset, a Fleet Air Arm (Navy Air Force) helicopter base.

This was bloody great, only six to a mess, in what seemed to be brand new accommodation blocks... with carpets, wow. We still needed to keep it clean, and there were still rounds to make sure we did, but it was a luxury.

We did not have to march anywhere unless it was a rare 'Divisions'. Divisions are where whole ship's companies fall in for a ceremonial

Parade. This happens once or twice a year on all ships and establishments.

I could live with that.

The Wardroom, where I worked, was up to the normal standard of comfort, with plenty of artwork as usual. I was given about eight cabins to clean each morning, and then served lunch, teas, and dinner, depending on what watch (shift) I was on.

It was a cycle, so everyone got the same time off work unless there was a function or a mess dinner when we were all required.

It was easy. I hated it as usual but, again, I made some great friends.

In the summer, which at this time it was, we would go into Weymouth when we had time off, chill out around the NAAFI, or go on a bender if it were a pay week.

I went sunbathing on the beach once and ended up like a lobster. In the morning, I thought I had prickly heat, it was unbearable, so I went to the Sick Bay, (Doctors). I got no sympathy at all and was sent to work. If I were to miss work because of sunburn I could be trooped as it is considered self-inflicted, so I got through the day, and the next day, until I was passed the worst and able to get on with life as normal.

This is where I first met Frank Flemming, one of the funniest men I have ever known. We became good friends. Frank will come up in this story a couple of times more. This man, or should I say at this time 'lad', had a rubber face, and he could make everything seem funny. He was a pleasure to be around.

The RN has a way of rewarding seniority. That is, from the age of eighteen, in four-year periods, up to the age of thirty, you would be awarded a stripe for good conduct. If you were not a Leading Hand or Leading Steward, which is the first step on the promotion ladder, (equivalent to a corporal in the Army or RAF), you would be called a 'badge man'. A one, two, or three badge man. They were respected and supervised the youngsters. When you were promoted to Leading Hand, you would be a one, two, or three badge Leading Hand.

When I first joined there were a lot of badge men. One of them, a very popular three-badge Steward called 'Ginge' Salisbury, had a serious drink problem. He was an out-and-out alcoholic.

He used to suffer if he did not get his regular booze fix, but as he worked in the Wardroom Bar this was not much of a problem, even at eight in the morning, when we started work, he was at it.

Ginge's money never lasted long for obvious reasons, so he regularly borrowed from everyone, this was a daily occurrence. But Ginge was as honest as the day is long, and every payday, every two weeks, don't forget, Ginge would get a pile of envelopes, put the name of the person he owed money to on each, with the correct amount of cash inside. He would then hand them out minutes after he had been paid.

That night he would buy everyone a thank-you drink in the NAFFI. The following day he would start borrowing money over again. He was a genuine character and, even with all his problems, a nice bloke.

I had my first experience of a 'Warrant Reading' at Osprey.

I will explain.

When someone commits an offence, one serious enough that the Captain, the Commanding Officer of a ship or shore establishment, is unable to award punishment, then a Warrant is sent to the nearest Flag Officer.

A Flag Officer is a Commodore or above. They are called a Flag Officer because they have a personal flag, which is flown when they are on a ship or in a shore establishment. The Flag Officer approves the recommended punishment by signing a punishment warrant.

The Warrant is returned to the ship, where there is normally a 'clear lower deck' command, which means everyone would attend the occasion.

The offender is then marched to the front of the entire ship's company, and the Warrant is read.

At one point, the offender's escort orders the offender to march one pace forward and they take off the offender's cap as he does.

It is humiliating. It is intended to be, especially if the offender is to be demoted, and more so if he is a senior rate (PO or CPO).

The occasion is designed to be a deterrent to others, amongst other things. Again, this is something I would need to organise in future years.

The payday I had been waiting for arrived and, as usual, we lined up to collect our pay. With our caps on we march up to the Cash Officer, salute, holding our ID card for inspection, and then repeat the last three numbers and the last letter of our official number. Such a '963L, Sir.' The cash Officer would place our pay (it was always cash payments back then) in our hands. Then we would right-turn and march off. If we did not do it properly a Regulator was waiting to point out our error rigorously, and usually loudly.

This time, I was getting my compliment pay. I was not a trainee anymore, so this trebled my wages to about twenty-three quid, backdated, to when I joined Osprey.

I now had around eighty quid in my pocket. A pint was only eighteen pence, so I was a very popular guy.

I needed some new clothes, which saw me visit the Naval Tailors, 'Bernards'. For five quid a month, I got fifty quid's worth of credit. So, out went the nylon shirts I joined with, and in came some cool shirts, slacks, jeans, and a coat... I looked the bee's knees.

Even the long days, when we had to serve a mess dinner, were fun at Osprey. Between courses, we would trot off to the NAFFI and quickly down a pint or two, or five in Ginge's case, before trotting back to serve the next course.

At the end of the night, when everything was stowed away, there was always someone who had 'rescued' a bottle or two of the officer's booze.

Happy days.

But for me, they were coming to an end. I was given a draft to my first ship. HMS Leander, which, as I pointed out earlier, was the sister ship of HMS Juno where it all started with my brother-in-law.

I was sorry to leave Osprey because of the good friends I made, but also because of the location, a seaside resort, you could not ask for much more.

In future years, Portland would send shivers down my spine because, if you are there on a ship, it can only mean early mornings, late nights, and endless exercises, but that was in the future.

Right now, I was off on summer leave, and then onto Plymouth, where I would join the HMS Leander before it sailed for Antwerp, my first foreign port.

Summer leave was great, I spent a lot of time with childhood friends Gareth, Jeff, and 'S'. One of them usually had a car, so it was down to Barry Island most weekends, to a disco we liked.

I'm unsure why we went there, it was a hell of a trek but good fun. They were two or three years older than me, so booze was again an integral part of our social life, and we made our 'Local' the Central Hotel, which was a bit of a dive but nice and friendly with the odd 'lock-ins'.

I also used the Royal Oak, but the beer was so watered down the locals drank bottled lager, but it was a laugh.

When the landlord and his girlfriend went out on a Saturday night, he left the keys with Len Fenley, another good mate, and of course, like all good teenagers, we took full advantage of the situation by having a little party before joining the Landlord at the night club.

HMS LEANDER

1973-74 - Aged 16-17

Your first ship is most important.

It's the pre-school for matelots.

It is where you learn to live in a confined space with up to fifty men.

It's where you perfect your personal hygiene skills and avoid the wrath of your messmates.

It's where you learn the language (The navy has an individual, particular, and peculiar language. It is commonly referred to as 'Jackspeak'.

It's where you tell jokes and play practical jokes, but most importantly it's where you learn to accept them when they are targeted at you. If you can give, but not take, you will be a 'Billy no mates', and have a short naval career.

You will hear a lot of serious and funny dits (stories) from the masters of bullshit. Remember them, because you will be telling the same 'dits' for the rest of your career.

Anyway, it was time to go back to work and this was nerve-racking. I was to join a real warship and work with experienced people onboard. As a sprog, who had only been in the RN, or the Mob as it is affectionately known, a dog watch -short time- it was a terrifying prospect.

I arrived in Plymouth, at the now-familiar railway station. Thankfully I had enough money left for a Fast Black (Taxi) to the ship. As the taxi approached the berth my butterflies grew worse.

The Leading Regulator (LREG) met me. I had not seen one of those since Pembroke. He was a big bloke but seemed OK, but you are always weary of Regulators.

On Frigates there is just one Leading Regulator, and one Master at Arms (MAA). The Regulating Office was also the MAA cabin, so there were no 'lie-ins' for him, as the office was always open. (*By the time I went onto my next Frigate, in 1990, the MAA cabin was separate from the office, I was the Master at Arms, and I did get some 'lie-ins'*).

I filled in all the forms needed, and the Petty Officer Steward, my boss, collected me from the Regulators Office (Reg. Office).

He was someone you needed to keep on the good side of. He was abrupt, 'old navy', and delegated everything. A Killick (Leading Hand/Steward) was summoned, who in turn handed me to one of the Stewards to show me around and help get me settled in.

A Killick is an unofficial name for a Leading Hand, this is because the Leading Hands rank badge is an anchor, and another name for an anchor is... you've guessed it... Killick.

I was shown to my bunk, which was in the middle of the mess square, unfortunately. A mess square is the mess's communal area. It is where the socialising is done. Those sleeping near this area would be last to get to sleep. There were twenty-five men in the mess. In bunks three high. Everyone seemed to be badge man or three badge killick, while I was only a sixteen-year-old sprog.

There were a couple of stewards and cooks around eighteen years old. But they were well established and in with the rest of the mess. I did not feel comfortable. This was the first time I was unsure about being in the Mob (RN). So much so, that I asked to leave the ship after about two weeks, and even requested to change branches to Seaman. Not only because I wanted off, but I wanted out of the Stewards Branch as well.

My Divisional Officer on the Leander was Lt Macgregor, who happened to be at Pembroke when Jock and I went on that bender.

Word soon got around the ship about that escapade. There was a little piss-taking but nothing more. It helped me fit in. So, in a matter of a few weeks, everything clicked, I started getting on with everyone, I came out of my shell and began to hold conversations with people, and even started giving some stick and taking the piss, which is the 'Navy way'.

Changing the subject slightly, it was around this time I was introduced to 'BABIES HEADS', the best steak and kidney pudding I have tasted in my life. It came out of a tin can and was part of the ration packs (Ratpacks) issued to men in the field. Ships kept a lot of rat-packs and when the 'use by' date was approaching they were given to the crew a treat. They held the tastiest filling in the world, and the pastry was as smooth as a baby's head, hence the name. They never lasted long, and they were few and far between. You could count on one hand the number of times I saw them on the menu in twenty-four years, but we would have eaten them every day.

Just a bit of more useless information I thought you would be interested in.

Anyway…

George, a badge man who always seemed a bully to me, began looking out for me. He was nothing like a bully. I supposed I felt intimidated by his size, confidence, and popularity. He, and Jock Mcguigan, a Stores Accountant and just as much of a nice guy, were like the mess 'Double Act', always joking, having a laugh and beer. He was a pleasure to be around.

Once, after being allowed a few beers in the mess, I fell asleep in a bit of a drunken stupor (I was still only sixteen). I woke in the middle of the night dying for a piss. When I came to my senses, I was mopping up my 'mess' in the corner of the mess using someone's white T-shirt.

Jock had hung the T-shirt up ready to wear in the morning. In the morning, I woke to his loud 'enquiries' into where it had gone.

There were even louder enquiries that evening when he found his wet, (now yellow) white T-shirt stuffed in a boot locker. I managed to keep this event quiet, until today.

I'm sure he would see the funny side; well, I hope he would have by now... surely?

Everything was great again, so much so, I even asked to extend my draft onboard. It wasn't granted but I would have happily stayed.

My social life was good, but one thing spoiled it at the time. I was still only sixteen, and a 'Junior', and 'Junior's' leave expired at 2359, Midnight.

I don't know why, but the RN does not have a midnight, it is either 2359 or 0001.

I never did find out about that.

It is the same with everything, you just do it, if you questioned everything, I suppose it wouldn't be a disciplined force, would it?

Anyway, on three occasions I was having such a good time ashore I did not want to go back to the ship at 2359, so I stayed ashore. The first time it cost me three days number 9s, the second seven, and the third ten.

There was a bit of a pattern forming here!

The first foreign visit for me was to Antwerp. It was uneventful, with the only highlight being one of the Store Accountants (SA) being arrested for taking the Belgium flag from a flagpole in the middle of the town. That was it.

We went back to Plymouth. But soon we were going on a three-month deployment to the Bahamas and the US. At first, I was dreading it because of what I said above, but once I had settled in, I couldn't wait.

Your first warship is a huge learning curve, learning how to do your job at sea, proper 'Action Stations', terminology, routines and more. On a ship, you get to know the older lads onboard, because in a shore establishment, most old hands are married, so you don't get to know them as they live ashore with their families.

The older men are the ones you learn from, and one of the oldest traditions everyone learns is how to sing the sea shanties (Ditties), or in my case how to join in, because I could never get to grips with all the words.

With a few beers down their necks, there was inevitably a singing session. I will never forget some of the timeless classic words such as:

"There's a moral to the story, the moral is this, always have a shifty before you have a piss, singing O tiddly O shit or bust, never let your bollocks dangle in the dust."

And:

"There once was a lad called Aladdin who had a magic lamp, he got it from a matelot who was fathoms up a tramp, he got it from a matelot to see what he could get, and he rubbed, and he rubbed, and he rubbed, and he rubbed, and he ain't got fuck all yet."

And everyone's favourite:

"And we'll all go back to oggie land, to oggie land, to oggie land, and we'll all go back to oggie land, where you can't tell sugar from tissue paper, tissue paper, from marmalade or jam."

Deep meaningful words, I think you'll agree.

I had settled in and would go ashore with anyone, anytime.

I wanted to go ashore with the lads the night before we deployed to The Bahamas, so, I invented a story that my brother was coming to Plymouth, and I would like to go out with him before we left.

I duly filled in my request form. (A request form is needed for anything you want.)

I handed it to the OOD, who was a good man and felt sorry for me, so he extended my leave to 0100. Only an hour extra, not much, but better than nothing.

As it turned out it wasn't enough, I got back on board at 0215. This was my fourth time being late on the same ship, which could mean deep shit for me.

After we sailed, I was up at the 'Captains Table' with my cap off, as you do at these tables, and in no uncertain terms I was told I was becoming a habitual absentee and a pain in the arse to the Regulating Staff (Ships Police).

If I continued with this behaviour, I was running the risk of being sent to DQs, which means Detention Quarters… Naval Prison… "On cap, Right Turn, Right Wheel, Quick March. Report to my office," said the Master at Arms.

The Master at Arms is the Chief Policeman and is feared and respected by all onboard. The MAA is also known as Joss, Jossman, or Jaunty.

Jaunty is a corrupt form of Gendarme, the French Police, and Jossman was the name of an infamous Master at Arms from many years ago.

I've had the official bollocking, so here comes the real one. And a real one it was, the Joss ripped me a new one.

He told me there is a good chance of DQs next time, but there is also a good chance of Second Class for Conduct. A punishment that everyone dreads, and most would rather spend time in DQs than ninety days of this punishment. Briefly, it consists of fourteen days No9s, followed by fourteen days No14s, which are No9s without the work. Then you muster at certain times of the day, have your kit mustered at regular intervals, and get one day's leave a week, and that's if you can find a Leading Hand to escort and stay with you, in uniform, for the duration of your leave.

No Thanks.

I was an old hand at Number 9s by now, but this was the worst yet. I was sent everywhere, but mainly to the engine room, where I painted or cleaned some greasy piece of machinery. I didn't want to do that anymore. I need to pull my socks up and get back on board when I should, or at least not get caught coming back late.

Our first port, on the way to the Bahamas, was Ponta Del Garda, The Azores. I would have loved to have gone ashore there, but I was far too busy with my No9s.

There is not much to do in Ponta Del Garda by way of entertainment for visiting sailors, except the bars, so in this scenario, a PO, along with two or three Able Ratings, would be sent ashore as a ship's patrol to stop any trouble and pick up any drunks etc.

Well, this was a real sleepy hollow, so quiet that the patrol got so bored they went for a drink themselves, which is a no-no, but when the patrol gets brought back to the ship drunk, they have a problem. And that they did.

The two Able Rates got a suspended sentence and the PO, was 'Busted', demoted down to cook, and sent to another ship.

And I thought I had problems.

'Scouse' Jones was a cook who always had a problem with someone.

One evening he returned on board alone, as usual, at about 2230. Some of us were having a quiet drink in the mess. Within fifteen minutes of his arrival, he almost fought with messmates before he got into his bunk.

George said to me, "We'll have him."

George was the badge man I was unsure about at first, but he became, a sort of, sea daddy to me, (took me under his wing). As I said, he was a big bloke from Newcastle, and he was pissed off with Scouse.

When Scouse dropped off to sleep, drunk, he dad his arse sticking out of the side of the bunk.

George said, "Watch and learn, and get up early in the morning to see the 'Scouse tosser' when he realises what he has done."

George got a Mars Bar from his locker, broke it in half and, very gently, tucked one half down the back of Scouse's knicks. It did not click with me at first, but then I couldn't wait to see him in the morning.

My bunk was opposite Scouse's. I was lucky enough to wake up as he realised something was amiss. He thought he had shit himself during the night, as the Mars Bar had melted into a mushy mess inside his kegs.

The look on his face was priceless.

He would not get out of his bunk; everyone was telling him to get his arse into gear or he would be adrift (late). But he wasn't going anywhere until everyone was out of the mess.

When he did get out of his pit, George, and Andy, the Leading Hand of the Mess, were waiting to pounce. When they did, they were calling him every name under the sun for dumping in his knicks. They kept it going for a good few minutes before they let him know it wasn't shit in his pants.

Scouse hadn't realised there was no smell, he just took it for granted he had a little 'mishap'. Maybe it wasn't his first time.

Scouse became very quiet after that.

Every week or fortnight, the ship would exercise 'Action Station', which is what we would be doing should we be involved in any conflict or battle scenarios.

On this ship, my job was to assist the firefighters in getting dressed and carrying any equipment they may need, a bit of a labourer.

I must say, at this time, and during my time on my next ship, HMS Tiger, we never thought for a moment we would be involved in a real conflict. It was a bit stupid really, we were in the Navy for God's sake, not on a P&O cruise line.

Halfway across the Atlantic, I had my first 'Hands to Bathe'.

This is the announcement made when the ship stops, and the crew are allowed to go swimming.

I found it strange to begin with.

I mean, no land in sight, and you know there isn't any for a couple of thousand miles in any direction, and suddenly someone decides it's a good idea to go swimming.

My first thought was, what about the sharks?

I needn't have worried; we had a marksman armed with an SLR standing on the bridge wing looking out for sharks, and ready to shoot if needed.

Thinking back now, it doesn't fill me with a lot of confidence, but then you just don't care. The ship being stopped gives the captain a chance to make his ship look nice, so the opportunity is taken to paint the sides.

Seamen sit on planks of wood dangling from a couple of ropes over the ship's side, painting their hearts away. On this occasion, the swimmers were called back onboard, to get going again we thought, but no, when we got onboard, we saw the painters on their planks of wood holding on for dear life, trying to keep their feet from going into the sea because sharks were circling.

They were pulled up sharpish and, once they had stopped shaking, we were on our way.

They don't call 'shark, shark' when we are swimming because of the panic it might cause, but the older lads knew what was happening and were the first out... Phew.

Thinking about it later, I did a bit of shaking myself, it could have been a very short career.

The next stop was Freeport, Bahamas.

A lovely Island with a big Casino. It was also the tax haven of an Ex-Steward who made good, he had something to do with Car parks, NCP, or something like that.

I never got to meet him, but he put a bar tab and a meal for about fifteen of us at the local Steak house. Excellent steak, it was the first time I ate a fillet steak, very nice.

I did go to the Casino, lost my twenty bucks, (that's all I had left), had a drink and went back onboard. Whilst in the Casino, I experienced the humour of the older generation of sailors.

A couple of 'Old Tar's' from a different ship, were in the Casino, in uniform (Half Blues) as we all were, when one of them said, "Hennessy, how are you? I haven't seen you for ages."

I'd never seen him before in my life. "Do I know you?" I asked.

"You are Hennessy, aren't you?"

"Yeah, where do I know you from?"

"'It doesn't matter if you don't remember me, but I'm hurt."

This got me going for ages, how did he know my name?

It was doing my head in trying to remember him, until Chaz, who I was ashore with, said Hey, you pillock, have a look at your belt."

Did I feel like a bozo or what?

Stamped across my belt, in bright white paint was my name, where it has been since my first week in Raleigh.

Everyone must put their name on their belts, and every other bit of kit they are issued with.

We were all red, me from embarrassment, everyone else from laughing.

Freeport gave me my first experience with Americans.

Wherever they are, and a Royal Navy Warship comes into port, there are loads of them, affectionately known as 'Grippo's', who want to take a sailor or two home for a meal, or out for the night.

There was a notice board with the names of hosts, and how many sailors they wanted to host.

Four of us volunteered for a couple in their sixties, who were putting on a BBQ. They picked us up, fed us, watered us, and brought us back to the ship.

What lovely people.

This happened almost everywhere. I don't know why, but it was genuinely appreciated.

Nassau was another port where we were anchored for the day, and a bunch of us went ashore. There is a local US naval base where we had some beer, pizza, and some beach games with the Yanks.

The wind blew up unexpectedly, and the Liberty Boats, the boats that take you to and from shore when the ship is at anchor and not alongside a dock), were unable to get alongside the ship safely, so the ship sailed without us, because it couldn't stay at anchor in rough weather as there was a risk of losing the anchor, and possibly running aground.

So, we just sipped our beer and waited for it to come back, which was about four hours later.

It was still quite choppy, especially in the small sea boat which picked us up. Two lads threw their hearts up on the way back to the ship, but we all made it, and every one of us was as sober as a judge after that short boat ride.

In the same weather, when I was working, I was sent to the galley to get a tray of eggs for the chef in the wardroom galley.

All cooks wear what are called 'steaming boots'. These are worn by cooks and mechanics because they were slip-proof, you could carry on with your work without fear of slipping or falling arse over tit. Stewards are not issued with these steaming boots, so must be more careful. Especially when collecting eggs from the galley in a force eight.

I managed to get to the tray of thirty eggs to the galley without incident, holding the tray on my flat right hand, whilst using the left to hold onto anything else.

For some reason, I grabbed hold of a handle, which happened to be the handle of a frying pan, as I did, the ship leaned to one side and kept leaning, as you can imagine, the frying pan wasn't much use in keeping me steady.

It joined me sliding across the galley from one side to the other, frying pan in one hand and eggs in the other. As the ship stopped leaning to port, it began leaning to starboard, I went straight onto my arse, sliding slowly to a halt against a cooker. I still had the frying pan in one hand and the unbroken eggs in the other.

I was chuffed to bits, smiling from ear to ear. As a mate helped me to my feet I was saying "Bloody hell, did you see that? Not one egg broken."

I turned to show everyone the tray of unbroken eggs, not considering I was not wearing non-skid boots. My legs flew from under me, the eggs went everywhere. Not one survived.

Hero to zero, in one slip.

This brings me nicely to seasickness and Karma, which I mentioned earlier.

The following day the weather worsened, quite a few hands were either in bed or in the heads suffering from seasickness. It never affected me, so when I saw Chaz kneeling with his head in the toilet I couldn't resist laughing and taking the piss.

Karma was to call.

The following day, at about the same time, in the same heads, was me, doing the same thing as Chaz the day before. And where was he, yep, in the same place as I was yesterday. It was his turn to laugh his socks off.

I never took the piss out of anyone after that, and I have never been seasick since.

During the rough weather, the ship sprung a leak. Not a good thing to happen, especially as we were so close to the Bermuda Triangle.

As it turned out, it was not as bad as it sounded, the leek was above the water line. It was where the four-and-a-half-inch gun had been replaced by an IKARA missile system at the front of the ship, the welding job wasn't up to scratch and, as the sea broke over the bows, it came through the badly welded area. We were quite safe but needed to take turns mopping the compartments until the weather calmed and repairs could be made.

As the bad weather disappeared, we were called to the aid of a banana boat which had a fire in the engine room. We sent a fire party over to get the fire under control, and once we got the banana boat close enough, we could use our fire hoses to drench the boat's upper decks, preventing the fire from spreading.

A few hours later the job was done, and the ship's company received a couple of quid in salvage money from that incident. Although it was a few years later.

I think I bought a Mars bar with my share.

Our arrival in Fort Lauderdale was quite impressive, especially for a sprog who had never been before.

When we entered the harbour, we were at, what is called 'Procedure Alpha', which means everyone, except those on watch, were lining the upper deck in their No1 uniform. There was a band on the dockside, and loads of public, including a lot of Grippo's.

Those who were lucky enough went straight ashore, and right into the arms of the enthusiastic Grippos. Some of us were on duty, but the Stewards and Cooks were allowed ashore after their duty watch.

There was a cocktail party for the Officers to entertain and socialise with the local dignitaries, as is the case in most ports.

This one is worth mentioning because one of the SAs, (Stores Accountants), Mike, was helping us out by washing glasses.

He got a taste for Horses Neck, which is Brandy and Ginger. It was being served from a litre water jug. Mike acquired such a taste for it, that before the cocktail party was over, he sat alone, drinking straight from one of the jugs. He was in plain sight of the officers and guests, so a cover-up was impossible.

He got done. He was lucky not to have had time. He got away with a big fine and fourteen days of No9s.

He never helped again, and the PO and Leading Hands were lucky not to have been busted for allowing Mick to help himself.

That is the danger when you are a 'superior officer', if you are aware, or present, during an illegal act by someone else you are first to get 'done'.

I didn't realise it at the time, but they were very lucky guys.

I should say, it is one thing going ashore and returning onboard drunk, which is on the lower scale of drunkenness, but then you have 'being drunk onboard', which is a more serious crime, and you could easily be demoted, or sent to DQs. The worst is 'being drunk on duty', then you can say goodbye to any rank you have and expect to do time in DQs.

We had a small dinner party to serve.

One of the Officers invited a family of Americans onboard for the evening. They are always impressed with us 'servants', and the Officers love to use us in this situation. But the Americans were nice people and, at the end of the evening, the father, as he turned out to be, told me to get the staff ready on the gangway at noon the next day.

He was to take us to his home for a BBQ. We were there at twelve on the dot when a big open-top Cadillac, or some other big American car, took the four of us to their modest home, one, with a driveway, pool, a choice of bathing suits, and a BBQ with the biggest steaks and prawns I had seen.

They invited some teenage family members to keep us entertained, who ended up taking us around town later in the evening. It was their 'Spring Break', so the streets and hotels were teeming with college students who, as part of an annual ritual, stay at Fort Lauderdale for two weeks in the spring. We had a great time, and it didn't cost us a penny.

Love those Yanks. They love the 'common' sailor and usually have no time for the Officers who, in those days, and for hundreds of years before, were always public-school boys and spoke with the most annoying 'posh' accent.

Some officers worked themselves up through the ranks, these were called SD Officers (Special Duties Officers). They were very rarely promoted higher than Lieutenant Commander though and were considered second-class citizens by most of the Wardroom, but there was much more respect for them from the ship's companies.

In recent years, it has been my joy to listen to Senior Officers on the TV who are speaking with regional accents. It makes me think of all the talent which was wasted over the years because they never went to public school or spoke like a normal person. That's the arrogance of the 'class system'.

During a day at a beach hotel, at the poolside bar, a man of about thirty started talking to us, we were in uniform of course. He turned out to be a Captain in the US Army who recently returned from Vietnam.

He did not go into any detail, but from what he said we knew it wasn't a picnic. With every bottle of beer, he toasted a friend who never returned. Not in a bragging, loud sort of way, but in a quiet thoughtful way.

And there were a lot of beers drunk that day.

He was a nice bloke and wanted to know all about us.

We told him what we did, and he couldn't understand why Naval Officers needed stewards, saying if his Army had the same, they would never be able to eat anything, because they wouldn't know what had been put in their food.

I must admit, though I never done it myself, I have witnessed some arsehole officers eating some disgusting things. I always tell my kids, "Never upset anyone who has access to anything you put in your mouth."

On our way back onboard one night, Trev, a cook, and I had a few bevvies, but not many Dollars left in our pockets.

A car stopped, and a man asked if we needed a lift, we thanked him and got in. I must stop at my place on the way he said, then made a detour. I was getting a bit worried, but Trev, a lot older than me, was chatty and having a laugh with our 'friend', who invited us into his house.

Trev accepted straight away. As soon as we went into his house it was obvious he had ulterior motives. There were pictures and ornaments around the house which could only be in a gay man's home.

I was shitting myself. I had never been in a situation like this before. I had never even met a gay man. I was making up all the excuses to leave and get back on board. I was duty tomorrow, felt ill etc. etc. Eventually Trev said we had better go. It was nearing 2359, so I had to be onboard anyway. Little did I know Trev had been in this situation before, knew exactly what was going on and took full advantage of the free booze, cigarettes, cash, and other trinkets lying around. Apparently, this happens sometimes.

"It's an occupational hazard", Trev said.

I also went on a trip to Disney World in Orlando.

As I was only sixteen, just a kid, this was a perfect day out for me. I had a fantastic time, as did all the sailors with me… of all ages.

The same goes for the visit to the Kennedy Space Centre, what a place. We went into the huge building where the rockets were assembled and saw the giant platform which moved the rocket to the launch pad, and some previously used capsules.

What a great day out.

I should point out, that between ports we were working, and the ship was taking part in exercises and trials for the new Ikara anti-submarine missiles.

On top of the drills and exercises, we had many trials people onboard, and they were victualed in the Wardroom, so that was extra work for the cooks and stewards, but it was OK.

Time seemed to go faster when you were busy, and we only worked during the day, whereas most other branches kept watches throughout the day and night.

The next stop was Baltimore.

This was another great visit, the same attention from the Americans, and we were invited to go and see the Baltimore Orioles Baseball team play.

We were led to our seats and given a bag of 'goodies', including baseball caps, baseballs, magazines and such. Unfortunately, it was wasted on us, we had no idea what was going on, and after about half an hour, we snuck away.

But the thought was there.

The next day I went on a bus tour of Washington. This was my favourite sightseeing destination.

We saw everything we had seen on TV and in the Movies. The White House, Pentagon, Washington Monument, Arlington Cemetery, the Kennedy graves, the Lincoln and the Jefferson Memorials.

It was an experience and a very cultured, sensible visit.

I took some great photographs and wish I had taken as much interest in the other places I visited during my career, but as I was growing up my priorities were more focused on fun, far less on culture.

Bermuda was another experience.

The highlight of that visit was hiring a moped, which is the done thing whilst you are there. I went sightseeing with Chaz and came back in one piece.

Others, however, would go on a pub crawl or a 'pub ride' and the MA (Medical Assistant) onboard was very busy with the amount of road and gravel burns there were.

When many of the bikers got to the dockside some of them saw it as another tradition not to return their moped to the rental office, but to put it on full throttle and watch it fly into the bay.

Yes, that common animal, 'The Idiot', is in all walks of life, more so in the Royal Navy.

Not long before we visited Bermuda, the Governor and his dog were murdered in his mansion grounds.

I'm not sure if the murderer was caught, or the reasons behind it, but we didn't let it affect our visit, it would take more than a sniper on the loose to do that.

You are probably pleased I managed to stay out of trouble and stick to my 'junior' status leave expiry time of 2359.

But I did say the least I could do was not get caught.

Each time someone goes ashore they must put their 'Station Card' in a little alphabetical box, so the Quartermaster (QM) and Bosun's mate (The seaman who looks after the gangway), can see who is onboard and who is ashore.

If you are an Officer or Senior Rate, then you get a pegging in and outboard, just put a peg in the right hole, 'Onboard' or 'Ashore'.

We needed to take care of our little station cards, and mine came with a big chunk cut off the corner. This was to highlight that I was a junior. So, if I didn't put the card in the box, they would think I was on board.

Easy?

No.

I had to get back onboard without anybody noticing, and as everyone knew everyone on a small ship, I had to take some drastic measures.

The gangways were always on the Flight Deck at the back of the ship. As the ship had ropes tying us up alongside, and they were at the front and back of the ship, the only thing for me to do was climb the ropes.

Not as easy as it sounds, but I became quite good at it. Although it wasn't an everyday occurrence, just on special occasions.

Again, as a dumb ass 'sprog', I had no idea of the consequences of this at the time, the main one being if there was a fire onboard, when they mustered the crew, they would think I was missing onboard and not ashore, because my card would not be in the box, all because I wanted some extra time ashore.

The fire party would then be obliged to look for me, putting themselves at risk. Time after time I kept proving to myself how stupid I was.

I had the experience of my first helicopter flight.

This was great, sitting next to the pilot in the ship's Wasp chopper, a bit hairy as well, the flight deck looked so small, and you wonder how the hell are we going to land on that? But all was well, and I enjoyed every minute of it.

There was also a submarine accompanying us on the trip.

They were carrying out an emergency surface. We were told it was going to happen on the starboard side, we waited for about ten minutes, not knowing what to expect, when suddenly, the sub broke the surface. It looked as if it was going to take off.

It was a hell of a sight.

My first deployment was almost over, but I still had another tradition to experience. 'Up Channel Night'.

This was the final night of a deployment when we would enter the English Channel for the last leg of the trip. For the lads onboard it was a celebration, a party night, which entailed saving beer from throughout the trip just for this night.

As we were only (officially) allowed three cans of beer per day, per man, (well, for those old enough to drink) Everyone would have a can or two from their ration stored secretly, somewhere.

It was illegal, but everyone knew it was done, cans were stowed behind false bulkheads and deck heads, and anywhere where it would not be found during rounds, or if there was a brief inspection.

After a few months, there was a fair bit of illicit beer around the ship. Everyone knew it went on, so there were the usual warnings from the captain to the crew, via the First Lieutenant and Master at Arms. All sorts of threats were mentioned for anyone who caused trouble or rocked the boat, so to speak.

I later understood the dread the Master at Arms felt, because it was, he who would be typing the charge sheets, taking statements and formulating reports, and potentially there could be quite a few legal implications for everyone onboard for allowing a drink-infused incident.

It has happened over the years, and always ends up with a Court Marshal, and headlines in the tabloids, with a few careers going down the Swannie.

But usually, there was no trouble. As expected, there was a lot of beer drunk, and a lot of sea shanties (ditties) sung.

I never experienced much trouble during 'Channel Nights', but they always happened, even when arriving back from the Falklands Conflict, which, of course, was something to celebrate.

Channel Nights are the grand finale of any deployment, and the longer the deployment, the better the Channel Night.

Nothing stops naval tradition.

All in all, a good first trip for me. How many kids at home now could say they had done what I had done, and seen what I had seen, all before the age of seventeen?

It was Christmas 1973.

I was on duty over the Christmas period, which turned out to be a great move.

Although it would have been nice to be home with the family for Christmas and New Year, being onboard is such a cushy number. As a Steward, you only had one Officer to look after. You needed to be there for his meals, and that was it. He would usually do his own thing in the evening, so plenty of time off. The Duty chef and I had a whale of a time.

On New Year's Eve, it was tradition to have the youngest onboard to ring the midnight bell. As I was the youngest, I had the privilege. It was explained to me it only was to be eight bells, and the QM instructed me thus...

"Two sharp rings, 'ding-ding', and no more than eight, OK?"

"OK," said I.

We had all been in the mess having a few beers before this, so I was well-oiled, so to speak when the time came.

I got the nod from the Officer of the Day (OOD), and away I went, ding-ding, ding-ding, ding-ding, ding-ding, ding-ding, ding... the bell rope was snatched from my hand. Apparently, a ding-ding is two bells, not one, obvious to everyone on the planet except me on that night.

Oops.

I did have the opportunity to go home for Christmas for three, days but there was no point because I would never get back in time.

Jeff, 'S' and Gareth had other ideas. They decided to pick me up in Plymouth and then deliver me back to Plymouth the day after Boxing Day night. I didn't have to leave too early because of the Sunday rail timetable. They were the best mates ever. They stayed for a pint in Plymouth, along with grabbing some fish and chips, before driving back.

Mick Timms was one of the Leading Stewards.

He was getting married in London and invited a bunch of us to attend. I had never been invited to a wedding before, so this was exciting stuff for me. Mick was a bit of a smoothy and so vain it was untrue. Hair, nails, and tan immaculate. He was the sort of bloke who would get right up my snoring organ in future years.

Anyway, we stayed at the Union Jack Club in the centre of London, which was specifically for serving and ex-armed forces. It was a bit of a 'cesspit' in those days, but now it is a nice place to stay. All we wanted was a bed for the night, so it served the purpose.

I can't remember where the wedding was, but it was a tube ride away. We downed a few beers beforehand and then went to the ceremony which, thankfully, was short and sweet, then onto the reception.

We were all in uniform and loved the attention. But Mick invited an Admiral Pope to the wedding, who he had worked for previously, and the man turned up, which put us on our best behaviour, at least for the first couple of beers. By the time the Admiral left we didn't give a toss whether he was there or not.

But it was a good wedding. We had a great time, and everyone behaved. But some of us were drunker than we thought. I don't remember leaving the wedding but remember waking up on a tube train with Jock McHale.

We stopped at a station, and I felt ill, so I got out of the carriage. Jock was looking through the window as I bent over to throw up. As I did, my cap fell off and landed on the floor in front of me.

I threw up in it. I looked up to see Jock laughing his head off as he and the train pulled away. I had no idea where I was, or which direction to go. I didn't have the common sense to wait for the next train, so I just walked until I thought I was close enough to afford a taxi.

Pure guesswork. I could have been going in the opposite direction for all I knew. Funny enough this worked, and I was back at the cesspit after a ten-minute ride, without my cap.

What a wedding that was.

Back onboard, looking forward to the next trip away, and not a care in the world.

I got called to the Master at Arms (MAA) office one Thursday morning.

He said, "Get your kit packed. You are going on draft tomorrow."

I was gutted.

I loved being on that ship and would have quite happily stayed on it indefinitely. Little did I know the MAA, or Leading Regulator (L Reg), was supposed to call me to the office weeks beforehand to tell me and have me sign the Draft Order. I had no idea I was due to leave and was, quite frankly, a bit pissed off.

Not that it made any difference. You don't point mistakes out to the Regulating Staff, and I didn't know any better anyway. I simply did what I was ordered to do.

I had heard about HMS Royal Arthur, a shore base in Wiltshire. Other Stewards told me it was a good draft, so I applied for it and that is where I was being sent. HMS Royal Arthur, Corsham, Wiltshire. Nowhere near the sea and a distinct lack of ships.

I didn't go straight to Royal Arthur. I needed to get off the Leander and get my leave in.

Everyone should join a new ship or establishment having used all their leave due. New bosses get a bit peeved when they must send someone on leave when they are needed.

Anyway, I got most of it in, and whilst on leave I went back to the ship for a day while it was in Portland. The lads sneaked me onboard to get some kip after a night out, before going on my way in the morning. It was the leaving do I didn't have time for before because of my quick departure. It was worth going back for.

HMS Leander

HMS ROYAL ARTHUR

1974- Aged 17

Royal Arthur is a Leadership School in Wiltshire.

It is where you are sent when you have been promoted to Leading Hand, or before you are promoted to Chief Petty Officer. I say promoted, but in the RN only Officers get promoted, NCOs get advanced until they are promoted to Warrant Officer, or as it was in those days, Fleet Chief Petty Officer.

I was still to work in the Wardroom, but it was a small quiet Wardroom with a good atmosphere. Again, everyone got on well and, having just come off a ship, I had some credibility at last.

Within hours of joining Royal Arthur, I was playing inter-departmental football for the S&S department. This was to become typical of the attitude within the camp.

The work was easy, and every break we had was spent in the restroom drinking tea and learning to play the card games you play in the Navy, such as Crib, Nominations, and Sergeant Major.

The NAAFI was well attended, and the civilian barmaids were nice but old. They knew everyone. The local town was Corsham. It was a couple of miles away. There were many other establishments around the area, all RAF and Army, and someone quite wisely built a nightclub in the middle, Flamingo's, or as it was more affectionately known, 'Flamin Jo's'.

As it happened, we did not use the nightclub much. We went to town on weekends and the odd mid-weeknight. The NAAFI bar was good, and we became regulars at the local bars when we did go ashore.

The accommodation was great.

It consisted of the usual long barrack-room-type buildings, but they were divided up into double cabins. If you were lucky, and most of us were, you had a cabin to yourself. Wow.

By this time, I was not a junior anymore. I was well into my seventeenth year. Well, three months into it. My leave now expired at 0100, but no one cared about that here.

This is a place where I was at my fittest.

The Leadership courses played sports every day, between four and six in the afternoon, as this time was the Dog Watches.

As they were held within the watch-keeping cycle, they were called the 'Dog Watch Games', and consisted of football, volleyball, and deck hockey.

Deck hockey was played in the gym using hooked sticks and hard pucks like they use in ice hockey. Steaming boots (non-slip galley boots) were used because they didn't slip, and they protected your ankles. The Ships Company provided two teams. After a while, I became captain of the junior team. As we, both teams, played every day we always hammered the course teams. I also played rugby for Royal Arthur, so I found it a great life.

Every so often we would have a big social evening in the main, huge gym. There were bars and a disco and or live music, along with busloads of girls from the local towns, Bath, and Chippenham. Between these events we would hold smaller ones in the ship's company NAAFI bar, they were well-organised, and great fun.

Part of the Leadership course was to spend a weekend orienteering in the Black Mountains. One weekend was organised for the ship's company to have a go and see what it was like. We had a short bus ride to the Base Camp in the Black Mountains, in Southeast Wales.

The camp was basic, with lots of bunks, dirty mattresses, and a galley. We were split up into our teams, and on the first night, we were shown the first point we had to climb, (using a map and compass,) which was a hell of a haul. We went back to the camp to get some sleep before an early start.

So, at four am, we began our hike.

We found the first point, no problem, as we were only there the night before of course. But I'm afraid a couple of hours of map reading doesn't go very far when you are on top of these mountains, freezing cold, and wet through. We carried on until about ten a.m. when Dinger said he thought he had a blister. That was it, we had an injured person with us, time to go down into the valley and make our way back to Base Camp, hoping that Dinger's blister would get a lot worse before we had to explain why we cut the walk short.

As it happens, going down the mountain was just as hard on his blister. When we got into the valley, a farmhouse we saw from above wasn't a farmhouse at all. It turned out to be a pub, and we desperately needed a rest and ingest some fluids. Only for medicinal purposes of course. This was the perfect spot we thought.

At 15:00hrs, a Land Rover arrived. It became clear it was expected at least one team would end up in the pub. We were playing darts when we noticed the Chief watching us from the doorway.

Silence. Until he said, "One for the road then."

Phew.

This was just a bit of fun for the ship's company. As long as we were accounted for, and not lost in the Black Mountains, everyone was happy. It would be a different story if we were on a course.

Careers relied on these courses, which needed to be completed before promotion, and any pending promotion would be put on hold until the course was passed.

A delay in promotion had a knock-on effect on other promotions and, of course, there was the extra money that came with a higher rank.

We had one for the road and returned to the Base camp, where we were volunteered to cook the meal for the returning teams.

I was a chef at last.

It was my second introduction to 'Pot Mess'.

I had it on the Leander when we were at Action Stations and exercised 'Action Messing'. Pot Mess and bread are delicious. All Pot Mess is, is everything and anything the galley has to hand. The best consists of whatever tinned food there is, beans, tomatoes, potatoes, peas, carrots (water and all), meat, and any leftovers from breakfast, a bit of stock or stock cubes if required. It thickens itself as it cooks, and that is it.

I even did it at home for the family in later years. Nothing is exempt if you can eat it, just throw it in.

After walking for over twenty miles in a day, a hot pot mess is what everyone appreciates, and they did, along with copious amounts of tea and coffee.

After supper and a shower, anyone who could walk went to the pub for a game of darts and a laugh. Unfortunately, not many teams wanted to stay up that late, so they went to bed early, but my team, for some reason, was ready for it.

It was a lot of fun, and if all the teams ended up in the valley in a pub, it wouldn't have been a big deal anyway. Some people were a bit pissed off they didn't do that, and some enjoyed the walk and the experience. Some of them were to do it for real in the not-too-distant future, as part of their promotion routine. I'm glad we had a chance when we did, and to have done it just for a bit of fun.

When you are based in a shore establishment you are allowed to buy 300 duty-free cigarettes per month, per person. These cigarettes were made for the Royal Navy and called RN. There was a blue line across the packet and a narrow blue line down each cigarette. They were nicknamed… 'Blue Liners'.

They were a strong smoke. It is rumoured they were made from the tobacco sweeping off the factory floor. Since I joined the Navy all my friends had been smokers. I wasn't. I'd experimented before I joined up but didn't like it. Since being in the Mob, and having all your mates smoking, I felt obliged to smoke as well and tried everything. Menthol, Cigars, Pipes, but I couldn't get the hang of it and was disappointed that I didn't like it.

The few of us who didn't, or couldn't smoke, used them as thank-you gifts or gave them to friends or family, which was illegal. You could expect a hefty punishment for doing this, or for smuggling more than your allotted twenty-five per night allowance, out of the establishment.

An Officer who lived in South Wales sometimes gave me a lift as far as Cardiff, where I hitched, or caught a bus, the rest of the way home.

He never asked for payment, like a donation towards his petrol, but one day, as I got out of the car, I said there was a thank-you gift on the back seat. When he saw the three hundred cigarettes, he went white.

"Oh shit," he said, seeing himself on a Court Martial.

I laughed, not thinking this Officer could easily have dropped me in the shit for doing it, but he never gave them back.

All he said was, "Thank you, but don't bother with gifts again."

I would quite happily spend my entire naval career at Royal Arthur. I enjoyed every minute of it, to the extent that once my grandmother phoned the Regulating Office (Police Office), she told them my mother had not heard from me for quite a while, and she was wondering if I was OK, and did I remember the way home?

I did try after that, even though there wasn't enough money for socialising and going home.

Dad helped when I told him I wanted to buy a motorbike, as this would get me home more often and would be cheaper in the long run. He lent me eighty quid, which was a fortune back then.

A mate had a bike, and he tried to show me how to ride it. It was one of those things I just couldn't do. My coordination was non-existent, and I couldn't ride more than a few yards without falling off or forgetting to break. It just wasn't going to happen. So, the bike-buying plan was binned.

I was seventeen years old, with eighty quid burning a hole in my pocket. A pint of lager was only around twenty-five pence at the time, and there wasn't much else for me to spend all that money on, well there was, but it wasn't as much fun.

I wanted to give it back to Dad, but it was too much of a temptation. I stretched it out for as long as I could. I could afford to go home more often. I even hitch-hiked to save money. Hitch-hiking was easy then.

Just hang your sailor's cap over your weekend bag. You always got a lift. The ease of this went out of the window as the IRA became more active on the mainland, and wearing your uniform was not allowed in public, nor was anything which could identify you as military.

Friends knew I was worth a couple of quid because of my dad's money, so I became an easy touch for a loan, but I always got it back.

That is except for one 'friend' who was trying to drag it out until I went on draft, which was, by this time, soon. I mentioned to a good mate, Jan, a three-badge killick chef, that I was still owed money. He was a biker and looked the part, long hair, well long for the navy, scraggly beard, broken nose, and tattoos. He was another one who seemed more like a bully until you got to know him.

Anyway, he had a quiet 'word' with this 'mate' of mine, and although I didn't get the money (because he didn't have it) Jan persuaded him to give me his watch instead, which was a good one, worth more than what he owed me, and I had it for years. Needless to say, he was never loaned anything from anyone who knew about his reluctance to repay.

So, the draft I mentioned was imminent.

There were two ships I was praying I wouldn't get, that was HMS Blake or HMS Tiger. Sister ships, which were the oldest and ugliest in the fleet... Sods law... I got drafted to Tiger.

I couldn't wait... Not.

It was tough and very sad leaving Royal Arthur. I didn't want to go, but you go where and when you are sent.

I had a great leaving piss up, and then I heard my draft was delayed and I would be joining Tiger in Cyprus, a week later. So, another leaving piss-up was called for, which I duly had.

As I said, I would have happily spent my whole career at Royal Arthur. I had a great time and made great friends.

I was to return on two occasions.

The first was as an RPO carrying out random searches with my drug dogs which I was to handle, and again in 2013, when the old place had been closed for nearly twenty years, and everything had become overgrown and covered in graffiti.

A very sad sight. It was surreal strolling around the places I used to walk through daily. Even standing in the now barely recognisable club brought back some happy memories. I hope it never turns into another housing estate because I would love to have another walk around the old place, but I know it is inevitable and soon it will be gone forever.

The following year I did go back to take some photographs, but the inevitable had already happened, it had been flattened, and old age housing was being built on the site.

The gatehouse was still there occupied by a security guard who told me I wasn't the first to be disappointed, as several other 'old boys' had turned up wanting to relive old memories.

HMS TIGER

1975-78 - Aged 17 – 21

It was the weekend I was en route to Tiger. I needed to be at RAF Brize Norton by Sunday night.

I arrived in plenty of time.

Being the shy, retiring person I am, I ate supper and went to my room, after a pint in the bar. In the bar, I met a couple of lads who were booked on the same flight. They were also joining the Tiger, and stewards, Mick Gritt, and Robbie Robins. I should have realised what was to come when in the morning both looked like death, after getting rat arsed in the bar. As it turns out, Mick was to become one of my best and oldest friends, while Robbie became a bit of a dick head.

I am still in contact with Mick now, but when he left the Tiger, he was drafted to HMS Heron, a Naval Air Station in Cornwall.

Mick was promoted to Leading Steward.

Now promotion and authority never meant a thing to Mick. They were things way down his list of priorities, so it wasn't a surprise when I heard he got pissed at an Officer's function he was supposed to be serving at but spent most of his time chatting to the guests.

His Chief was not amused, ordered him out of the Wardroom, and told him if he got his head down, he would not 'troop' him in the morning. Well, Mick lived ashore, so had nowhere to sleep, but a friend offered him his cabin for the night. Mick knew where his cabin was, and he was led there by his mate who let him in and locked the door. Being locked in wound Mick up so much that he decided to get out and resume where he left off in the Wardroom. He opened the window and slipped out.

The last time he went to his mate's cabin it was on the ground floor, since then he had moved into a cabin on the first floor. Mick broke an ankle, was trooped, and was demoted to Steward. Not a good day for him, but he didn't give a dam.

That was Mick.

The Tiger was a big ship with four Sea King helicopters on the back, housed in a huge hangar, which was the eyesore of the ship. It was originally a Cruiser with six-inch and four-inch guns forward and aft.

The aft guns were removed, being replaced with the flight deck and hanger. It was an old ship, but well looked after. She was based in Portsmouth, so this was the start of my Portsmouth connection, which lasted until I left the mob twenty-two years later.

We. That's me, Mick, and Robbie, who were directed to our mess when we arrived onboard. There were about forty men in the mess, which had a bathroom with two showers and three sinks, a luxury unique to the Tiger and her sister ship Blake.

They were also called the 'night heads' because, in the middle of the night, it was a two-day camel hike to the nearest toilet, so we used the showers.

The other stewards seemed OK, but there was one who always created an atmosphere when he was in the mess. Jim Dodds, a huge Glaswegian who was an Acting Local Leading Steward. This is a temporary rate which could be revoked at any time. His leadership skills were based on intimidation and bullying, and like all bullies, he had his little band of followers, and there was a big divide in the mess. It did not feel good. The first real bad feeling I'd come across since joining the RN. I soon realised which side of the divide I wanted to be on.

It was not Jim's.

The ship was on its way home to Portsmouth, with just Malta, and Gibraltar visits to go.

A few of us went ashore in Malta, as you would expect. I hadn't been to Malta before but the place to visit was 'The Gut'.

The Gut is a narrow street in the centre of Valletta, the street's real name was 'Straight Street'. I have no idea why it was called 'The Gut' by sailors.

There were bars on each side of the street, full of women whose sole purpose was to get you to buy as many 'Sticky Greens' as possible. A 'Sticky Green' is a drink bars serve the girls. It is sickly sweet, sticky and, well, green. There is no alcohol in a sticky green, and the girls earn a commission on each drink a sailor buys them. The girls would do anything, and I mean anything, to keep encouraging someone to buy a drink.

Often that encouraging activity was carried out under the tablecloths.

The local wine in Malta is called Marzovin. It is cheap. It tasted cheap. But after a couple of glasses, it became somehow palatable. I don't know how much of this I drank but I felt OK. I returned onboard without a problem and was almost required to be a cell sentry, as one of our lads needed babysitting after returning onboard paralytic, but as I was on duty the following day, so I was let off.

The Mazovin took effect when I was asleep because I had the mother of all hangovers when I woke.

I was sick, had a banging headache, sweating, you name it, I was suffering from it. It was the worst hangover I have ever had, and I have never had one like it since.

I learned one of the great lessons whilst growing up in the RN. Don't get pissed on something you know nothing about.

Malta had a huge connection with the RN, there was a Naval base there, and local men had been recruited for years to serve in the RN, there were some on board the Tiger.

The Maltese were usually stewards or cooks, and the PO in charge of my watch was Joe Ferugia, a lovely man who was constantly walked over by the lads, because he had little or no leadership skills, but everyone loved him.

The Killicks would take charge and give him the credit for a good job well done. This was not because we loved the man, it was quite selfish. We maximised our time off because we ran the watch, and no one was any the wiser. Joe, in turn, got loads of time off in his hometown of Valletta. Even the Chief was happy because everything was running smoothly.

Everyone won.

Gibraltar was uneventful; the little British 'Rock' is renowned as the last watering hole before hitting the home port after a deployment. There are more bars on this three-square-mile piece of land than anywhere else, and we must have hit most of them.

There are also (usually) more arrests in Gibraltar than in the other ports put together. The Police wear British uniforms and drive British cars, but English is their second language.

All Gibraltarians call themselves British because they benefit more from being British than Spanish. However, there is a blatant dislike towards British servicemen, and this was never more evident than through the actions of the Gibraltar Police.

It is well known many Gibraltarian car owners can get a re-spray, or money for repairs if they accuse someone, normally a visiting sailor, of damaging their car. Visiting sailors because they will sign anything rather than be kept behind when their ship sails, for a court case. Especially as they would need to pay for their transport back to the ship.

So, compensation is always on the agenda. Any unaware sailor could be arrested for leaning against or staggering into a car, and the list of damage from the owner is always forthcoming. And like all other ships, we had our share of accused sailors.

There were some very nice-looking motors in Gibraltar after the Tiger visit. All at our expense.

Gib to me, at this time, was just an island full of bars and only good for getting pissed. I had no way of knowing that one day I would live on 'The Rock' for two years, and then I would see it in a completely different light.

Generally, working in the Wardroom was easy, but in the mornings, as usual, you had cabins to clean which was the pits. After a couple of months, I asked for and got a job change to the bar, which was a lot better but required working unsociable hours.

When the food stewards finished the bar steward's work began. It was something I needed to learn but I didn't want to do it for long.

It had its perks though.

The odd bottle would disappear and find itself in the mess for a special occasion. In fact, at one time I had five different spirits in my locker. A stupid thing to do, because when we had Captain's Rounds, the Fleet MAA, who accompanies the captain on his rounds, always tried random locker drawers to make sure we had locked them.

I always left my locker open, and once during rounds, the FMAA tried to open the lockers on each side of mine. Thankfully, he gave mine a miss. I then started keeping the bottles under a bunk. I was on the top bunk, so couldn't keep them under mine, so it had to be the bottom bunk belonging to a nice quiet lad, Benny Goodman.

Well, he was nice and quiet until he found out I was stashing the booze under his bunk, he went uncharacteristically ballistic. He had a point I suppose. So, we had a cocktail party in the mess to get rid of the booze. Benny wasn't too unhappy with that. He never said no to a few drinks.

The good news was everyone, but Jim and his cronies had a good laugh. Thankfully the Jim Dodds era didn't last too long. In the first couple of months, Robbie was to take his PPE for Leading Steward. This is a Pre-Promotion Exam, which he passed and was duly promoted. Now Jim, for some reason, could never pass his PPE and was duly reverted to steward to make room for Robbie.

Jim never accepted Robbie as his supervisor, who was, quite rightly, getting in the habit of telling Jim what to do.

Robbie went a little too far on one occasion, which resulted in him getting a right hook from Jim, and flying through the service hatch which connected the Wardroom to the Pantry. From thence forward, the hatch was to be known as 'Robbie's Hatch'.

Jim could and should have had time for that, but it was hushed up the way departments usually try to hush things up to keep it in-house. But there was good news. Jim was soon drafted to a shore establishment in Scotland.

The atmosphere changed overnight.

It wasn't long after Jim was in the News of the World after hitting an Officer on a Minesweeper. The officer was also in the habit of telling him what to do. It is said Jim took offence at being told to clean up some drunken Officer's piss stains in the Wardroom. I don't know what happened to him, but I imagine he did time and got kicked out.

Jim's 'Cronies' were very quiet after he left, and soon left for some 'shore time'. I extended onboard for twelve months, and life became a soap opera.

3L2 mess, HMS Tiger, was now a pleasure to be in.

We were on a tour of the UK.

We had a day at Falmouth when everyone had to be back onboard by 20:00. So, we went ashore at 12, noon and stayed there. You tend to drink more, and quicker when time is limited. It was an interesting day. We caused a fight between two lesbian lovers when the pretty one of the two fancied 'Alfie' Bass, who was a moron, but a good-looking moron.

We went for a swim to the floating platform just off the beach. I was knackered when we got back to the beach, and Mick Gritt thought it was funny to put his foot on my head as the waves kept coming in. He then bragged that he saved my life - because he took his foot off my head.

It wasn't just our group who were having issues. Many were sent back to the ship by the Police for all sorts of reasons and, after we sailed, we were informed that we were banned from Falmouth.

Not just 'us', our little group of run ashore buddies, but the entire ship's company. They banned the whole bloody ship. They must have had a total sense of humour failure.

I visited Falmouth twice after that, on different ships, the latest being in 1991 and they were still talking about HMS Tiger then.

What an impression we left.

Then we stopped at Liverpool, where a run ashore with Mick Gritt nearly turned nasty.

We were in a floating nightclub, an old barge or something, and got talking to this scouser with the most horrendous broken nose. We were looking at it all the time when he was talking, and I suppose, as he was this big ugly giant with a nose that was practically at right angles to his head, we looked very meek and intimidated.

He could see this and said to us, "Listen you two, you shouldn't be worried about me because I've got this nose," he said, "You should be worried about the bastard who gave it to me".

Good point, well put, I thought, but it didn't change a thing he was still this big ugly giant with a broken nose who, thankfully, turned out to be quite harmless, to us, anyway.

We left the nightclub, hyped up by the booze and the violent stories the scouser was impressing us with, when along a dockside road we saw a couple arguing, well it looked as though the woman was getting a bit of a clout.

I went to a small building site just to our right, as Mick, standing about twenty yards away from them, shouted at the bloke to leave her alone.

"Who the fuck do you think you are?" came the reply.

At this point, I found what I was looking for, and came out of the building site with a short four-foot scaffolding pole tapping it on the tarmac. This was it; we were going to save the girl from a beating from her boyfriend, or husband, and be the heroes of the night.

Nah., she started throwing stones at us, swearing, and telling us to mind our own fucking business.

The bloke just let her get on with it.

Me and Mick looked at each other and shrugged. I threw the pole away and we did exactly what the 'lady' told us to do... Fucked Off.

On my watch, there was a Petty Officer in Charge (George,) a Leading Hand, and about six stewards. We all got on great, we knew where we stood with the Killick and PO and generally had a good laugh with them, but you couldn't get too familiar, especially when there were others around.

They say familiarity breeds contempt, and it does. You needed to appreciate they were 'superior officers', and to be contemptuous, or insubordinate, would damage their reputation and credibility if they let it get out of hand, so there was always that respect. It's one creates offers a better working atmosphere. Let's face it, if one of the stewards screws up it would ultimately be the PO who took the rap for losing control.

So, one day in Liverpool, our PO, George, got us all together and informed us we would be working at an officer's private function for a few hours on one of our days off because he had volunteered us to do so.

Evidently, the officer wasn't a bad bloke, and he was doing him a favour. Bearing in mind we were entitled to charge a fee for private functions, we were not too pleased.

George was a good bloke and knew we would all do it, but it didn't stop him from getting some stick from us. Bugger contempt and insubordination.

I said to George, "George, if I called you a twat, I would be in serious trouble, wouldn't I?"

"Damn right," he said.

"But if I thought it, it would be ok?"

"You can think anything you like, Taff," said George with a smile.

"Well, I think you are a twat," I said, to roars of laughter.

Thankfully George saw the funny side, and after throwing a few knives and forks at me, we all did as we were told, as usual.

For some unknown reason, I began calling Mick, Churchill, or Winnie. It started to catch on. I can't remember why, or what happened for it to start, it's not like he was fat and smoked cigars.

One day, after a couple of weeks of being an ex-prime Minister, Mick got around to asking me why I called him Churchill, and right off the top of my head, without thinking about it I made a connection.

I said "Come on Mick, can't you see it? Churchill = Winston. Winston = Winnie. Winnie = Winnie the Pooh. Pooh = Shit. Shit, Gritt, get it?"

I was quite proud of my speed of thought. It never happened before, never happened again.

Coincidentally, my youngest daughter, Emily started calling me Churchill. I thought it was because I had charisma, was a natural leader of men, quick-witted, intelligent, and the sort of person who could be called upon to lead the country at a time of war.

NO.

It was because she thought I looked like Churchill the dog. The one featured in the Insurance adverts.

Nicknames seem compulsory in the forces, particularly in the Royal Navy. It's very unusual for someone not to have one.

There are the usual regional nicknames like Scouse, Jock, Taff, Brum Geordie etc. Then there are the historical names which may come from someone famous if your surname matches, like 'Benny' Goodman, 'Bomber' Harris, 'Harry' Worth, 'Brigham' Young etc. and then there were names which, for whatever reason, automatically go with certain surnames like. 'Smudge' Smith, 'Bungy' Edwards, 'Nobby' Clark, 'Buck' Taylor, 'Topsy' Turner, 'Daisy' Adams, and many more. And there are names which were simply made up. If someone was a Cohen, then he would be christened Manny even if he was a Catholic. The surname of Kerr or Carr would, unfortunately, be 'Wan'. Doon, would be 'Ben', see what I mean, very few people are known by their real names.

Things got crazier on the Tiger with the wonderful group of characters we had onboard. Every day was like an episode of a soap opera.

We called at Rosyth in Scotland, a Naval Dockyard. Taking a run ashore to Dunfermline for a night, where were offered a lift from a guy we met in a pub, (Déjà vous).

There were about seven of us, but he had a van, so we went for it. It was only a florist's van, wasn't it? The final giveaway that this bloke was bent, was when he got in the back of the van with six of us, leaving 'Flory' Floyd in the front to drive. I had just turned eighteen, and this was still a nerve-racking experience. But some of the older lads took it in their stride, and when this bloke said he needed to stop at his shop for a minute, they were all for it.

We staggered into his shop. Someone put the kettle on, another, Mac, put this very nice camera around his neck.

"I was just going to buy a new camera,'" he said. The bloke, in his fifties, was laughing as well. He came onto one of the lads, can't remember which one, but for his efforts, the flower man was laid out. I should say we were not happy with this, and the guilty party got a clip himself later.

The man was put into the 'Prone Position' so he wouldn't choke, but we expected he was playing dead until we left. Before we left, we helped ourselves to a few bunches of flowers. I don't know why, and his van was left in one piece... about a mile from the dockyard.

I was shitting myself because of what was done. The older lads had no such worries.

There was no way this bloke was going to call the police and tell them he had invited seven young sailors around to his shop without telling them his motives and revealing he was gay. They were right. Nothing was ever heard about the incident.

Trev must have been right... It was an occupational hazard.

On the same night, on the way through the dockyard, I did one of the stupidest things I have ever done (besides getting married). Throughout the dockyard, there are many pylons holding flood lights, to which there is a ladder right to the top.

Two of us raced to the top. A pylon each, up we went.

As we got to the top, an MOD police car turned up and the officer asked the other five lads what they were doing hanging around the dockyard with bunches of flowers. They said nothing about us. Just mumbled some crap and wandered off.

I must have sobered up by then, because I realised what I had done, and then knowing I had to get back down from this bloody platform. I was a shivering wreck. Somehow, we both made it down safely. Thank God.

But I can't pass a pylon to this day without smelling roses.

We caught up with the lads and went onboard with the flowers. We thought they would brighten up the mess.

Mick hadn't come with us that night because he was on duty. He was fast asleep when we got back to the mess that night. He couldn't believe his eyes when he woke in the morning. There were Dafs, Tulips, and Roses everywhere. They were hanging off overheads, in his bunk, some were in the mug of water he had beside his bunk. What a night that was. The mess never smelled so good.

Things were great on board; I loved every minute of it. I had great friends.

It was just the job that spoiled a perfect life.

Although I didn't want to leave the ship, I wanted to leave the job and applied for a change of branch, to Stores Accountant. To show my keenness, I spent some of my time in the department to learn the ropes. But this was forgotten, brushed under the carpet. I was getting annoyed I might leave the Navy because I couldn't do this job for another twenty years, no matter how easy it was, or how quick the promotions. It was not a job I was proud of, and the older and wiser I became the more I hated it.

I was becoming annoyed that I joined as a steward because I could never delete it from my history. I needed to think of something to get me out of the branch.

In later years, when asked what I used to be before becoming a Regulator, I would say, "Sorry I don't talk about my past," as a bit of a joke, but as soon as you say that people would say "Aah, a steward were you?"

In the meantime, there was the 'Brewery Run'.

An invitation from the Tenants Brewery in Edinburgh for a group of us to have a tour of the brewery, followed by some hospitality in their bar.

This was to be the first and last time I went to a brewery.

The tour lasted about fifteen minutes, and the hospitality around four hours. We all poured ourselves into the bus to get back onboard for a shower, before going ashore again with the lads who never made the brewery.

Who was I trying to kid?

I woke up at three in the morning, still wearing my No1 uniform, wondering where the gorilla was. The gorilla is always blamed for breaking into your room, house, or mess, throwing all your clothes around and shitting in your mouth.

On this occasion, I could only blame him for shitting in my mouth, as I was still wearing the same clothes, I went ashore in.

Happy days.

One of the funniest things I saw was by a lad called Gerry, he was only about twenty but didn't have a tooth in his head.

He was from Yorkshire and had a broad accent to match. He was a quiet lad and a bit of a loner, He had 'found God', so he was also very boring.

One night, when he was having a couple of beers, he was becoming quite an extrovert, he got his guitar and was playing and singing, and generally having a good time with the rest of us. Then, out of the blue, and totally out of character, when things were becoming quiet, he went to his locker, put on his flat cap, and took his false teeth out. He then sat in the middle of the mess square and sucked on his gums, saying, for no apparent reason, in his broad Yorkshire accent…

"When I was a lad as big as me dad, and me dinner all covered in gravy, I said to me dad I must have been mad to join the fucking navy,"

Not funny?

It was hilarious, but I suppose it was one of those times when you must be there to appreciate it.

There were another couple of verses, but that first one has stuck in my head all this time.

It was always nice to get back to our home port of Portsmouth.

We knew the pubs well and, after a skin full, we usually ended up in one of the two nightclubs the Naval community used. The best, or worst, depending on how you looked at it was 'The Bistro Club', referred to as 'Beasties'. It was an absolute dive in every respect, you had to keep moving or your feet would stick to the carpet.

The other, 'Johanna's' wasn't much better, a little cleaner but still a dive. There was a plastic palm tree in the centre of the seating area. It was usually surrounded by a mist because lads would rather have a piss around the tree than go to the toilets so, as you can imagine, it began to stink after a few gallons of the Navy's best urine.

We also like the local Indian and Chinese Restaurants and Takeaways. My favourite takeaway was the Chinese. They did the best spareribs and BBQ sauce in the world, and they had loads of bags of prawn crackers hanging on the walls and shelves.

We didn't know what they were at the time, so we used to order the spareribs and ask for a bag of 'Them,' pointing at the prawn crackers, to dip in the sauce. If someone took orders in the mess for a takeaway it was always spareribs and a bag of 'Them', or a chop suey and a bag of 'Them'. That's what everyone called them, 'Them'.

The ship was asked to make a dream come true for a young boy who had written to 'Jim'll Fix it', a TV show, hosted by Jimmy Saville.

The boy was asking for a ride in a helicopter. The lad came onboard with a camera crew and minders, and we, the stewards, won the job of keeping them fed and watered.

As a reward, a group of us were invited to London to see the show being recorded. A good day out, and we went backstage to meet Jimmy Saville himself. (Which is now something you do not brag about). I always thought he was a bit creepy when I saw him on TV, and nothing changed those thoughts when I saw him in person.

We had a couple of hours to get ripped off in Soho.

In uniform, and in a strip club, we ordered one drink each and they were only half pints. Each half pint cost almost a fiver. In today's money that is a fortune, back then it was a mortgage.

We made a noise, saying we weren't going to pay that much. But when the 'heavies' turned up, who were used to these disputes, they said pay up and they will let us walk out unaided.

Pay up we did.

On another occasion, we were invited to go to a recording of 'Top of the Pops.' I think 'Black Lace' was the only band we had heard of the rest were videos, and a couple of Americans singing things like 'Honey, I miss you', or something like that anyway.

We were herded from one end of the studio to the other, all to give the impression of a larger audience. One of the lads, a stoker from another department, asked Noel Edmonds (The DJ) a question about a character on his morning radio show on Radio 1. Noel wasn't very nice to him, waved him away, and said, "Shut up and dance."

The stoker had to be held back, he was going to blat Noel. When we heard what Noel said we all wanted to 'blat' him.

We all left early after that, and that was the last of the invitations to TV land. We didn't bother with Soho again.

We 'popped' across to Europe, paying a visit to Malmo, where I experienced my first and last 'Live show'. It was amazing really, especially when one of the girls got one of our crew up for some fun. Unfortunately, he wasn't having that much fun and couldn't live 'up' to the girl's expectations. She was merciless. Her little finger was being waved to everyone.

I don't think he ever lived that down.

Then onto Kiel, via the Kiel canal.

Nice place, but not a lot to do except the usual. Unfortunately, one of the electricians overindulged with alcohol. He fell between the ship and the dock and wasn't seen again. Very sad.

On occasions like this, it is traditional to sell the deceased man's kit in an auction onboard. This can raise a lot of money for family and next of kin. The auction lasts for ages because everyone keeps putting the items of the kit back to be re-auctioned. In the end, the family gets all his kit as well as the money raised.

I missed a 'belter' in Hull. I was going home for Easter early because I was on duty over the festive period.

Remember, I said that was the best thing to do over Christmas. It's like having two leave periods. Although it's always nice to be home, it was getting to the stage where all my mates were working, and some had regular girlfriends.

I wasn't ready for that yet I'm afraid, but it was only a matter of time before I got a 'normal life'.

There was a great crowd in the mess, and we always had fun whatever we were doing, even when we went ashore when things were really quiet, we found ways to have a giggle.

One time that springs to mind was when five of us were sitting in the Park Tavern in Portsmouth. It was dire, dead. We were sitting quietly, deep in thought when Pete Scott offered me a cigarette and said "Cigretski?"

"What?"

"'Cigretski, It's Russian," he said. God knows what deep thoughts he was having.

Anyway, we laughed, and then the five of us couldn't stop laughing as we invented our own 'Russian language', which was any word ending in ski, ov, or ic.

Here are a few words from the English to Russian Crap dictionary:

Helloski	= Hello
Bollokovski	= Rubbish, or telling off
Dicov Headovic	= Idiot (Dick Head)
Pissovski	= Go Away
Fokovski	= Go Away

Tosserbolokov = W*&k*r

To name but a few.

Summer leave came quickly, and seven of us decided to hire a canal boat for a week. I don't know who suggested it, but it sounded like a good idea.

There was me, Mick, Flory Floyd, the appropriate adult, Jonah, a mistake because he had the smelliest feet in the world, Walter Scott, who was a good friend and a great laugh, and lastly, and very least, Sid Scott.

I think Flory felt sorry for him, and they had a bit of history like joining up together or something like that, he wouldn't have been asked to come by anyone else.

We were in Portsmouth Harbour station, waiting for a train and having a few beers. There were quite a few in the buffet and we were having a good laugh with everyone. We owned holiday T-shirts, ones we made especially for the canal boat trip. They were to be a sort of 'uniform'.

For some reason, Jonah gave his T-shirt to the son of a couple we were talking with. I gave mine to one girl of a bunch of girls, and someone else gave theirs away. All the T-shirts were disposed of before we even got on the train, what a waste of money and a good uniform. We had such a laugh in the station buffet we put it onto our pub crawl route a few times, but it was never the same.

We caught a train to Birmingham, then caught a fast black (taxi) to the canal marina, where we were given a twenty-minute instruction on important things, like how to drive the boat, and how to empty the toilet.

Then we were flying solo.

It took us two hours to go a mile, steering by rudder is not the easiest thing to do, you go from one side of the canal to the other, and it seems impossible to go straight. It took a while, but, eventually, a few of us became pretty good at it.

It turned out to be a fantastic holiday. Stopping outside any pub we fancied, staying the night before moving on in the morning. It was through design that every time it rained it was Sid Scott's turn to steer. Sid was obviously bullied at school, and it carried on, in a nice way, whilst he was on the Tiger.

This story sums up Sid.

Six of us went ashore to Old Portsmouth, a nice area of Portsmouth where we normally behave ourselves. We were buying rounds, and it needed to be pointed out to Sid that it was his round. He knew what we drank (all the same I think).

As he got up to get them in, he said "I'm having a Pie, does anyone else want one?"

Bloody hell, good one Sid, we all put our hands up, he must have come into some money. Sid came back with a tray of six pies, dished them out, and sat down to eat his. We all looked around to see who was bringing the pints.

"Where's the beer, Sid?".

"I didn't get any beer. You all said you wanted a pie instead."

We looked at each other, and as if a mental message was sent to everyone at the same time, we

picked up our pies and threw them at him.

That's Sid for you.

Sid went to steer in his southwester, whilst the rest of us had a cuppa and a game of cards. Thirty minutes into the game, Sid came and sat down, watching us play cards. What's wrong with this picture?

We all knew, but couldn't figure out what was wrong until Mick asked, "Who's driving, Sid?"

"I don't know, don't care. I've had enough of steering on my own in the rain."

As he finished speaking, we were thrown off our seats as the boat hit the embankment. We were very good to Sid, he was clearly not happy with the situation, and we didn't want to make things worse by doing something like throwing him in the canal. So, we talked, agreed on some compromises and promises, and made sure everyone was happy with the way things were going to be from now on.

That night, after a few beers, we threw Sid into the canal.

Mick was always the first to get the beer out and usually got pissed first, but he kept drinking. He was well-oiled when we were coming up to a lock. I pulled into the bank, letting Mick off, to go and operate the lock. He needed help giving the bows a push-off from the bank. He used his hands instead of pushing with a foot, forgetting to let go. Watching him stretch out with his feet on the bank and hands on the boat was so funny. The inevitable happened, with a loud cheer and round of applause from us, and everyone who was watching. When he got out of the water he continued to operate the lock, what a hero.

The canal boat was the best holiday I had. At our age, it didn't get better than being away together, having a good drink when we wanted, and having loads of laughs.

After the canal boat holiday, we went our separate ways for the remainder of our leave. But were soon back on board in Portsmouth. I have never been in many jobs where I have looked forward to going back to work, but it was as exciting as looking forward to going on leave in the first place. I didn't realise it then, but I was a fortunate lad, and in a position not many people often find themselves, ever.

One of the funniest things I saw, was on a quiet Sunday afternoon in the Park Tavern, Portsmouth. Me, Mick, and Florey sat in silence facing the bar, there was just us and one bloke at the bar, when this couple walked in, dressed to the nines, with long overcoats, shiny shoes, and jewellery. The man swaggered in as if he were the local Mafia and the woman called and waved to the bloke at the bar. "Darling, I haven't seen you for ages, what have you been doing with yourself?" They both loved themselves dearly.

He sauntered to the bar, looking around 'Casing the joint', as she continued her chat with her friend, her back to her boyfriend, 'The Don' (get it? ... Mafia... never mind).

Now, her hair was like the 'Beehive' style from the 60s, combed up and out like a big stick of candy floss. The hubby, still looking around cooly, nodded to the barman as he ordered their drinks. As he did, he smoothly opened his cigarettes and put one in the corner of his mouth, flicking open his Zippo lighter, flicking it a second time to light the wick.

He then turned around, so he was facing towards the back of his Mrs. Her hair must have been saturated with hairspray, because her hair caught fire, the flames almost hitting the ceiling.

The Don started patting her beehive, trying to put the flames out. At this moment she had no what was happening, and was knocking his hands away, telling him to bugger off... until she smelt her hair burning, and the heat must have hit her.

For a Mafia Don, his attitude changed immediately. He turned into an apologetic whimpering wimp. She ran out (not on fire now, by the way) pushing him away, and yelling for him to "fuck off, you stupid bastard."

It is funny how a little flame can change attitude and language so much.

We, like the three monkeys, watching were mesmerized. We never uttered a word, just looked at each other and took a sip of our beers. We were soon in stitches though, once we realised what we had just witnessed.

Larry Parry (his real name) was getting married in Canterbury, in Kent. Some of us were invited.

What a great weekend.

Me and Mick teamed up with Larry's mates and had a fantastic time, a laugh a minute, and the same with pints. Everyone enjoyed each other's company and sense of humour. But little did we know that Simon Solari's wife, who was also invited, was taking notes. When she and Simon got married a few months later, Mick and I were left off the list because she thought we would be inappropriate guests. We had a good laugh and took no offence, probably because we agreed with her.

But Larry's wedding was a great day, and we did not spoil it. He and his wife loved us being there and we got on great with her father, which Larry was happy with, of course.

Angie, Larry's wife, was a lovely girl but not the brightest of buttons. They seemed a lovely couple, which they were at the time, but years later, after bumping into him on the Forces Reunited website, he explained that it didn't work out. They divorced and settled down with new partners, as many of us did after marrying too early and for the wrong reasons.

Larry was the focus of one incident which happened in The Bistro Club, Southsea, one evening.

As usual, we had been in town most of the night, ending up in the club. No one seemed overly drunk, just 'happy', no arguments or disputes, simply a bunch of mates together having fun.

Then suddenly Larry swung his glass at 'Walter' Scott, (canal boat), a good mate and very popular, another one of the mess comedians. The glass sliced a chunk out of his chin. The Police, and then the RN Provost were called. Larry was arrested and investigated by the RN SIB (Special Investigation Branch).

We were interviewed as witnesses, and all said the same. We had no idea why Larry did it.

Larry went through the trial procedure. He was lucky just to get a suspended sentence, and that was mainly because Walter appeared as a witness for Larry, and his statement was considered.

This was a strange incident because even Larry didn't know why he had done that, but he always regretted it and was quite embarrassed if it was mentioned.

Simon went on to work on the Royal Yacht.

He was offered a job by Prince Charles, which Mrs Solari must have loved. The last I heard of Simon was when I read in the News of the World that one of Prince Charles's staff, (Simon), left his wife after having an affair with a woman staff member. I emphasize a 'woman staff member' because you never know with the Royals, do you?

Whilst Simon was on the yacht, we met in Portsmouth, and he invited me on for a drink. It was a floating Palace.

But the most impressive 'item' was in the crew bar.

It was only brought out on special occasions and then shown only to people who could be trusted.

It was (supposedly) one of the Queen's turds, Freeze-dried.

It looked like a fossil. Ostensibly acquired years before, by one of the plumbers who had nothing better to do. It was mounted on a plinth under a glass dome.

Very tastefully done.

I'm still not sure if it was real.

Tiger was put into a dry dock for a refit.

We were to paint anything which needed painting and refurbish whatever needed refurbishing.

I thought this would be a good opportunity to get off the ship for a while, so I volunteered to be temporarily drafted to a career's office.

The maximum time I could go was three months. I was sent to the Cardiff Careers Office.

This is where it all began.

There was only one of the Staff who was there when I joined up. He was a Royal Marine Warrant Officer. He remembered me. It was a good break as all I did was address envelopes and be a 'Gofer', go for anything.

My time in the Careers Office passed quickly. I spent the first month at Cardiff, the second at Merthyr Tydfil, and then back to Cardiff for the third month.

One time at Cardiff, it was the time of year when the Navy had loads of promotional stuff like beer mats, playing cards, pens etc. to be distributed as the staff saw fit.

There was a Submariners Association in Pontypridd, at the Criterion pub. I know the pub. A school friend's grandfather used to run it. Anyway, I was given the afternoon off and told to drop two bags of 'goodies' off at the pub.

I went in, dressed in uniform, and was going to leave the bags with the barman, but he insisted I wait for the landlord so I could give them directly to him.

The landlord arrived and he took me into the back bar. There were submariners' photographs all over the walls. He pulled me a pint, and we were chatting about the wars when another ex-submariner came in, then another. Soon the rum was broken out for 'Splice the Main Brace', the term used when the ship's company were given their daily ration of rum.

The tradition finished the year before I joined, but it is still done on special occasions. We must have had eight to ten tots. It was time for me to go home, and go home I did and, without a word to my mam and dad, I went straight to bed.

The staff in the career's office knew exactly what was going to happen to me, and they were surprised I made it to work the following morning.

It was time to go back to the Tiger in refit.

Before I left Cardiff, the Officer in Charge, and a couple of the Chiefs, took me out for a pint. What a great surprise that turned out to be.

The Officer, I can't remember his name, was a member of the Cardiff Rugby Football Club, so we went there for a couple of pints.

As a Pontypridd boy at heart, and a lifelong Pontypridd Rugby Club supporter, arch enemies of Cardiff, this didn't impress me. But when we got inside it didn't matter which rugby club you supported, because half the Welsh Rugby team were there, JPR, Gareth Edwards, Phil Bennett, the Davies's, the Pontypool Front Row etc. That was a hell of a leaving surprise. Unfortunately, they weren't there to see me off. It was just coincidental I'm afraid, but it was nice anyway.

Christmas on the Tiger was a laid-back affair, very easy and cushy with no major dramas.

In the New Year, it was suggested I attend HMS Dolphin, in March, where there was to be a PPE for Leading Steward. The preliminary Professional Exam (PPE) is what you need to pass before going onto promotional courses. As soon as you pass the PPE, if you have the appropriate NAMET score, you can be promoted, if there is a vacancy.

I don't know where this came from. There is no way I was giving the impression I liked being a steward or wanted to make a career out of it. But when thinking about it, if by some fluke I passed the exam and became a Leading Hand, it would be a huge pay rise for me. I could put up with it for that.

But first I had to do something about my NAMET score, or it would be a waste of my time. Remember my NAMET was 4-9, I needed a 4-5 before I could get promoted. So, I started learning maths with Florey Floyd, and a couple of others in the mess.

I was learning more from them than I would have if I attended the classes. So, come the time of the exams, I asked the Education Officer if I could sit them. He wasn't happy I hadn't attended any classes, but as I saw him every day and handled his food, he let me take the exams.

Four weeks later, when the results were in, I knocked on his door to get the results, for curiosity's sake rather than the excitement of passing. When he saw me, he gave a wry, I told you so, smile and an "Aaah, Hennessy."

I knew I had failed and was waiting for the old "I told you to attend the classes" lecture. His face dropped when he looked at my score. He then looked at me in amazement and said, "You've got a 4-5." That was good enough for me.

Result.

So, come March, the three of us went to HMS Dolphin, where the PPE orals were held. HMS Dolphin was a submarine base in Gosport, within Portsmouth harbour. There was no significance the PPE was being held there; it could have been anywhere.

There were about ten of us. I was the fourth to go in. After a couple of hours of waiting, I found myself sitting in front of a Supply Officer, a Fleet Chief Steward, and a Chief Steward. They spent forty minutes asking me questions like sketching and describing the working parts of a plate, and what meat would you eat with mint sauce… A little exaggeration, but you know what I mean. What are the contents of a Russian Salad was another, I recall. There were also some questions regarding bar work, cocktails, and the bar books we would be using, of which there were about six, numbered 1823 to 1828 inclusive. *(All books and logs are known by their numbers in the RN).* Also, my favourite (not), is napkin folding.

On completion it was, "Thank you very much, we will let you know."

So, it was back to work and forget about it. Four weeks later I was called into the Chief's Office and told I passed my PPE. I wasn't doing cartwheels or anything, it was the money I wanted, not the 'Prestige' of being a 'Leading Steward', because there wasn't any, but the pay rise was significant and very handy.

Thank you very much.

Easter came around and, as usual, I worked over the Easter period and took late leave.

When I returned there was a banner across the mess door saying, 'Congratulations Leading Steward Hennessy'.

Shock.

My first promotion and I was not a badge man yet. I was only nineteen years old, and my initial thought was of another pay rise, the biggest a naval rating would get at one time, and then I thought this is when things get serious.

Now I need to start taking charge of people, and more worrying was I now had to start taking responsibility, not only for my actions but for those whom I supervise.

Then I thought... get the beers in... let's go ashore... let's get 'bladdered'.

I'll get serious tomorrow.

I also found a good friend from HMS Osprey who was now in the mess, Frank Flemming. The funniest man I have known. Whatever the conversation he has you laughing, even the faces he pulled were hilarious. On top of that, good news, I was given a job change to the pantry, which means no more dressing up and serving the 'grunters' (Officers) their meals. I was now in charge of the washing up, and the food which was passed through 'Robbie's Hatch' to the stewards inside.

I worked in a T-shirt and working trousers.

What a day.

I needed to go through the usual formalities before I became a 'Leader'. I had to request to be advanced to Leading Steward, hopefully, get recommended by my Divisional Officer, and go to the Captain's Table for him to promote me.

Captain's Tables are not only for Trials and punishments, but also for good things like promotions, and medal awards, even where some complaints are heard. I completed these steps and was issued my Leading Hand badge, which is a single anchor.

I dutifully stitched them onto my uniform and started my new job.

The new job suited me down to the ground.

No more direct contact with the 'grunters'. I was in the position, if I wanted to, being able to 'doctor' the food of the wasters in the Wardroom, the ones who didn't know how to treat people correctly.

I must admit I made some weird sandwiches for this type of Officer, but I never put any bodily fluids in them. I left that for someone else. With that in mind, my best advice to my kids is "Always be nice to people who have access to anything you put in your mouth."

I know I have said it before, but you can't say it enough times, and it teaches them to be polite and respectful.

I had two deployments on the Tiger, the first was to the West Indies, and then down to Brazil. This was an experience.

One of the 'runs' which was memorable was Barbados - Nelson Street, the Red-Light District of the Island, which doesn't need any explanation.

Me, Mick, and Pete Scott (not to be mixed up with Sid Scott) were going from bar to bar when we came across Jonah, and Ben, another two of our lot.

Johnah was sitting on the curb with his head in his hands.

"'What's up Jonah?"

He explained he had negotiated a deal with one of the girls in a bar. It was, that if he paid for two shags, he could have one for free (and you thought Tesco's thought of that?)

"Bargain, Jonah. So, what up?"

"I've had the two shags I paid for, but I can't get it up for the free one. I'm gutted." He was inconsolable.

"Go and ask her for a credit note, or give the free one to Ben," I jokingly suggested.

"'God, yes," he said, "great idea." And off he went.

I saw him the following day and he had a black eye. It seems the lady didn't give credit, and the offer was not transferable.

We spent a couple of days in Puerto Rico, at the US Naval Base, 'Roosevelt Roads'. It was not far from San Juan. We were in a bar where there were a lot of US servicemen, there were about eight or nine of us, and we had downed a few beers, believe it or not.

Now, an old Naval tradition is, sometimes, to make a spectacle of yourself. One of our favourites was when we left a bar, to do as the Seven Dwarfs, it doesn't matter how many of you there are.

When you are ready to leave someone stands up and sings 'Hi Hoooo'. Then someone else stands up and sings the same, this is done five or six times in a row, and while each is singing, everyone gathers at the same place in the bar and slowly gets down on their knees, walking/marching out on your knees singing "Hi ho, hi ho, it's off to work we go, with a shovel and a pick and a walking stick, hi ho, hi ho, hi ho, hi ho…" This is repeated over and over, at the same time we are marching on our knees in a line, arms swinging and bent at the elbow, smiling and waving at everyone as we go.

Well, the Yanks loved this.

They got up and applauded. Not only that, but they started joining in, I mean on their knees behind us, it was like a dwarf conga. There must have been thirty in the line.

The next bar was a couple of doors away thank God. We normally get up when we get outside a bar, but this time we couldn't, not with all the Yanks following us in the line, so we carried on. Our knees were knackered.

That was it for the night then, at every pub we visited we did the dwarf exit. Soon the Yanks were doing it on their own. In the end, we just let them get on with it.

The funny thing is, at the enlisted men's club on the base the following night they were all into it. It got a bit boring then, and we were pissed off coz it was 'our thing' not theirs.

We had a good sulk.

We got to hear about some darts players in one of the hotels giving exhibitions. Alan Glazier and Leighton Reese were the famous ones of the era. Leighton Reese was from Pontypridd; he'd recently won the World Championship.

I remember my father saying he knew him from the Workmen's Club and Horse Racing trips. Also, my brother, who was a bit of a darts player, had been beaten by him a few times, and played against him in the local 'Super League'.

I told the lads in the mess about this. I don't think they believed me, so a trip to the hotel was organised. I was duty, so wouldn't get there until after everyone else, after I finished work.

When I arrived, the lads were talking to Leighton Reese and began pointing at me. I'm sure they expected me to be made out to be a liar. I introduced myself to Leighton, telling him about my dad and brother. Not only did Leighton confirm he knew them, but there were a few more people in Ponty we both knew. I still don't know whether he did know or remember my father and brother, or was humouring me, but he was a good sport anyway.

We had a great night, including a few games of darts, I invited them on board the following day, but they had a full programme so couldn't make it.

A tradition of the RN, in warmer climates, is to have a BBQ, Sports evening, or Sods Opera, on the Flight deck of a ship.

We had a Sods Opera, which is an amateur style 'sketch show'. Most messes create a comedy routine and perform in front of the crew on a makeshift stage. I wouldn't say there have been any major talent discoveries at Sods Operas, but they are very entertaining for the crew, and normally it gives them a chance to take the piss out of the Officers.

We also had a boxing competition, one which anyone could enter. There were a few good boxers onboard, one or two boxed for the Navy.

There were also some very bad ones.

The most entertaining bout was between two heavyweights. One was Jan, a seaman who had quite a few competitions under his belt, and another was a cook, Dickie. He had never boxed before but said he watched it on the Telly and thought he could do it, so wanted to have a go!

Round 1 - after a few seconds and a couple of 'wake up' jabs, which caught him by surprise, Dickie was worried and panicked, he started lifting his knee and pushing with his gloves to defend himself, as you would see a child do. Then he started kicking out with his foot.

The Ref shouted for him to put his leg down, Dickie turned his head, shouting back "It hurts", and as he did so, Jan put an end to his agony and laid him out.

The Doc was called to check on him and wake him up. He got a standing ovation from the crowd, and as Dickie didn't have a brain cell in his head, he thought it was for doing a good job.

Bless.

The next visit worth mentioning was Rio De Janeiro, for another nighttime, red light district, fun-packed visit.

But we did add some culture and visited 'Sugar Loaf Mountain', the statue of Christ the Redeemer on Mount Corcovado, which overlooked the Maracanã Football Stadium. At the time, the largest football stadium in the world.

Copacabana Beach and Ipanema Beach were the places to be during the day, for obvious reasons. But one of the most fulfilling things I did was to volunteer to help at an orphanage.

About twenty of us went to this little group of buildings, they were about a two-hour ride inside the jungle. We painted walls and woodwork, fixed furniture, and anything else which needed doing. It was a great experience.

The highlight of the visit to Rio was what the cook's mess did.

On the first night, some of the ship's company went looking for, and found, Ronnie Biggs, the Great Train Robber.

He was wanted by British authorities at the time. They spent the night on the piss with him and invited him on board for a visit the following day.

Ronnie did come on board.

Our Captain knew nothing about it until it was in the British Press when he was informed of it by London. According to the press but not confirmed, whilst he was on the ship, which is a little piece of British territory, anyone on board could have made a citizen's arrest. It was a bit of an embarrassment for our Captain and Government, but a bit of a laugh for the crew.

The cooks pleaded ignorance, and they denied any knowledge, but I know it to be the truth.

It was later confirmed, in 2008, by a friend who was the Leading Hand of the cook's mess, and who had retired from the Police force as a Sergeant.

It was he who invited Ronnie Biggs into the cook's mess.

At sea, we were to cross the equator.

It is a huge tradition to hold a 'Crossing the Line Ceremony', which will I go into again when speaking of my time on the Hermes, but this was my first time crossing the line, so, as a first-timer, I was stood in front of Neptune *(not the real one, just someone dressed as him)* who judged and ordered that I be given the most foul tasting medication, a concoction of god knows what, and then dunked in the pool provided.

For undergoing this treatment, I was given a certificate signed by Neptune *(not his real signature)* and an exemption from going through the same judgment again. It is purely tradition and a lot of fun. Every ship in the mob does this. I hope they will always continue to do so.

On our way home, we stopped briefly at Dakar in Senegal, West Africa, for refuelling. We let some of the locals on board to help us get rid of the garbage.

It was a twenty-minute job.

In return, they were given a meal. Our meal trays were moulded metal, pressed into three sections, one for holding a cup or bowl, say for soup, a main meal area, and a dessert section. These guys had no idea what they were eating, and they couldn't grasp the concept of what the different 'bowls' were for on the tray.

Their food, main course and dessert, ended up mixed in all the compartments. When it came to gravy and custard, which were in two big urns, the custard won every time. Every one of them covered the whole meal with custard. It must have been the bright colour which attracted them.

The Tiger took part in the Queens Silver Jubilee in 1977.

The ship, along with many others from our Navy, and other navies from around the world, lined up in the Solent, waiting for the Queen to sail past on the Royal Yacht.

It was a hell of a sight, with the ship's companies lining the decks of the ships and giving her the customary 'three cheers' as she passed. Just one part of a year of celebrations for the Queen.

She hosted a huge dinner in the hangar of the Ark Royal, where stewards from around the fleet helped serve the meal. About four were chosen from the Tiger.

I was gutted I wasn't one of them... was I hell; by this time, I was well and truly against the sea-going waiters. I gained no pleasure from serving some posh nosh to a hanger full of privileged people and their hangers-on.

In one of our locals, The City Arms, we became involved in a tasting trial for Pot Noodle.

This is one of my claims to fame.

They were very crafty, because they waited for us to down a few pints before feeding us, and everyone knows everything tastes better after a few pints. So, their survey was a little floored in that respect.

In the same pub, on another occasion, a film company was making a short alcohol educational film for the Royal Navy. They wanted a full bar, so they paid for the drinks for an hour or two whilst they filmed the two main actors.

It was stop, start all the time. Cut, action and all that luvvy crap. We were getting a little pissed off because 'for continuity reasons' they wanted us not to drink between 'takes', and to stay in the same position. I mean, they didn't want us to move our feet even.

We were right behind the two actors, and we decided we didn't like their rules, so, every time there was a 'cut' we would slowly, as not to be noticed, swap places and exchange drinks, anything to screw up their 'continuity'.

An amusing afternoon was had by all.

Next, we had a seven-month deployment to deal with.

I was going out with Kim at the time. As we hadn't been dating for long, I think it was fair to say it wasn't going to survive my seven months away.

We stopped writing to each other halfway through but resumed our relationship when I got home. We married and had three great kids.

But that's another story.

Before we went on deployment, a bunch of us were out in Southsea. We were in a Taxi on the way to the 'Himalaya' Indian Restaurant.

The driver asked, "Have you heard Elvis is dead?"

We thought he was telling a joke.

Frank said to the driver, "Go on then," as if to say, tell us the punch line.

But it was no joke. Elvis had died.

In the Indian restaurant, they played non-stop Elvis songs. We did the same the next day on board.

Sad days.

Our first stop was Gibraltar, known for drinking and not a lot else, as I mentioned previously. Well, that's what I thought until I lived there a few years later.

The pubs and the 'Rock Race' were the attractions. It's a bit of a ritual and you need to be fit to have a go. The rock is extremely steep, and the roads/pathways that wind their way up the Rock are long. Needless to say, quite a few of us went for the pub option, which has its own type of risk.

You must go up some quite steep roads to get to many of them, the music can be very loud, and you could end up in court for leaning against a parked car.

There is always a resident Regiment at Gibraltar, they have nice barracks and a club out of town. We were given an open invitation to use the club when we wanted.

We had a good night playing pool and darts on one occasion, but I was pissed off when my new tungsten darts disappeared. I demanded their return, telling everyone what a bunch of thieves they were. Not the right thing to do when you are outnumbered and a squirt of a bloke anyway.

They took pity on me and apologised. It didn't make any difference, I was off.

I left, giving all sorts of hand signs to our Army friends. The following day, just before popping ashore again, I found the darts in the breast pocket of my denim jacket.

Ah well, shit happens.

Istanbul next, before we transited the Suez Canal.

We were the first British warship to do so since the Suez crisis. It seemed strange that a huge ship was sailing in such a narrow channel with nothing but sand on each side.

There was also a nuclear submarine in our flotilla, but because it was nuclear, it was refused passage through the canal and needed to go the long way around, via South Africa. They earned their submariner's pay that month.

We allowed a traditional 'Gully Gully' man on board. Gully Gully men are Egyptian street magicians. This one entertained us on deck, while a few of his mates sold us the usual tourist crap.

We went on to stop at Jordan, where the king of Jordan came onboard to have a go in one of our helicopters.

Then Iran, where it took us half the night to find somewhere that sold beer, and then we had to find somewhere to drink it.

It was there we held a seven-a-side rugby competition. Me, and a chef friend, were reserves. We weren't in the rugby 'click,' so we spent the afternoon in the beer tent (beer supplied by the ship).

It was after this, that a group of us wannabe rugby players, started training in earnest. After the circuit training run by the PTIs every afternoon, we went into a little hot pipe space below our mess and did another half hour of training. It was a sweatbox. But it got us noticed, and although we still weren't in the 'in crowd', we did get a few games.

Karachi, Pakistan was next. The thing I remember was, as we sailed into the harbour, we could see a haze above the city... and then the smell hit us.

I didn't go ashore there.

Bombay wasn't much better, but I did go ashore.

I had a drink in a local hotel which wasn't bad, and then we went for a tour of the city in a rickshaw-type vehicle. It was a grim experience, with lots of poverty, and people going to the toilet on the side of the road.

What made an impression on me was when we went through a market area and saw a stall with a woman kneading a huge lump of what looked like dough. As she kneaded the dough you could see things crawling over it. She just kneaded whatever they were into the dough.

We didn't eat any of the street food.

In the evening, we asked a taxi driver where the best place was to go for a drink and entertainment.

"I will take you to 'Club 375'," he said.

So, six of us got into the taxi, and off we went. Strangely, we were leaving the city and heading for the suburbs.

We were about to tell him to stop and take us back to the city when he told us we were there. The street could have been any suburban street in most parts of the world. As we got out of the cab five women came out of No 375 to greet us. It was a private house with music, booze, and dancing.

It turned out to be a great night.

Onto Freemantle, Western Australia.

We were at sea for a couple of weeks, so now we were drinking powdered milk in everything. All we wanted was a pint of cold, fresh milk. That's about all there was, nothing much to liven up the evenings for a bunch of young sailors.

I think it was Freemantle when we held Divisions. We all dressed in our best tropical uniform. Divisions are a bit like a passing out parade but without the passing out. Unless it's too hot, then quite a few pass out, literally.

Anyway, the idea was to check everyone's best white uniform for topical use. I got mine laundered, but I didn't try it on until the last minute, when I did the jacket was about three sizes too big. By that time, I had no option but to wear it, so I came up with an idea... I can't believe I got away with it.

You see, on parade, you are inspected, firstly from the front, and then the inspecting Officer walks around and inspects you from the back.

When he was at the front, I was standing to attention pulling the excess material to the back, so it tightened at the front and looked pretty good. When the officer went around the back, I pulled the material to the front.

Job done.

The lads thought it was hilarious and were impressed I got away with it.

During the deployment, there was a darts and crib league between the messes. We became good friends with the lads in the cook's mess, which worked out to be very beneficial to us, because if we were short of beer or wanted more for a birthday or something like that, then the cook's mess always had beer to spare. They hid it behind wall panelling, as it was illegal to store beer.

We were issued three cans of beer per man, per day, and had to drink them that day, or they were taken off the next day's issue. But the cooks were good at amassing beer and selling it at a profit. We had many a good game's night against these lads.

Three of the cooks I knew well on the Tiger were later to lose their lives during the Falkland conflict onboard HMS Sheffield and Coventry.

There were quite a few cooks lost after ships were hit by Exocet Missiles, which caused the name of the missile to be changed by us to 'Exochef'.

They would have appreciated the humour.

Sydney was another matter.

We were a short distance from Kings Cross, the 'Soho' of Australia but with no rip-offs. None we noticed anyway. We were to be there for six weeks, over Christmas and New Year.

So, Me, Frank, Lee, Andy, Smudge, and Botty, yes Botty, took a week's local leave and stayed in a Bondi Beach Hotel for Christmas.

Botty, by the way, was what they call 'a bit of skin', a young lad who doesn't shave and has a face as smooth as a baby's arse. He had the piss taken out of him because he was the next best thing to a woman onboard an all-male ship.

This was a piss take, of course, in Nelson's Day they meant it, but here it was a bit of fun, and because of his young looks he was christened 'Botty'. We had a great week.

We went to a dinner at a posh place in Sydney where 'The Stylistics' were the entertainment. We saw the first showing of 'Star Wars' in a movie theatre on George Street. The best film ever made we thought at the time. This uncharacteristic 'normal' behaviour was balanced with visits to Kings Cross (Sydney's Soho) and quite a few all-night sessions.

One morning at the hotel, the cleaner knocked and opened our room door. She was about to say, "Good Morning," but changed it to, "Good God" when she smelled and saw the state of the room.

She promptly closed the door and disappeared.

The three of us embarrassingly shouted to her, all at once we chorused, "We'll do it" (the cleaning).

We did, and she received a good tip at the end of the week.

In Kings Cross, there was a show full of Transvestites, very funny, and the men were attractive I suppose. But one of the lads, 'Snowy' Winter, thought they were better than simply attractive. Before we sailed from Sydney, he went missing.

Word has it he deserted so he could be with one of these she-men. He was the only person I know who met Elvis Presley, he went backstage to meet him in his dressing room in Las Vegas, what a claim to fame.

By the way, he was never caught.

A bunch of us went to a friend of a friend's house which was close to where the ship was berthed, at Walamaloo. Now, what was a rather scruffy dockside is, I have been told, a yuppie area full of overpriced fancy houses and apartments.

Anyway, this friend's house belonged to a married couple, they were the hosts, lots of booze and food, and generally a good night. That is until the husband confronted one of the cooks who was with us, Johnno.

Johnno, come to think of it, disappeared for a while, and we were wondering where he went.

Hubby said, "You screwed my wife."

Oooooh shit, not a good thing to do Johnno, we all thought, and stood there staring, mouths agape, waiting to see what was to happen next.

"Now, what do you think I should do about that?" hubby asked, menacingly.

Now, Johnno deserves a medal for his nerve, calmness, and speed.

He said, "Well, why don't you piss off, so I can screw her again?"

As you can imagine, that was the end of the party. No blood was spilt, both men were kept from killing each other, and Johnno was quickly ushered out of the house. As a matter of fact, he was ushered out of the country and back onboard the ship.

Hong Kong saw me sober at 'Pinky's'.

Pinky's' is a famous, (*well, famous in naval circles*), tattooist. I was about to have eyes tattooed on my arse when I came to my senses. But it was an experience being in there. There were loads of sailors having tattoos on all parts of their bodies.

Do you remember what RN cigarettes were called and why?

They were called 'Blue Liners' because they had a thin blue line running along their length.

Well, I witnessed a blue line being tattooed along a man's penis.

His manhood was placed into a frame, a box-type contraption, to keep it straight whilst the buzzing needle set to work.

There was also someone having a butterfly put on his 'todger'.

Why?

What was wrong with these people?

Hong Kong was also where Taff Richards, Leading Steward, gave Mama San (Madam) some lip in her bar and was thrown out by her. He went arse over tit, ending up in the gutter with a gashed eye, which needed a couple of stitches.

I have no idea what was said, but she was a big girl and ugly as sin. I think Taff got a bit personal, so she did the same to him.

Things were good, but despite having a great time on board I knew it wasn't going to last and thought I should start thinking about my future.

I wasn't satisfied with my career path, so I developed a bit of a plan.

First, I put in my eighteen-month notice, which was everyone's right by this time; you no longer needed to buy yourself out of the contract.

I was called into my Divisional Officer's office to talk about it.

I told him I liked the Navy but couldn't keep doing the job I was doing. He asked me what I wanted to do. I told him I wanted to be a Regulator (Naval Policeman).

I'm not sure where that came from. I had thought about it on occasion but not to the extent of changing branches. Anyway, I said it aloud, so I was committed.

The DO arranged for me to spend time with the Regulators on board, and if I still wanted to change after spending some time with them, he would sign my request to change branch and rip up my eighteen-month notice.

The Fleet Master at Arms at this time had a bit of a reputation for being a nasty bastard. He was big mates with The Commander (Executive Office), who was king of the nasty bastards and who once stopped our beer ration, (three cans per day), over the Christmas period in Sydney.

It only lasted a week or so, because the NAAFI profits went down so much that he had to lift the ban. He was given the nickname of 'Beano', Be no beer, be no leave, be no fun, be no moral.

Anyway, the Fleet Master at Arms turned out to be helpful. He was keen to see my request forwarded for approval. I spent a lot of time in his office and was given things to learn for the course, should I be accepted.

Things happened quickly.

I volunteered to take charge of the Colours Party at sunrise and sunset. The Colours Party is a small platoon that marches around the flight deck, stands to attention, and salutes with rifles when the Ensign is raised at Sunrise, and lowered at Sunset.

I was the platoon leader giving the orders, I took this seriously. So that was it, that's what I wanted to do. My boss signed the request and the FMAA endorsed it.

It was now a case of sitting back and waiting.

But general life went on in the meantime.

Singapore was another memorable visit.

The Naval Base in 'Singers' is one where ships frequently visited. The main attraction in the city was Boogie Street. This is where everyone congregated for the midnight procession of Kathoey (Ladyboys), the 'She-Men' of Singapore.

What a sight, if you didn't know beforehand you would never tell they were men unless you get a good look at the Adam's apple (women don't have one).

They would spread themselves around the tables and chat with everyone, trying to get sailors to buy them drinks, and to tempt them away for a night of passion.

They were nice people... but not that nice.

There was a famous/infamous flat-roofed concrete block at one end of Boogie St. This block was the public toilet, the roof of which, on many a night, became the stage for drunken sailors to perform the 'Zulu Warrior' and 'The Dance of the flaming arseholes.

'Zulu Warrior' is a form of striptease executed in front of a crowd of sailors standing on the street below, who chanted the immortal words "'Haul 'em down, you Zulu Warrior, haul 'em down, you Zulu Chief, Chief, Chief, Chief. Alay Zumba, Zumba, Zumba, Zum," repeatedly, until the stripping sailors were naked.

'The Dance of the Flaming Arsholes' is slightly different.

Usually performed by two or more sailors, who would prance about the toilet roof, often to the same chant, but this dance saw the participants sport a rolled-up newspaper wedged between the cheeks of their arse, or sometimes inserted right into their recreation spaces. The said newspapers are set on fire. The dancers prance around until one of them bails out before getting third-degree burns to his backside.

The winner is usually rewarded by the spectators throwing the remains of any alcoholic beverage in their glasses over the performers.

This is intended to extinguish any still burning newspaper, although, on many an occasion, the odd double brandy, or other volatile liquid might be used.

It is one of those things you need to witness to fully appreciate. Remember, this strip is performed by two men in front of hundreds of other men, for no other reason but to show off...

They were real 'showmen'... Respect.

I got a call early one morning in Singapore, after a good long night out.

I was to play rugby for the group, (the 'Deployment' of ships we were with), which was quite an honour and a game I had to play, hangover and all.

Thinking about it, this is the only 'representative' match I played, and I must say, it was one of the best games I have played.

Because of the heat, most of us were substituted, so we only played a half each. I was glad to get off at half-time. I was dehydrated before we started due to the hangover, and the sweating I did for the forty minutes I was on the pitch was nobody's business.

At half time I must have drunk four litres of water and juice, which was provided for us at the game. Then I went around the back of the stand and threw up until the end of the game.

I asked for a little more notice if I was to play again.

We visited the world-famous 'Raffles Hotel' to sample the world-famous cocktail, 'Singapore Sling'. It was nice but expensive. I thought it tasted like a soft drink.

There were peanuts everywhere, bowls of them on all the tables, the shells scattered over the floor. This is something else Raffles is known for.

I revisited Raffles thirty-five years later. The cocktail was still overpriced, still tasted like a soft drink, and peanut shells were still covering the floor the floor.

I received the shocking news that my request to change branches to Regulator had been approved, and a course was allocated for me. I honestly didn't expect to get onto the course. I was as excited as I was shocked. Now I may have to work for a living, so I must tone down the partying.

Manila followed, with much the same sort of bars, women, and booze. It was extremely humid, but nothing to write home about.

Now and then the ship needed to be re-supplied. This was by two Royal Fleet Auxiliary (RFA) ships which followed us everywhere. One for fuel and one for stores, food liquids etc. This was undertaken at sea and is called Replenishment at Sea (RAS).

This was always a pre-empt to a week of partying for our mess because the NAAFI beer store, was through a hatch in the middle of our mess, so all the beer had to pass through our mess and our lockers.

There were always two or three of our lads in the line when the crates of beer were passed along, and now and then an odd crate would leave the line and disappear into one of our lockers.

Some of these crates went to the mess beer boat (a fund from beer sold in the mess), and some were kept by the lads in the line, one of whom was usually me, Frank, Lee, or Andy.

We lived in a quiet corner of the mess called a 'gulch', this is where we had our little invitation only, parties. Nothing loud or mischievous, just a crate or two of beer drank with friends while chatting.

All very civilised.

Me and Frank were the regulars who gave out invitations to the 'privileged few', or anyone who fancied a bit of a party.

Frank was the entertainment; his favourite was to make everyone make an impression. He was good and did loads of well-known personalities, the others could usually manage one or two, but I was the worst of the bunch, every time we played the silly game my Barney Rubble lost the game for me.

"What's up Fred," was all I could manage. It was a pathetic excuse for a Barney Rubble, but it usually got a (sympathetic) laugh.

Another lasting memory of Frank was one of his worst jokes, funny but terrible. It was the time of pioneering heart and lung transplantation.

Frank's question was, "What is the worst thing about a heart and lung transplant?"

We stated the obvious, not realising, at first, it was a joke, until he told us the worst thing about a heart and lung transplant was, "Coughing up someone else's phlegm."

Well, anything to do with bodily fluids gets my stomach turning, and between gagging, I was calling him all the names under the sun. He was laughing his socks off watching me trying not to throw up.

Is this the behaviour of someone about to become a Naval Policeman? This is where the navy's philosophy, 'it takes a thief to catch a thief', makes sense.

If you don't get caught you can make a pretty good Regulator.

I was to fly home from Malta as part of the advanced leave party. They enabled the ship's company to go straight on leave when the ship docked in Portsmouth.

A couple of nights before I flew home, we were having one of our social gatherings in our 'Gulch,' and because we were going our separate ways once we returned to Portsmouth, it extended into the early hours.

This was illegal as bars closed at 2300hrs, and we were only entitled to three cans of beer per man per day, but it was like an early 'up channel' night.

The Duty Regulating Petty Officer (DRPO) carried out rounds of all messes sometime after 2300hrs, but we all forgot about that.

At about 0100 RPO Henry Millington came in quietly and slowly, pulling back the curtain to our 'gulch'. He caught us red-handed. We were drinking. He got the four of us to bang to rights.

I was a Killick, so I could have been busted and had my Regulators Course cancelled. Thankfully, Henry was a nice sort of guy, he said, "I'll be back in five minutes." Which meant you had better be gone by the time he returned.

We were all tucked away and cleaned up within two. He came back. All he said was, "Taff Hennessy, see me in the morning."

I was summoned firstly because I was the Leading Hand, and secondly, because I was selected for the Regulators course. I had a lot to lose. I reported as ordered, expecting the worst.

He ripped me a new arsehole before sending me on my way, thankfully with my course intact. He often reminded me of that incident in future years. He was to become an Officer and one of the better ones at that.

I have been stupid in my time but that takes the cake... We should have remembered the DRPO did his rounds after 2300.

That was the end of the deployment, back through the Suez, the usual visits to Malta, and Gibraltar. I flew home from Malta to get my leave and then to work over the main leave period. This was a bit sad because many of my good friends were leaving the ship.

Frank was leaving, and he was leaving the Navy too, shortly after his leave.

The night before we were playing pranks on each other. Emptying his pillow of feathers and filling it full of shaving foam. I, in turn, had my bunk filled with feathers and other sophisticated pranks. So, to remind him of me when he got home before we left the ship together, I opened his neatly packed kit bag and dumped quite a few feathers inside, hoping he would see the funny side when he got home.

It worked out better than I could imagine.

At the dockyard gate, the MOD police frequently pull people to check their bags and to ensure they aren't smuggling cigarettes or booze out of the dockyard.

My prayers were answered. Frank got called in.

I couldn't stop laughing when I looked into the search area, there was a 'plod' with his arm in Frank's kit bag, feathers were flying everywhere. I nearly died laughing. I could see Frank was trying his best to not laugh, but when he saw me looking, he lost it and nearly cried as he laughed his head off.

That was the end of another happy episode of my life in the RN.

But things changed from this point forward, I was never to have the same good friends as I had up until then, probably because the people I would be working and socialising with were nearly all married, as I was soon to be. Plus, there were so many who were solely career-orientated, the ones who put career before friendship much of the time.

I wasn't used to that mentality, and could never get into that frame of mind, but changing branches was the best thing I could have done. I could not have stayed in the mob as a steward for any amount of money. But I did stay in contact with some of the good friends I made.

Around this time, I was going steady with Kim, soon to be married, to some of my mate's disgust.

I am not sure whether it was a coincidence, but I became a serious smoker at this time.

You cannot join the Navy as a Regulator (Reggie), you need to complete three years of man's service before applying. Man's service begins at eighteen, so the two-and-a-bit years I served before my eighteenth birthday did not count. It was a case of a poacher turning gamekeeper, or it takes a thief to catch a thief, as I said earlier.

I think if you were allowed to join the RN direct as a Regulator/Policeman then your typical sailor would run rings around you. By the ripe old age of twenty-one, I had seen it, done it, and got the tee shirt.

I had (just) got my three years in when I applied. I passed out as a Leading Regulator on my sixth anniversary of joining the RN. I was a 'no badge' Leading Regulator, which is quite young for any branch never mind the Regulating Branch.

The nickname for the Reggie's, amongst other things, was 'Crusher.' They were often pictured as not-so-bright, hobnail boot-wearing, thickos. Thankfully, that was no longer the case, but the name lived on. All part of that Naval tradition I speak of.

As a Regulator, you are the Police of the RN. It is said they are not called Police because the job was to regulate the behaviour of the crew, and we couldn't be in a position where we could arrest the captain of a ship, or so the story goes, but not confirmed.

At the time I became a Reggie, the vast percentage of the work was administrative. Anything to do with movement, drafts, leave, sickness and so on, the paperwork was the responsibility of the Regulators. There was also discipline, which meant investigating offences, interviews, framing charges, and formulating reports when required. I say when required, because in the early days, if someone was in the shit (trooped) there weren't any reports for minor or naval offences, you framed the charge - told the Officer trying the case what happened - give the lad, or his Divisional Officer (DO) a chance to say something in mitigation, and then find him guilty and punish.

Easy.

Another responsibility was mail. Mail has one of the biggest effects on a ship's company's spirits, more so than almost anything else, especially when at sea. It was responsible for many Regulators being 'busted' for getting it wrong.

So, off I went to HMS Excellent, the home of the Regulator.

HMS Tiger C20

HMS EXCELLENT

1978-79- Aged 21

I joined the RN regulating School at Whale Island/HMS Excellent, in Portsmouth, a month before my course commenced.

Whale Island is only two hundred yards from the mainland. It is a manmade island, constructed during the Napoleonic times by prisoners, and prisoners of war. It is also the home of Seamanship and ships' husbandry, and where Divisional Officers are trained.

For those four weeks before my course started, I was making tea and coffee for the instructors and watching the classes in training double everywhere, that is, instead of marching as a platoon, you ran (jogged) as a platoon.

I also witnessed the panic before the morning parade took place to look immaculate for the inspecting Officers. The Regulating Officers all rose through the ranks. As they had been through the school themselves, so there was no 'blagging' them like you would any normal Officer.

This gave me a fair insight into the course, and plenty of time should I wish to back out. That wasn't going to happen. I was not going back to stewarding.

This was the turning point of my career.

It was going to be serious stuff from now on.

I needed to grow up and progress as far as possible in my career. The better I do, the higher my wages. But I'm not going to give up all the fun and my friends, just be a bit more mature about it.

As it happened, most of the fun and friends disappeared, but I did grow up... a lot.

The course started, we were given many warnings to behave ourselves, be immaculate at all times, and work as a team, etc. etc.

Our instructor was RPO 'Jumper' Collins, he was one of the first of the drug squad, which was put together in the late 60s and early 70s to combat the escalation of drug use in the country, which was sadly reflected in the RN.

His favourite subject was discipline, although he was a bit lacking in the admin department, so sometimes, we would get another instructor for those subjects.

This got us thinking, if he could make it into the regulating branch, then so can we. The other instructor was also a bit lacking - about a year later, he was arrested for impersonating a doctor and making 'House Calls'. It must have taken some nerve or a severe mental illness.

Smartness was always a big thing.

We had inspections every morning. Part of our No1 uniform was a lanyard, a piece of thin rope for want of a better description, which goes around the neck, sometimes we wore it and sometimes we didn't.

We were supposed to be wearing it one morning, but I wasn't. Jumper inspected us and didn't notice, the Training Officer inspected us, and he didn't notice, so I got away with it... had I hell!

The Officer in Charge of the Regulating school was standing twenty yards away, at right angles to our platoon. He noticed from that distance and angle I wasn't wearing my lanyard.

Bollocks.

Not many trainees get trooped (charged) on the Regulating Course. But I did. I got an admonishment, which was a slap on the wrist. It was not as bad as the ribbing I took from the other lads in the class though.

We had exams each week. Things were going well. If you fail just one of the exams, you are off the course. We were to lose two lads by the end of the course, which is better than average.

We had other duties to carry out, as you do anywhere in the RN.

Our duty consisted of cleaning the school classrooms and getting picked up by the Naval Provost (Patrol) in the evening to go out on patrol with them. Our job was to assist the 'real' Regulators get the odd drunken sailor off the streets and break up any fights.

During one of the patrols, we were involved in getting a drunken sailor out of The City Arms Pub in the centre of Portsmouth. He was creating a nuisance of himself. As we were about to put him in the back of the van, he went mad. Three of us eventually got him in, but he managed to grab hold of the LREG in charge. He got a grip on Butch's nuts and wouldn't let go.

As I was closest, I rammed my fist into his nuts and grabbed them. It had the desired effect. He let Butch's go.

Butch didn't forget, the following day he went to the school and told the Training Officer how I helped when I got stuck in.

Theoretically, I assaulted a man who was in our custody, but everyone was happy with that. They call it 'using the minimum amount of force necessary' – works for me.

Butch didn't have to tell the school about the incident, or my involvement but I was grateful he did.

The course was intense and hard work.

We learned about Naval Law, Criminal Law, definitions of different crimes, and how charges are framed because of knowing the definitions, the administration, mail, and general leadership. After eight weeks, which seemed like an eternity, came our passing out.

The highlight of which was receiving our 'Crown', which is the Branch Badge of the Regulator. This was a short ceremony with a passing out parade. What a huge sense of relief and achievement.

I felt fantastic. I could not believe I was not a steward anymore.

On completion of the course, we were sent to RAF St Athens, just outside of Cardiff, where we learned how to drive. Those who already held a driving license were taught how to drive HGV's.

I failed my driving test and needed to return to Portsmouth to carry on with my duties. But I was to return and pass the second time around.

Now I was in the Regulating Branch, where there are exceptions to the CPO and PO rank rules. There are no CPOs in the Reg Branch, they are Master at Arms, and the worst thing you could do is call a Master at Arms 'Chief'.

"I've never been a Chief, never have been, never will be," was the normal response, spoken in a loud, raised voice.

The same for Regulating Petty Officer, he is an RPO, not a PO, and you would get the same response if you called him a PO, a response I would give when I achieved these ranks.

It was a bit of fun really, very funny when a lad calls you a Chief and everyone around him cringes, knowing what is to come, and then the look on their face when they realise what they said.

Priceless.

But there are the smart arses who call you PO or Chief just to get a reaction. I've seen these guys smiling as they walk away.

But they paid in the end.

I was proud of my achievement because I was only twenty years old, and I had no Good Conduct badges. The stripes are awarded after four years of (man's) service. So, I was a 'No Badge Leading Regulator,' the like of are few and far between.

A change of branch

RNPHQ - HMS NELSON

Portsmouth 1979 – Aged 21

At the RN Provost Headquarters (RNPHQ, or Unit), I was integrated into a watch and began the patrolling of the streets of Portsmouth.

This wasn't the extent of our duties, it just seemed like it. Every so often, we would pick up a deserter who had been arrested by the Civil Police. On one occasion we went to Dover, where a deserter got arrested as he was coming through Immigration.

All deserters are placed on the Police National Computer, so he was picked up quite easily when on a visit to Belgium. When we arrived at Dover, there was this smart gentleman in his forties, who looked totally out of place in a cell and would look totally out of place in the Navy. As it happens, he deserted in the early 60s after falling in love with a Belgian woman. He settled there and never returned to the UK.

He even spoke with an accent because he hadn't spoken English for so long. It didn't seem right, but we had to take him to cells in HMS Nelson, to the RNPHQ. Fortunately, everyone was sympathetic. He was soon signed off from being a deserter and allowed to carry on with his life.

Another deserter was a man called Tony Damon, he deserted six years previous and joined the Foreign Legion. The only reason he came back was because he had a bad landing on a parachute jump and damaged his back, and the Legion were going to put him behind a desk.

The only thing he had with him was his Foreign Legion cap and two scars below his eyes, where he said he was pistol-whipped for not learning French fast enough.

He seemed a nice bloke. He was a Marine Engineering Mechanic before he left, and he resumed this career when he returned. When he had done his time, he returned to the RNPHQ as one of the 'messmen' (helpers). He showed an interest in becoming a Regulator and formed a relationship with one of the WRN Regulators, Karen. They later married.

More about him later.

The duties were long hours, sometimes hard work, and sometimes funny.

The civilian youth in Portsmouth had a sick pastime, they called 'Skate Bashing'. A Skate is their nickname for a sailor, so as we were on the same radio frequency as the civil Police and had a good relationship with them, it was always a joy when the 'Skate Bashers' were involved in a fight, which we usually helped the Police to break up.

On one occasion, we were parked in our van, in a side street opposite one of the local bars used by sailors. To our left, on the pavement was a big hole left for the night by workmen. It was dimly lit.

We sat in silence, looking ahead in a bored trance, when a man, about twenty years old, obviously a civilian who could only be described as a thug, or a 'Skate Basher', walked across the road from right to left in front of us. When he saw us, he started hurling abuse, waving two fingers and making any other obscene gesture he could think of.

As he was entertaining himself, he didn't see the hole in the pavement and fell straight into it, headfirst. Well, that broke our boredom. We were in tears as this idiot crawled out of the hole in silence and slithered away.

When we picked up a drunken sailor, or anyone in the military for that matter, we had to take them to the cellblock called Recess, and then call out the Officer of the Day (OOD).

The OOD would question the man, and if he formed the opinion that he was drunk, he would sign a drunk certificate and the man would be banged up for the night.

If the OOD didn't sign the form it wouldn't change the fact the man was drunk when we picked him up, so a report would be sent to the ship anyway.

One night, driving along Southsea front, we saw a man who was walking like Bambi on ice, obviously drunk, but because he had long hair, we weren't sure if he was a sailor. So, we stopped and got out of the van.

I said to the lad "Are you navy mate?" he kept walking, turned his head and said "Negative." It was a nice try, but how many civilians say 'Negative'?

We got him back to Recess and the OOD was called. We got the lad to his feet when the officer arrived, who then started asking him questions to see if he was drunk.

"Where have you been tonight?"

"'Park Tavern, City Arms, Mucky Duck, some other places," the lad slurred.

"'What have you had to drink?"

"Ahhh, beer, lager, cider, Guinness, and some whiskey," he replied, giving it a lot of thought. "Anything else?" asked the OOD.

"'No thanks," the drunk said, "I've had enough."

"Where do I sign?" said the OOD.

Unfortunately, some Regulators get pissed with power, as happened on this embarrassing occasion, embarrassing for me anyway.

The driver of the vehicle is always the one in charge, and Smudge is in the driving seat. We were parked up when an old buddy of mine staggered past.

I said hello, and we started having a chat, he'd had a few, and Smudge formed the opinion he had drunk more than enough, so he got out of the van to arrest him.

"You have got to be joking," I said, "he's a mate. We'll give him a lift back to his ship."

Smudge, the man in charge, insisted and we ended up taking the poor bloke to Recess. Fair play for Thommo, he said "Don't worry about it,

Taff. I can see it's not your fault," and went without a murmur. I felt bad about that, and soon after I took him out for a pint and we both got hammered. Things weren't right between Smudge and me after that, as you can imagine.

It highlighted the fact you don't get the same calibre of friends as a Regulator as you do in 'normal' branches.

The RNPHQ was on the first floor of the Gate House There was a window which overlooked the car park, from where you could shout down to the lads rather than use the radio.

I was in reception with Whiskey Walker, a senior Reggie who I got on well with. The Boss said to him shout down, tell Griff to get back up here, I want to speak to him.

Whiskey was right to it, he ran over to the window and put his head through it... I mean, he put his head through the windowpane. The glass shattered.

Whiskey was on his knees holding his head, and I was on my back laughing for Wales.

Whiskey eventually becomes an Officer.

I was on duty at RNPHQ when the IRA killed Lord Mountbatten, in Southern Ireland. They blew his boat up.

It wasn't long before the jokes appeared.

Q. What's white and travels at 200 miles an hour?

A. Mountbatten's plimsoll.

As it happens, Monty was a well-respected member of the Royal Family, and he famously captained HMS Kelly during the Second World War. He wasn't one of the Royal who was given their rank, he had earned it in every sense of the word.

A huge state funeral was arranged and, as it was the middle of a leave period, everyone was involved in recalling crews, delivering messages, and giving lifts to those who couldn't make it back to work.

The Civil Police were our contacts in different areas of the country, and they helped enormously in delivering messages. It was a sad occasion watched by millions.

Bob Doyle, who was the Training Officer at the Regulating School, was the Officer in Charge of the Pall Bearers.

It is something he is extremely proud of doing.

It was an experience working at the RNPHQ, but life is full of statements and report writing, and it tends to get you down a bit. So, to continue my training on the administration side of things, I was drafted to HMS Sultan, the Marine Engineering School at Gosport, on the other side of the harbour from the main dockyard.

HMS SULTAN

1979/80 - Aged 22-23

Sultan was a considerably steep learning curve. There is a lot of admin to learn and remember.

There were approximately ten Regulating Staff, led by the Fleet Master at Arms (FMAA), Jimmy Green, who was the youngest person to be promoted to FMAA. He was a good bloke. We had our mess (club), as all Regulating Staff did in all establishments at the time, and it was well supported.

It was traditional to have, as honorary members, the Chief Cook, Chief Steward, and Chief Caterer, who would all use their position to the mess's advantage.

The Chief Caterer at this time was Mick, he was the SA on the Leander, the one I mentioned earlier and who got a taste for 'Horses Kneck'. It was he who was drinking it from litre jugs if you remember, which was a slight hiccup in his career, but it didn't hold him back.

After six months of learning the admin side of the job, I was moved to the Discipline Office, where the discipline MAA was Pete Shackloth. He had served his time, and he was now waiting to leave the Navy. He said he was looking forward to going to Horticultural College. He was a good teacher. I learnt a lot from him.

One morning, the Duty Regulating Petty Officer had reason to place a stoker in cells for the night. He went home to his married quarter and his wife had cleared out all the furniture whilst he was out.

He was pissed and causing a nuisance of himself. The provost picked him up and delivered him to Sultan as it was a domestic situation, which is why he wasn't taken to Recess.

I immediately recognised his name. It was Tony, the ex-Foreign Legion chap.

The routine is for the MAA to have a chat with anyone who has been held in cells before sending them back to their department. I let him out of his cell, and we exchanged pleasantries. He was standing at the MAA's desk, and I was sitting at mine when he lost it. He wasn't violent, but he went into a rage of abuse to the MAA and spoke mostly in French.

I was waiting for him to become violent, but strangely enough, the MAA shouted, "Get back in the cell." Which he did.

I couldn't believe it. That's where he stayed until he was administratively discharged from the RN, which means he was taken to the main gate and set free as an undesirable.

I escorted him to the gate; we shook hands and he just walked away. He couldn't settle down to married life, or the boredom and lack of risk and excitement in the Navy, so he took to drinking big time.

I later heard he went to Germany where he worked as a mercenary. Then I also heard he gave himself up to the Foreign Legion.

Who knows?

I spent less than a year at Sultan but learnt a lot from the staff.

One was 'Rocky', a late joiner to the RN, and at this time he was an RPO. He lived down the road from me and was into cars. He was a car mechanic in 'real life'. I called on him a few times to rescue me in my 'bangers'.

He was also into darts. We played for the local pub together, so it was an easy decision to apply for the Aircraft Carrier, Hermes when Rocky and the boss got drafted there. Jock Docherty, also a Leading Regulator, applied at the same time. We were both happy when we got the draft.

Rocky was an extrovert and a bit of a big head.

He thought he was a karate expert, probably self-taught because he always felt that he knew a lot about everything.

Jock was a Glaswegian, and you needed to listen intently when he spoke, or you would lose the gist of what he was saying.

He was christened Captain Concrete by some of the crew because he hardly ever smiled and was always serious, or at least he gave that impression.

He became a good mate and turned out to be a good laugh.

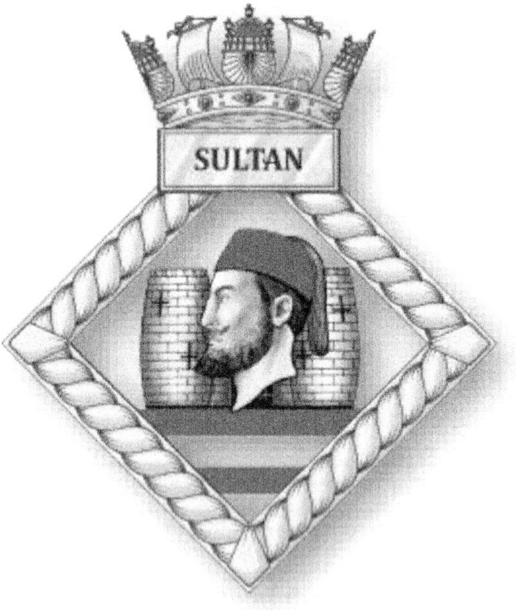
SULTAN

HMS HERMES

1980-82-Aged 23-25

We joined the Hermes while she was in refit, the flight deck redesigned for use by the Harrier Jump Jet.

It had the slings and nets, used by previous jets removed and a ramp put on the front end to make it easier and more economical for the Harriers to take off, but they would always land vertically.

We had three offices, the junior Rates Office, where I worked with Rocky, a senior rates Office, which was combined with the Discipline section and housed the Boss's desk, and there was the Mail Office.

Jock was the Mailman, but he was often helped by whoever was available. Another member of staff who joined during the refit, to make us up to compliment, was Dave Leeming, who became the Discipline RPO, very sour-faced and hated everyone. But socially he was a nice bloke.

Last, and the very least, was Brian McKay, the third RPO. He was an old Granny. He complained about everything.

The five of us were in a small mess, which we refurbished and built a bar and lounge area, very nice. As we didn't know each other, we elected Brian to be our Mess President, as he was the most senior. All messes have someone in charge to take responsibility for everything that goes on in their mess, good or bad.

In one of my first conversations with Brian, he mentioned he was divorced and had a son. He was telling me about the boy, and when I asked the boy's name he said, "His mother wanted to call him Wesley."

I sighed in sympathy, asking what they ended up naming him.

"'Wesley," he said.

"Nice name," I replied.

Rocky was an Atheist and took pride in telling everyone. One of his good friends and golfing partner was John Ryan, a Catholic Priest, and it was his quest to get Rocky to see the light.

It never happened, but he had some fun trying.

He liked his booze did Father Ryan, as he proved when he Christened my two kids on board. We had a hell of a party after the Christening, and he became a good friend to all of us.

We were duty RPO (even though Jock and I were not yet RPOs), every five days, and part of our duty was to take care of any disciplinary incidents and to carry out rounds of accommodation with the OOD at 1830, and again after 'Pipe Down' (lights out), which could be any time after 2300.

On my first rounds, we went into the steward's mess around 0030hrs. The Duty RPO goes first, followed by the OOD. As I opened the door to the mess, I could see there were some lads playing cards for money.

Gambling in the RN is strictly forbidden, it leads to all sorts of money problems and theft. So, as I walked in, I stalled for a few seconds, so they could get the money off the table and act, at least sort of normal.

They shifted their money, and I said in a tongue-in-cheek sort of way, "You are not playing for money, are you?" to which the Leading Steward at the card table said, "Only for 5p's."

What a plonker.

He said it in front of the OOD, so now I had to troop him. I gave him such an earful for being a tosser. He ended up getting a big fine, and the poor lads he was playing with got a handful of Nn9s each.

This is why, when asked what I did before I became a Regulator I say, "I don't talk about my past," rather than admit to being a Steward.

After trials and 'work up', the Hermes went on a short deployment, firstly to Gibraltar where some of the 'Gibbo's'(locals) were waiting to have repairs done to their cars, (remember what I said about them earlier).

We then went to the US and Bermuda. Rocky was a bit of a motorbike freak. He and a bunch of others were allowed to take their bikes onboard, where later they were to leave the ship in Jacksonville, to take a bike ride through the Blue Ridge Mountains of Virginia, rejoining the ship in Norfolk Virginia.

All right for some.

We were in the US to show off the Sea Harrier Jump Jets to the Yanks, and by all accounts, they proved to be a big hit.

One of my favourite stories was a dog fight going on between an F14 and a Harrier. The F14 was chasing the Harrier and thought it was about to 'for exercise' blow the Brit up when the Harrier stopped.

The F14 flew past at 700 MPH (ish) and the Harrier sent a Sidewinder (heat-seeking missile) up the Yank's arse.

A few days before we got into Jacksonville Florida, we did an exchange visit to the USS Forrestal, one of their smaller carriers but still a lot bigger than us. I was lucky enough to fly over to her, spending some time with the USN Master at Arms (MAA).

Very interesting. They were dedicated Police, with no other duties. They continually patrolled the ship and had a drug dog on board who worked continuously.

There was always someone in the 'Brig', and you could be committed to the cells for almost any offence. One of the MAAs was Scott, who spent some time in Hawaii He worked undercover with the Police Department. He had a few attempts on his life and a visit to his family home by some of the drug dealers.

It is truly a different world.

He was kind enough to invite us to his home in Jacksonville.

Other parts of life on an American ship are very different from ours too.

They had a burger bar on the go 24/7, and their food was great, steak and shrimp meals, something we rarely saw, and ice cream on tap. But their ships were dry, which means there is no booze on board.

Give me mince pies and fish and chips any day, along with a cold can of beer to chill out with at night.

It was a good day for us on the Forrestal, but a better one for the exchange Yanks when they came on the Hermes.

There is a strange tradition in the RN that when you have an American sailor in your mess, you get him pissed, and on this occasion, there was no exception. We heard later there were no vacancies in the cells that night.

A good day was had by all.

We were in Jacksonville for five weeks.

During that time, we went to Scott's place for a meal and a few beers. We then invited Scott and his wife, and any friends he may like to bring along, to a social evening in our small mess. From that evening came an invitation to Scot's friend's place, for a BBQ.

It turned out to be a great few weeks.

We did go ashore and did normal things too. On one occasion, I went to a local bar on the back of Rocky's bike. We had a couple of bevvies before deciding to drive on to the next bar. Everything is so spread out transport was essential.

I jumped on the back of his bike, he revved up to pull away, taking his feet off the ground as you do, but the bike was in sand, so the wheels simply spun, going nowhere fast.

The bike, with us still sitting on it, as if in slow motion flopped onto its side, taking us down with it.

I couldn't get up for laughing.

Taff Wannacott was an Able Seaman and the office runner.

He worked for us because he was pretty much useless at his job. He was a character and very funny. He was one of the Ship's Company who arranged to have his wife come out to Florida for a week. This often happens when a ship is away for a few months.

Anyway, he hired a car for the week. The car was an automatic. He hadn't driven an automatic before, so the first time he got to drive was when he picked it up to drive it to his hotel.

The second time he drove it was outside the hotel reception where he parked it. He selected his gear, turned his head to the rear because he was reversing out of the parking space, accelerated, and drove through the hotel reception window and into the foyer.

Wrong gear. Thankfully no one was hurt. He did get another car, and the rest of his leave went without further incident.

It was a very eventful few weeks where a bit of everything happened.

Dave was our liaison with the local Police.

They asked if we could help them trap some drug dealers who were peddling to sailors in the area. They thought British sailors in town would be a target for them.

Me and Jock were the youngest, which, according to the Yank Police, meant we were more likely to use drugs, and therefore a more likely target. So, we went out for the night with the police, they would send us to the bar with a few bucks to buy a drink, and then wait to see if we were approached.

If we were, they would spring into action.

We must have done about eight bars, one or two drinks in each meant we had a very good cheap night out, a tour of the town, and we didn't get stuck in the middle of a gunfight with 'Miami vice'.

I was volunteered to escort one of our guys, a prisoner, to Washington and hand him over to the RAF police, who would then escort him to the UK where he was to spend ninety days in detention.

That was another day out. Spoilt because I lost my ID card, which cost me one day's pay, which is the standard fine for losing your ID.

Finally, four of us went to Disney World in Orlando.

We had the ship's minibus for two days, yes, we had a minibus on the ship, it was bought by the Welfare Fund to be used for leisure and sporting activities.

We travelled down the coast of Florida, stopping at various parks and beaches, a day in Disney World, overnight in a hotel. We didn't have a single drink; we were all too knackered.

Back to work the next day.

This is why I joined the RN.

A short stop at Norfolk, Virginia was uneventful but memorable.

There must have been six of the biggest ships in the world there, all the size of, and including, the most famous Carrier Nimitz. What a sight.

Back to sea.

As we were passing St Thomas, Virgin Islands, one of our helicopters was going ashore for some reason, so it was decided this was a good opportunity to get some mail off.

I have said how much of a morale boost receiving and sending mail is, and if there is an opportunity then we usually take it. It was my turn to take it ashore, just one bag, along with all the relevant paperwork, simple.

I was kitted out with a flyer's jumpsuit and helmet. As we were landing at the airport, the pilot said he would drop me off and come back to pick me up later.

That was news to me. Thanks.

I was dropped off. I found the office at the airport which accepted the mail, got my signatures and was away to the Post Office to pick up any incoming if there was any for us.

I wasn't exactly dressed for walking around town. I looked a bit of a burk, but it had to be done, so I got a taxi there and back. It was a wasted trip because there wasn't any mail for us, and there wouldn't be because it wasn't a planned dispatch place, but I had been told to check anyway.

I waited for the Sea King Helicopter to come back, and I waited and waited, and waited.

No sign of my lift back to the ship.

'Information' called the tower for me, but they had no idea where the chopper was, or when it was coming back.

How could they forget me?

Thirteen hours later, without warning, it arrived, stopped, waved for me to get on board, and left as if there wasn't a problem. But once the pilot got the take-off over with, he apologised.

The chopper had broken down on an Island.

They had to wait for another chopper from the ship to arrive with engineers, and then they had to fix it.

He said they would have been an hour earlier picking me up if they hadn't forgotten about me. They were well on their way, heading back to the ship before the ship asked them if there was any mail... whoops!

During my first year on the Hermes, I was admired for my ability to sleep anywhere at any time. If we broke for coffee, I would sneak fifteen minutes should I feel the need, anywhere any time.

In recognition of my talent, I was declared 'Golden Blanket' Champion 1981/2. The staff awarded me a certificate, stamped and signed by all department administrators.

That certificate and the South Atlantic medal, what a year.

Whilst we were in the West Indies, Jimmy Green, the boss, was replaced by George Drury, a lot older and 'old school' which meant he was more of a 'Crusher' than Regulator.

The old 'Crushers' were best known for using their muscles and not their brains. But once he proved to everyone who was the boss, he was okay and often came into our mess to have a drink with us.

One of my 'duties' was to keep his fridge topped up with beer and lager. The NAAFI Assistant Manager, Dave Llanwerne was a good mate, he used to put the boss's cases of beer in a cigarette box and hand it over the counter to me. Just to hide the fact the boss was getting more than his daily allowance.

But often the prick used to write on the front of the cigarette box. 'Beer for the FMAA' he caught me every time. Not that anyone cared or would question why the boss was getting the extra beer. The rest of the Reggies had the same unofficial privilege.

We were members of the PO's mess but still had a bar in our small mess. Perks of the job. Even Jock and I had the privilege of being a member of the POs mess even though we were of a lower rank, by virtue that we were Regulators made us senior to the usual Petty Officer.

This was resented by some but accepted by most.

The Hermes was given the chance to test the very new method of quitting smoking.

Nicorette chewing gum.

Loads asked for samples and most of us were given a couple of weeks' worth. Enough, apparently, to be able to stop.

After a few days, most of us had the same problem, we needed a fag to get rid of the horrible taste and we all agreed… it was crap.

The weather was getting bad in the West Indies. You know it is bad when a Carrier as big as us is being tossed around like a rubber dingy.

To this day, I don't know if what happened is true, but the story goes…

A signal (an RN communication like a telegram) was passed around the ship. It was from Northwood, the RN's big HQ, and it stated that the Hermes was to send its condition and exact coordinates to Northwood every hour whilst it was within the bad weather area.

We were in the Bermuda Triangle at the time. Not a nice feeling.

No one admitted to this message as being a hoax. Then again, I never heard of it being confirmed as a genuine message either.

It was home for Easter… and an unexpected turn of events.

A week into my leave, Rocky, who lived up the road from me banged on my door one morning. I wasn't on the telephone, and he had got a call for both of us from the ship.

There was a General Recall, Fleet wide.

The Argentineans had invaded the Falkland Islands.

I'll be honest here; my first thought was "What the hell are the Argentineans doing in Scotland".

I, and quite a few others, had not been taking notice of World News, and we had no idea where the Falklands Islands were.

But we were soon to find out.

We went straight to the ship, where they were already taking on stores and ammunition. The Regulators grabbed the leave passes of everyone who was on leave, and if we couldn't contact them by phone directly then the Local Police were called and asked to deliver the message.

Just as they did for Lord Mountbatten's funeral.

We did that for forty-eight hours straight. Lorry loads of supplies were being delivered continuously and everyone was involved in getting those supplies on board.

The decision was made by Thatcher to send a Task Force, and we were to sail as soon as possible. Those who could be spared were allowed home for a last night before we left.

When I left my wife that morning, I told her I would see her in a month.

"Two weeks there, and two weeks back. It will all be over by the time we arrive, anyway."

That's what I thought.

Hermes was the Flag Ship, which meant we carried the Task Force Commander, Admiral Sandy Woodward.

This was good and bad news.

We would be better protected because of this. We were already a priority target for the Argies. Funny enough, the same thing goes even if he wasn't onboard because we were an Aircraft Carrier.

We sailed at 1000 hours, and what was waiting for us on the way out of the port was never, in a million years, expected.

We were leaving in 'Procedure Alpha', everyone on the upper deck in No1s. As we turned into the channel to leave the narrow harbour mouth, we saw a large crowd by the railway station and Gosport Ferry on the Portsmouth side waving us off, then I noticed the Gosport side was full of people waving too.

They were on the 'Old Portsmouth' walls, (known as the wailing wall) and opposite in HMS Dolphin (Submarine Base) and when we sailed through the narrow harbour entrance, we could see the beach and roadways, for as far as you could see along Southsea, were full of people cheering and waving flags. It was the most amazing sight, and anyone who tells you they didn't shed a tear would be lying.

The following day was the start of intense periods of training in our Action Station duties. My duty was as an Incident Board Marker and communication in one of the section bases. Ship are divided into sections; each section has boards with charts of that section of the ship. If there were any damage in a section it would be indicated on the charts.

Fire, flood, smoke, hole in the ship's side, times and any other details. This information was passed onto HQ1 where the command would have an overview of the status of the entire ship.

Every day a different scenario was exercised, and in every scenario, there would be the order 'Hand's Stand To', which meant we were about to be hit, and everyone was to sit down and hold onto something solid. At first, the thought that we may get hit, or even sunk, wasn't a consideration. Maybe we weren't taking it seriously but the further south we travelled, and hearing on the BBC news every day that the Argies, by all accounts, thought they were on the Falklands to stay, made us change our attitude.

As time went on, to our surprise, there didn't seem to be any sign of the situation resolving itself, but I still never thought that it would come to blows. All those with beards were told to shave them off because if there was a chemical attack a beard would prevent a seal from being made around the face by your gas mask.

Men who had had beards for fifteen or twenty years were shaving off. They were not recognisable. Rocky was one of them. They were allowed to keep a moustache until we got a bit further south.

We had a BBQ on the flight deck after a week, to give the crew a break. There was some beer, not too much, and loads of people dressed up. Rocky, being the extrovert he was, had kept a moustache. He borrowed a couple of belts of bullets from the aircrew, which he wore crossed around his body, and he found a Mexican hat from somewhere. By this time there were film crews and reporters on board, and he was interviewed as a Bandito General Galtiarie. (Argentinean President). It was very funny and was shown on national TV… with quite a few bleeps.

We were to cross the equator, even a war wouldn't stop the age-old tradition of the Crossing the Line Ceremony.

King Neptune's court was open to judge all those who had not crossed the line before. The Reggies were the King's Police of course, and we dressed up as Gestapo with rubber truncheons. We belted anyone whose name was called and put them in the 'Dock'.

First up were two BBC reporters, Brian Hanrahan, and Peter Nicholson. Both were good sports and got clouted quite a bit. They were covered in all sorts of goo, and sticky stuff the cooks had knocked up. This went on for a couple of hours, followed by a beer in the mess.

In the morning it was as though it hadn't happened. It was back to drills and exercises.

We arrived at Ascension Island, off West Africa. A British Island with an RAF base and runway. We anchored and hadn't been there more than an hour when Action Stations were called.

For real.

Now there's an odd feeling doing it for real.

We sailed within thirty minutes. It was called off after a couple of hours. Someone had detected what they thought was a submarine in the area, and as Argentina had invaded the Islands of South Georgia, also in the South Atlantic, using a submarine; we thought this may have been them.

There were other ships anchored and, a thorough search had been carried out by them. Nothing was found.

From here on we were to always be on high alert.

We would always be accompanied by a 'Goalkeeper', a frigate sailing around us constantly to take out any missiles which may be heading our way. Or, to put themselves between the missile and us.

For this reason alone, HMS Broadsword Ships Company were our heroes.

We were getting closer to the Falklands.

The exclusion zone had been drawn up, and as we sold some of the Argentinean Frigates to them, identical to some of our own, we had a big black line painted down the middle from funnel to sea.

We heard of a lot of merchant ships being commandeered to bring supplies and troops and to be used as Hospital Ships. The Royal Yacht was supposed to have a wartime role as a Hospital Ship, but we would have needed a tanker to supply their fuel alone as it was different to the warship's fuel, or so they say.

On the Hermes, many of the Junior Rates messes were below the water line, so, in case of a strike, they had to be moved to a higher deck, which meant dining rooms and passageways. This included the Marines and SAS who were onboard waiting to deploy.

On top of this overcrowding, we were put on rations, no more helping yourselves at mealtimes. We didn't know when the next time we could be replenished could be.

The ship's companies were all in Defence Watches. Two watches doing six hours on and six hours off.

If you were not manning essential equipment (Radar, Sonar etc), you were cleaning. If you were off watch you would be eating or sleeping. The ship's policemen were also keeping watches. Discipline needs to be maintained, especially during war. We would carry out rounds, ensuring restricted areas were locked and secure, and there was no one below the water line, but the biggest workload was processing the disciplinary action required by departments whose personnel had been breaking rules and regulations.

One of the most serious offences during conflict is sleeping whilst on watch, although we had every sympathy with the stress and strains everyone was under, sleeping on watch could cost lives especially whilst manning radar or sonar etc. So, we were kept busy formulating reports and framing charges, and then, when we were called to action stations, everyone on or off watch went to their action station.

Well, I thought, this might take longer than the two weeks I told the Missus.

I must be captain of the understatements.

This was confirmed when we were told that the Argentinean Cruiser Belgrano had been torpedoed and sunk by one of our submarines, with a huge loss of life.

BLOODY HELL. This is serious now.

They are going to fight back after that little incident, I thought. See what I mean, captain of the understatements.

And they did fight back. Soon after, HMS Sheffield got hit by an Exocet and sank.

Brian Welsh, the Master at Arms on the Sheffield died. He was the only Regulator to lose his life in the conflict.

We had most of the injured brought onto the Hermes. When one of them woke, he was told where he was. He said it was the last place he wanted to be, as "They will be after this one."

Action Stations happened many times a day. The Argie aircraft were getting close, and after the Belgrano, aircraft were their main method of attack.

Their Navy was pulled out of the area and returned to port.

HMS Coventry was next to be hit and sunk by an Exocet. In these two ships, three of the cooks I knew from the Tiger died.

Sad times.

During this tense period, life went on to a certain extent, we needed to chill out a little, more so the boss.

I was still picking up his beer for him, and on one occasion I went into his cabin to put it into the fridge when we had a 'Hands Stand To'.

This could be it; the Argies were getting closer and closer. The boss came in, and he must have thought the same. We were both sitting on the deck, waiting, when he handed me a beer and just said, "Cheers."

Nothing happened, thank God, not to us anyway but it was a huge pause for thought.

In that same attack, the merchant container ship Atlantic Conveyer was hit by one of the Exocets. It was close to us, and it was thought one of the missiles locked onto the Atlantic Conveyer because it was the bigger target.

It wasn't protected with a 'Goalkeeper' and didn't have any deterrents like chaff. (Foil launched into the path of the missile to give the impression of a different, bigger target)

Five or six people were killed, including their Captain, and as the ship was full of Helicopters and critical supplies its loss would have an impact on the outcome of the conflict.

Every so often we would get some mail, which was sent to us on any ship or aircraft bound for the Falkland. It would turn up with loads of bags missing. The paperwork wasn't so important now, as long as we got some mail, we were happy. If they found the missing bags that was a bonus.

In any other situation, there would be people all over the world looking for the missing bags. But here we were grateful to get anything, any time.

Families were sending boxes of 'goodies', chocolate, cigarettes, cakes, drinks, sweets etc, and by the time it arrived most of the mail was covered in chocolate or sticky coke. It took a while for the Forces Mail Services to get it right and keep the letters separate.

But it was always appreciated. We were sent booze, magazines and newspapers from big companies. Schoolchildren sent letters and women sent photographs, all to cheer us up.

It was a nice feeling to be appreciated like this.

There was a ship's newspaper called 'The Hermes Herald' printed every day. It was full of poems, jokes, observations, and anything else contributed by the ship's company, along with news from BBC World Service, or news signals sent by MOD in London.

During a couple of quiet watches, I decided to contribute one or two things, but in case it wasn't printed, or was a load of crap, I didn't tell anyone what I had done.

Until now.

I just signed it, T NSE. Taff Hennessy, get it? Henn(N) es(S) sy(E). So, here are my two contributions to the Hermes Herald.

COULD THEY BE HUMAN

I started my service of just one short year

No trouble, no fighting, no bloody fear

The orders came for the biggest assault

Can't anyone see it wasn't our fault?

The General said we must hold our ground

Although he had realised to die, we are bound

We will fight for our country with body not soul

We will fight though we know there is no goal.

On this Island of hell, we must save face

Not for the General but our families' disgrace

They hear the war stories that are not all true

If the privates were Generals no fighting we'd do

The food is short and the weather is cold

But our enemies come they are brave they are bold

The closer they get the harder they try

Soon it will be my time to lay down and die.

That was the first one, and if you didn't guess it's what I had imagined one of their privates would have been going through. I was a bit pissed off when it got to the second one. Our ships were taking a bit of a battering, and I was a bit flippant.

THE LAST WARNING

They've pushed us back or so they say

Can't get near come what may

Back at home the Argies cheer

What a load of Diarrhoea

Argentina, don't you know

That our fleet will grow and grow

It doesn't matter what you say

The Brits, my friend, are here to stay

The 'Shiny Sheff' a lucky shot

Don't you know that's not all we've got

Frigates, Destroyers, Carriers two

Thank the Lord I'm not you

You've had a taste of what's to come

Now take a hint, get up and run

Don't be foolish and hold your ground

Or even hide coz you'll be found

Now our boys will be playing blinders

A thousand pounder a few Sidewinders

That's what our Harriers carry

And they're after you, you twat, Galtieri.

I know, I know, I'll never be the next Dylan Thomas, but I tried.

There were one or two more published which were very witty. Here's one of my favourites:

THE HERO OF THE FALKLANDS WAR

"What did you do in the Falklands?" said the little boy to his dad

"Well thinking back son it's the best time I ever had."

"But, what did you do Dad? I'm interested tell me more"

"Alright, relax son and I'll tell you about the Falkland Island War."

"I was a chopper pilot, who nearly sank a sub,

Then I re-took South Georgia just in time for grub.

I just jumped inside a Vulcan to bomb an airport.

In MY Harrier I shot down two fighters whilst I was an escort."

"That's amazing," said the boy to his father with a look of awe,

In the Falkland Island war

"I put on my combat jacket and with a rifle went ashore.

I recaptured the Falkland Islands and took 5000 prisoners or more.

The Queen at the Palace thanked me, the crowds of people roared.

And that's the story son, of the Falkland Islands War."

Just then Mother walked in with a steaming pot of tea,

Father rose and went to the toilet for a much-needed pee.

"Oh Mother, isn't Dad brave, he's told me of the war.

He's told me of the things he did

In the Falkland Islands War"

Mother put the pot down, sadly stared up at the roof.

She said, "Sit down my little darling, I'd better tell the truth."

"Your dad was on the Hermes, fuel and ballast was his game

He was a DB Stoker, his only claim to fame

Now dear, drink your tea up your dad is just a bore

What he said was waffle,

About the Falkland Islands War."

Unsigned

And finally:

STATE 3 CONDITION MUSHROOM

I think I'll read the Herald

I think I'd better wait

I'll hear the news at six fifteen

It's much more up to date

It's just like that September

Absurd how time stands still

They're bound to make a pipe soon

I don't suppose they will

I think I'd better stroll around

Perhaps it's best to stay

I think I'll have a whiskey neat

I can't this time of day

I think I'll have another smoke

I don't know what to do

I promised to ring someone up

I can't remember who

They say it's been averted

They say we're on the brink

I'll wait for the new statesman

I wonder what they think

I hear the nation's keeping cool

The public calm is fine

This crisis can't shake England's nerve

But it's playing hell with mine.

Signed   Midicus Nauticus

(With apologies to Sagittarius)

The Argie Pilots were brave.

They were getting closer and closer but the Harrier Jump Jets, though not as fast as the Argie jets, were far superior in combat. The 'Kill count' was well in our favour. But they kept coming. Many times, during Action Stations, I thought I was in the wrong place. I mean literally.

The Exocets were launched from aircraft, ships, and in the Argies' case from land. (We had the same missiles). They skimmed the sea, about two metres above the waves, so when it hit a ship, at the largest mass, which was in the middle of the ship, it would go through the hull and then explode, causing a big hole just above or on the water line. So, we would have the explosion, fire, and flood at the same time.

My Action Station was amidship and on the water line. Not the best place to be. We were cursing the French by this time as the Exocets, and the fast aircraft were supplied by them. Rumour had it they were selling arms to Argentina whilst the conflict was in progress.

We had SAS onboard for some time.

They used to disappear for a day or two and come back for a break before being sent somewhere on another mission. One morning a team had returned onboard and went to breakfast in our dining room. You could tell they were knackered and needed food and rest.

We were exercising portion control by this time. Food rationing. One of the guys picked up a spatula at the service area and put two eggs on his plate. The young cook behind the counter slapped the bloke on the back of the hand with his serving spoon and said "Oye. One egg."

This SAS guy was gobsmacked, I don't think he knew if he wanted to laugh or kill the cook. As he was thinking about it the PO cook grabbed the lad from behind and threw him into the galley. The PO said, "Carry on mate," to the stunned soldier. I don't think the young lad knew how close he came to death.

In the same galley and pantry, one of the Leading Cooks started keeping a diary but a unique diary. He started drawing daily events on the walls of the galley and pantry. He wasn't a fantastic artist. What he did was very understandable, and relevant to any action that occurred each day. I'm not sure, but I think the walls were removed and placed in a museum or kept at the RN cookery school.

I would be interested to know where they are now.

Dave Llanwerne, the NAAFI Assistant Manager lived in a mess with his staff. They had quite a few spare bunks, so it was used by the SAS for their comings and goings.

I was having a beer with him, in his mess one evening, when he had a bunch of these guys there on a break. We were all chatting, and I asked if they had anything to do with the Iranian Embassy Siege, they all groaned, and one said that's all anyone wants to know about. It wasn't them; they were off watch for that incident.

The following day, these same guys were in a Sea King helicopter being taken ashore for another sortie, the weather was so bad the helicopter went down. It was flying low and hit a wave. Everyone onboard was lost.

I was talking to a fellow Welshman, Taff Harry, one day, he was the Petty Officer Radar Operator in charge of the Radar in the Operations Room, where the Captain and Admiral spent most of their time.

He told me, in layman's terms, that we went to Action Stations and there were three 'Blips' on the Radar screen, all Exocets.

A lad of eighteen was on duty, and it was his responsibility to give a continuous narrative to the Admiral on what the missiles were doing. The captain and anyone else was listening in silence to this young lad. For each Exocet, he gave the speed, direction, and altitude, one at a time, repeatedly.

He was cool, calm and very clear in what he was telling the Command. One of the Exocets disappeared.

The first missile ditched and off the screen he reported.

The second was taken out by a Seawolf Anti-Missile Missile (Thank you HMS Broadsword). Second Missile destroyed and off the screen he reported.

The third Exocet changed direction, finding a bigger target, which was the Atlantic Conveyer. He reported this, confirming all missiles were now off the screen.

The Command team then directed their attention to the Atlantic Conveyer.

The young lad stood up and asked Taff, "Was that OK, PO?"

"That was brilliant," said Taff.

The lad fainted.

The conflict was well underway.

It didn't look good; we were losing too many ships. Sunk or damaged by bombs. We would have lost more if the Argentinean bombs were not set to explode from a higher altitude, which resulted in a lot of unexploded bombs on our ships. One or two exploded whilst being disarmed, then the loss was total.

The land forces found themselves trekking further than they thought because of the loss of the helicopters on the Atlantic Conveyer.

Then the RFA Sir Galahad was bombed close to the coast before the Welsh Guards were sent ashore. There were many dead and injured, including the land force Commander Colonel H Jones, who was later killed in close combat.

The only good news seemed to be the Harriers still winning their battles. They had only lost one aircraft, and that wasn't from combat.

Three Vulcan Bombers famously flew from England laden with bombs. They refuelled enough times to get to Port Stanley Airfield without stopping, to put the airfield out of action.

They did damage, but it was not as much as planned.

The Argie aircraft doing the damage were coming from the mainland anyway.

So, a Sea King helicopter was gutted of all equipment, leaving just a shell and enough fuel for a one-way trip to Argentina.

Several SAS were flown to the Argentinean mainland, where they reported military aircraft movement to the Fleet, this gave us more notice of their arrival.

The helicopter was flown onto a Chilean beach where it was set ablaze. The crew gave themselves up to the Chilean authorities. They were repatriated to the UK soon after.

A cover story was invented. No mention of the SAS involvement. I saw the helicopter and it was gutted to give a maximum range, there was nothing left in the cab, and even the seating was removed.

As a result of that operation, HMS Hermes sailed closer to the Argentinean coast than any other ship. She became more vulnerable than at any other time. Ironically, it was joked that the Hermes was the Simonstown Flotilla because, at all other times, we were probably closer to the South African coast than the Falkland Islands. A Flagship must be protected.

Frigates and Destroyers were sent daily down 'Bomb Alley', a narrow channel of water off the coast near Port Stanley, where they bombarded Argie's positions and incurred a lot of damage in the process. I felt for the men on these ships. I was grateful I was on the Hermes.

The land forces started getting results. Each day we heard about Argentinean forces surrendering. It was all up to the Army and Marines now. The Argies were well equipped for the winter, and it was only a few weeks before the snow would come. Then, within a couple of weeks of being beaten by the weather, and probably the Argies, the Argies surrendered.

You needed to be there to experience the feeling of complete and utter relief. I can only imagine what the Land Forces felt.

But their job wasn't over.

They had thousands of Argentinean forces to disarm, feed, and contain. Although it was a lot easier and safer than the situation, they had previously been in.

A couple of days after the surrender, I was in a team of five, all from different ships, sent ashore to ensure the fleet started getting their mail. I said it was always a priority, didn't I?

After a three-hour flight in a Sea King, we were dropped at Port Stanley Airfield and left there.

For the first time, I saw the aftermath of a war.

There were many aircraft parked up. Shot to bits when the Harriers paid a visit. The buildings were all but demolished. The Argies had been escorted away.

There were some RAF people, so we bummed a lift into Port Stanley where the Headquarters were. We found the Headquarters and were told first to find the Post Office, where we would be setting up the Fleet Mail Office, and then find a bunk on the RFA Sir Belvedere, which was now alongside in Stanley.

They gave us a shot-up Argentinean Ambulance to use as a mail van, ordering us to report to the HQ each morning, when they would try and let us know when a chopper was arriving, or leaving, and what ships mail we needed to get ready.

We got a bunk on RFA Belvedere and met the choppers coming and going until the Army took over.

It was an experience and a privilege to be ashore at that time.

A couple of days after we arrived, we met a helicopter from the Hermes. Onboard was Jock Docherty, he was sent ashore to relieve me. To be honest, I was a bit pissed off because I was enjoying the experience and I had done most of the hard work.

I would be even more pissed off if Jock got the credit for it.

Thankfully, Jock saw it the same way, and if I was happy to stay, he would return onboard, which he did. I think he was more than happy to return because he was cold and miserable when he got off the chopper, but smiling when he got back on.

We saw a lot of prisoners waiting to be sent home, there were piles of weapons everywhere, and their vehicles were being used by everyone, civilians included, who eventually inherited all the 'Jeep-like' vehicles and trucks the Argies left behind.

There was a horse racing track which was full of 'fox holes' dug by the Argies waiting for the Brits to arrive, and we had a drink in 'The Globe', one of two pubs in Port Stanley.

It was freezing. I gave a thought to the Land Forces and the conditions they had to endure and was very grateful they were on our side.

Another three-hour flight and I was back on the Hermes.

It was warm and so was the atmosphere. We were still waiting for word on when we were going home. It felt like an age before we were told we were on our way.

We were to stop at Ascension again before the final leg home.

Jock and I were asked to sort out who was going home from Ascension to take leave and be ready for duty when we got back into Pompey.

This was one time I didn't want an early leave. Remembering what leaving Portsmouth was like on the way down, I said I would prefer to stay onboard.

Jock was happy to go home.

Sorted.

There were a few parties on the way home, and we had a break from Action Stations.

Two weeks after leaving the Falklands we were anchored off the Isle of Wight, waiting for the big arrival the following morning, and it was a big arrival.

Procedure Alpha again, of course. I was way up in the superstructure by the funnel.

Hundreds of small craft were following us, tugs in front and behind, with huge arcs of water spraying from their firefighting hoses. As we approached Southsea, I saw the whole beach was black with people waving.

The feeling I had leaving was fantastic; multiply that by at least 100, that's how good it felt when we returned.

Wherever I looked people were waving and shouting and singing. During Procedure Alpha, everyone stands to attention in silence. This one was different, all the crew were waving and shouting, and as we got closer to our berth, we began picking out family in the huge crowd on the dockside. There were TV cameras and the Royal Marine Band to welcome us. The ship was low in the water and covered in rust.

She looked absolutely beautiful.

That was a great homecoming, but what was unexpected for me, was when I went home to Ponty to see my parents, there were loads of family and friends to welcome me back. Jeff, S, Gareth, and many other friends put on a 'do' in the Central Hotel, my local.

It was all unexpected and fantastic.

By the time we went back to work, it felt like nothing had happened, we still had a job to do.

Many people were affected by their experience in the Falklands but being on the Hermes we didn't experience the 'hands-on' combat and engagements other servicemen experienced. Unlike an old friend, Dave, the other Regulator on the Sheffield (The MAA was Killed), suffered mentally for a long time. He left the Navy because of the traumatic experience.

The only thing that made my stomach turn for a long time was whenever the Action Stations Claxton went off. It is not worth mentioning considering all the other suffering some people probably still feel.

Regulating staff
HMS Hermes

THE FALKLANDS CAMPAIGN

The following is the diary written by my friend and colleague **RPO Rocky Hudson**, who kindly allowed me to copy his diary and reproduce it here. *(I didn't have the foresight to write one myself.)*

Too bloody lazy more like.

FALKLANDS DIARY 1983

2nd April 1982

I received a phone call at 0800 from FMAA Drury, recalling me from leave, along with Taff. I was not too chuffed. I was about to set off on a long-awaited camping trip to France with Joe a few hours later.

Although nothing was said, I suspected we may be on our way to the Falklands.

I called into Microfiltrex to let Mary know. She cracked up as expected.

After the ship took on vast quantities of ammunition and stores, I managed to go home on the Friday and Sunday nights.

Mary and I went to the Middlecroft and had a good night.

Everyone was talking excitedly about the invasion. One or two of the civilians said they wished that they were going.

I wished they were, instead of me.

John Lee even bought me a double Rum after time, which must go down in history as a great one-off. We went to John Lauries afterwards, where we saw off another couple of bottles.

Sailed for the South Atlantic at 1030hrs, in the now usual Procedure Alpha. It was astonishing and I wouldn't have missed it for anything. The crowds were out in their thousands waving their banners and Union Flags and cheering, an amazing show of patriotism that left us all with a lump in our throats.

The crowds stretched all along Southsea Beach. A mini armada of small boats followed us out of the harbour. I think at that moment we felt extremely proud of ourselves.

One task group is already on its way from the Mediterranean, where they had been taking part in the exercise 'Spring Train'.

At this stage we were trying to convince ourselves it was going to be easy; all reports suggested their planes were no match for our Harriers, and their navy would be easily dealt with by our nuclear submarines. They had already been deployed.

The Argentinean army consists of mainly conscripts who do twelve months of National Service. Reports of more than nine thousand troops were considered an overestimate.

As events show, the report about their navy being dealt with by our Nukes was dead right, although rather than sink them, they just frightened them off.

The Argie air force was the biggest threat in the end. They gave an excellent account of themselves, although they were destroyed by our Harriers in combat, despite being far superior in numbers.

The army, as forecast, did not have the stomach for a fight, despite outnumbering our troops 2:1, being better equipped and in good tactical positions. Our casualties, in the end, were far lighter than anticipated. We lost three warships, one civilian ship, and one landing ship. Several more ships were damaged.

WARSHIPS

ACTIVE, BRILLIANT, GLASGOW, SHEFFIELD, ALACRITY, BRISTOL, HECLA, YARMOUTH, AMBUSCADE, BROADSWORD, HERALD, COURAGEOUS, ANDROMEDA, CARDIFF, HYDRA, ONYX, ANTELOPE, COVENTRY, INTREPID, SPLENDID, ANTRIM, DUNBARTON C, INVINCIBLE, SUPERB, ARDENT, ENDURANCE, LEEDS C, VALIANT, ARGONAUT, EXETER, MINERVA, ARROW, FEARLESS, PENELOPE AVENGER, GLAMORGAN, PLYMOUTH

RFA's

APPLELEAFE, FORT TORONTO, SIR BEDEVERE, STROMNESS, BAYLEAF, OLMEDA, SIR GAWAIN, TIDEPOOL, BLUE ROVER, OLNA, SIR GALAHAD, TIDESPRING, BRAMBLELEAF, PEARLEAF, SIR GERAINT, ENGADINE, PLUMLEAF, SIR LANCELOT, FORT AUSTIN, REGENT, SIR PERCIVAL, FORT GRANGE, RESOURSE, SIR TRISTRAM

CIVILIANS

ABELONE STAR, BRITISH TEST, IRISHMAN, ST EDMUND, ANCO CHARGER, BRITISH TRENT, JUNELLA, STENA S'SPREAD, ASTRONEMA, BRITISH WYE, LYCAON, TOR CALEDONIA, ATLANTIC C'WAY, CANBERRA, NORLAND, TYPHOON, ATLANTIC C'VAYOR, CONTENDER B, NORTHELLA, UGANDA, BALDER, CORDELLA, NORDIC FERRY, WIMPEY

S'HORSE, BALTIC FERRY, ELK, PICT, YEHUIN, BRIT. ENTERPRISE, EUROPIC FERRY, QE2, YORKSHIREMAN, BRIT.ESK, FARNELLA, RANGATIRA, SCOTISH EAGLE, BRIT. DART, FINNANGER, SALVAGEMAN, GEATSPORT, BRIT. TAMAR, GOOSANDER, SAXONNA, VINGA POLARIS, BRIT. TAY, IRIS, SHELL EBURNER, BRIT. AVON, BRIT. IVY, BRIT FERN

During a passage filled with action stations and emergency stations, along with a lot of very hard work to bring the ship to a very high state of readiness, the spirit of the ship's company was fantastic. Anyone who didn't know we were heading for war would assume we were on a normal deployment.

Newspapers were few and far between, but a brief of the world news was given day on video and each time a possible negotiated settlement was mentioned a cry of derision rang around the ship.

The general feeling was, that we would rather fight than let the Argies get away with their aggression.

11 April Sun.

As a slight break from the routine was a flight deck sports afternoon Organised with a BBQ and booze on the flight deck. Just for a laugh, I dressed as an Argie bandit complete with a bandolero of 30mm cannon shells, provided by Mick Gribbens.

Photographs were taken by the national press, and I was interviewed by a BBC reporter and video crew. Although my picture appeared in newspapers at home and abroad, the interview with the BBC was not shown, probably due to me expressing my view in guttural terms.

A great day was had by all although, of course, it rained.

16 April Fri

Crossing the line today, and guess who King Neptune was, yup me, with Taff Davies as my Queen (Yuk).

It was the Commander who volunteered me, due to my previous acting experience as a bandit. He didn't know I hadn't crossed the line myself, but the boys did and sorted me out later.

I knocked up a costume in a couple of days. It looked OK. The ceremony was a scream and was filmed by the BBC and ITV.

This time I made the telly.

Brian Hanrahan, of ITV, got a right going over, he was a great sport and had already let the ship's company snip off his beard for charity, along with several Chiefs and POs.

In the end, John McKay had a punishment warrant read out for me and I was duly sentenced to be rubbed dubbed and scrubbed for having the cheek to play King Neptune.

They gave me the works.

17 April Sat

Arrived at Ascension Island at 1200hrs, one day early. Took on FOF1, Admiral Sandy Woodward. We did not know how long we were staying, but we thought we would sail on Monday. We spent almost twenty-four hours ferrying stores around the fleet.

18 April Sun

1000hrs, action stations - due to a report of a periscope sighting at thirty miles. The fleet carried out an emergency departure and we were underway in thirty minutes from cold. A remarkable feat by the Stokers.

Our Seakings were launched. They found the contact, but it did not answer their calls to identify itself, but it sped away at a great rate of knots. We surmised it was either a Russian Nuke or a whale. The fleet stayed at sea, heading south to the 'Total Exclusion Zone' (TEZ). The poor Chinese were unhappy because they didn't want to go. The NAAFI staff all had a chance to return home but they all declined.

21 April Wed

1130hrs. Action stations due to an unidentified aircraft at 200 miles. A Sea Harrier was sent to intercept the aircraft, which was an Argentinean 707 in military colours. The Harrier chased it off. It was a recce plane which made an almost daily attempt to recce the fleet but was intercepted at 200 miles each time.

23 April Fri

The first tragedy of the campaign. A Seaking helicopter, of 826 squadron, crashed into the sea. PO(AC) Kevin Casey was missing, and presumed dead. A massive search was made by every available helicopter but to no avail. I had to pick up his belongings and there was a great sadness throughout the ship. He was married with two children.

24 April Sat

The re-taking of South Georgia was the first major event of the war.

Antrim, Endurance, Brilliant, and Plymouth attacked an Argentinean Guppy-class submarine. It was forced to beach at Gritviken, after being hit by AS 12 missiles fired from the Brilliant's Lynx helicopter.

1445hrs. Naval gunfire support preceded a landing by the SAS. Forty troops went in. The Argie garrison surrendered after two hours without any casualties. Around one hundred and fifty prisoners were taken. One prisoner was shot dead by a Marine who thought that he was trying to scuttle the sub.

The Argie propaganda machine was reporting severe fighting on the Island and kept it up until we gave them the prisoners back.

I don't know how they explained that one away. Some of the prisoners didn't want to go back, a trend that was to repeat itself after every surrender.

Most of the conscripts were no trouble but some of their special forces were belligerent, and one tried to strangle an AB who was guarding them.

1 May Sat

Admiral Sandy Woodward's birthday was celebrated by a flypast of a Vulcan bomber from the Ascensions. It dropped 21 x 1000lb bombs on Port Stanley Airfield on the way over at 0740hrs. The Vulcan had flown from the Ascensions by refuelling in the air three times. Fuel is supplied by Victor Tankers.

1050hrs. Our Harriers attack the airstrip with 1000 lb'ers and cluster bombs, to make it unusable by fighters. One of our Harriers was hit by AAA, he had a nice 20mm shell hole in his tail but got back OK.

1145hrs. We knew we had annoyed them when a Super Etendarde attacked us and launched an Exocet missile.

We were at action stations when the Commander announced 'Exocet launched, target Hermes'. Half the ship's company discovered, at that precise moment, that adrenalin comes in brown lumps, the other half hadn't heard the pipe (announcement). I was rather glad to hear that it was adrenalin as I thought I'd shit myself. The missile was, apparently, launched out of range and, thankfully, fizzled out before it got near us.

1300hrs. Action stations again, but the aircraft turned away when confronted by our Harriers at about 120 miles.

Attacking Mirage jets were intercepted by our Harriers, and our first kill was recorded by Lt Bertie Penfold of Hermes. We then discovered both Glamorgan and Arrow had been hit. Luckily only one rating was injured a seaman from the Arrow who was brought to Hermes for an operation to remove shrapnel from a stomach wound.

His words on recovering were, **"This is the last place I want to be if they are all after this ship."**

A big kill for us. The Valiant put two Mk 8 torpedoes into the Argies' second biggest ship, the General Belgrano. World opinion turned slightly against us as she was outside the 200-mile exclusion zone, along with two destroyers.

She was sunk as she was trying to outflank us but was an obvious threat as she was armed with Exocet, as well as 15x6 inch, and 8x5 inch guns.

Whilst on patrol, a Seaking helicopter was fired on by two Argie gunboats. The Coventry's Lynx joined in and sank one of them with a Seaskua missile, the other being allowed to escape, but the cheeky sod took a potshot at Glamorgan, so the Lynx put a Seaskua into her as well.

2100hrs. Confirmation the Belgrano had sunk was greeted with a loud cheer. I spared a thought for the ship's company who perished, but not in the least sorry she had sunk.

4 May Tue

A Vulcan bomber again attacked Port Stanley airfield followed by Harriers.

1415hrs. Hurried action stations, heralded an attack by Super Etendarde and Mirage jets.

There was some confusion caused, which resulted in them being reported as friendly and Invincibles CAP (Combat Air Patrol) was not airborne.

HMS Sheffield took a direct hit from an Exocet missile, and after several hours of frantic firefighting, she had to be abandoned. The injured were brought onboard along with some shock cases.

One CPO was very badly burned about the face.

His No 8's were burned into him. Whilst fighting the fires a torpedo attack was made on her and the Ardent, who was alongside assisting.

We legged it at a great rate of knots to escape torpedoes being fired at us.

1615hrs. Three Harriers attacked Stanley Airfield. Lt Taylor was shot down by AAA.

1700hrs. Sheffield abandoned with at least twenty of her ship's company dead, and another twenty injured.

6 May Thu

Two of the Invincibles Harriers disappeared whilst on patrol in very bad weather.

It is assumed they crashed into each other. The rest of the day was very quiet due to the weather.

7 May Fri

1800hrs. Action stations due to aircraft at seventy-five miles. Invincible CAP launched, but after a long search, nothing happened. These sudden attacks play on your nerves a bit after a while.

8 May Sat

Action stations, due to a submarine contact. These are the moments when you can't do a bloody thing except wait. The Seakings were launched but found nothing.

9 May Sun

1400hrs. Two Harriers returning from a bombing mission were fired upon by a fishing vessel. They returned fire with a 30mm cannon, two Harriers joined in with bombs. The vessel was abandoned with one fatality. Seventeen prisoners were picked up and taken to Invincible.

The captain of the vessel Narwhal was an Argie Lt Cdr and he confirmed it was a spy ship.

The Argie propaganda machine of course told another story, alleging our Harriers shot up an innocent fishing vessel and then fired at the survivors when in life rafts.

How they are going to account for their safe return I don't know.

The SAS were dropped onto the Narwhal to try to get the ship underway as a prize, but she was too badly damaged, so they blew her up.

1130hrs. Coventry splashed a Puma helicopter with her Seacat system. Two Skyhawks were reported missing by the Argies in bad weather.

10 May Mon

0702hrs. Sheffield sank whilst under tow to South Georgia, due to bad weather conditions. I'm glad she sank; it would have shocked the people back home to see her like that.

11 May Tue

Alacrity shelled an Argie gunboat/supply vessel that had been running supplies between east and west Falklands. There was a terrific explosion, which indicated she was carrying explosives or ammo. The ship disintegrated and so could not be identified.

12 May Wed

Action stations due to air raid warning 'red'.

Glasgow had an incredible escape when she was hit by a bomb which went in one side and out the other without any injuries. Speaking of the 826 squadron, one ditched, but everyone was saved.

13 May Thu

The SAS were due to go on a mission that was cancelled for no apparent reason.

14 May Fri

Invincibles' Harriers bombed the airstrip, we went in close to give them air cover and left at dawn at a great rate of knots before the Argies woke up and got a sad on.

15 May Sat

0230hrs. Seakings of 846 sqdn landed sixty SAS on Pebble Island, where Argies had built an airstrip and fuel dumps. They only faced token resistance. Two of the men were slightly injured.

A very successful raid which claimed eleven aircraft, mainly Pacara anti-insurgency aircraft and one Skyvan. Fuel and ammo dumps were also destroyed.

16 May Sun

1130hrs. Action stations. Aircraft at 150 miles. CAP launched, but after an hour nothing happened, and we fell out.

Two Argie supply vessels were attacked by our CAP. Although they were not seen to sink. One crew was seen taking to a life raft.

17 May Mon

Action stations, air raid warning red but nothing happened, we were probably out of their range.

2230hrs. One Seaking, of 826 sqdn ditched due to engine failure. Due to the missile threat, it was too risky to recover, so Alacrity was called in to sink it with shell fire.

All the crew were safe.

18 May Tue

Canberra, Intrepid and Fearless arrived. We took on more Harriers and GR3s (RAF Harriers) bringing Hermes up to a strength of twenty aircraft. Our helicopters were farmed out to make room.

21 May Wed

D DAY.

The weather this day was lovely and sunny. The events of the day were everything but.

0230hrs. A Vulcan bomber raided Goose Green airfield. The SAS and SBS were landed.

0730hrs. A full-scale assault began at Port San Carlos, with several thousand troops landed, spearheaded by the Para's and Commando's.

The enemy was not expecting a landing from there and put up no resistance. The bay was very small and the assault ships, particularly the Canberra did well to get in and out.

A large force of warships was in the area to give gunfire support and air defence. There was also massive air cover from Harriers.

As expected, the Argies mounted massive air attacks with wave after wave of Skyhawks and Mirage jets attacking the fleet. They took their toll. Five warships were hit, with Antelope, and Ardent severely damaged, and Argonaut and Antrim taking on unexploded bombs.

Our group included Invincible, Glasgow, Coventry, Arrow, and Alacrity, in the area known as 'Yellow Brick Road' so called because it is defined on the map as a broad yellow road. We thought we were out of range of Entendarde and Mirage but were wrong, although it was still a lot safer than Bomb Alley.

During the assault we also lost two Gazelles and one GR3, however, we splashed five Mirage and eight A4s, one Puma, and one Chinook.

After two hours a bridgehead of ten square miles was established. Stores and equipment were being landed, including Rapier anti-aircraft missiles, light tanks etc. Air raids continued throughout the day without much further damage. It was a very hard day, one which left everyone emotionally drained.

The objective had been reached but at a cost, one we found hard to accept.

22 May Sat

Antrim removed her UXB and got underway to join our group.

Argonaut had sustained severe machinery damage and lost all power. She has 2 UXBs but her weapon systems were still operational, so she was staying manned to fight on.

Four GR3s bombed ammo and fuel dumps at Goose Green, Lt Frederickson and Lt Hale attacked a fast patrol boat, which they severely damaged and it was abandoned. Argonaut's UXBs were being tackled by experts.

CinCFLT signalled: Please thank your Harrier pilots and crews for their efforts yesterday. The attrition they inflicted on the Argie must have hurt them terribly, but we must keep it up. We are doing our best to strengthen the bridgehead and will be working in the happy knowledge that you are nearby shooting both sitting and flying birds.

23 May Sun

Ardent, which had been hit on the 21st, sank. Again, the ship's company took it badly, anger and a certain amount of bewilderment at the tactics being employed led to irrational gloom.

It was announced later that Argonaut had managed to get some power on one engine, and although she still had two UXBs onboard, she could now leave the area. At this news, the ship's company cheered and visibly bucked up.

Monsoon, an Argie supply vessel, which was running supplies around the Islands, was attacked by Brilliant, it ran aground and was abandoned.

1245hrs. Action stations, low-flying aircraft, maybe Super Entendardes. Our Lynx was launched with its deflector, and chaffe was fired. During the day there were continuous attacks on our forces ashore.

Antelope splashed two A4s but took two UXBs onboard, with the loss of one hand.

1700hrs. Action stations due to reported Super Entendardes. Chaffe was fired, but nothing more happened.

Reports show that today we got five Mirage, three A4s, two Puma and one Bell Huey 206.

2330hrs. Harriers attacked Port Stanley airfield. Seconds after take-off one Harrier exploded and Lt Cdr Batt of 800 sqdn is presumed dead.

One of the UXBs on Antelope exploded, killing a bomb disposal expert. She was abandoned and the crew was taken to Intrepid.

24 May Mon

Still launching CAP and coordinating ships' movements, it is estimated the Argies have lost at least twenty-five per cent of their Air force, but they launched more raids on the ships in Bomb Alley.

Antrim and Glasgow went to the tug and repair area (TARA)

Sir Lancelot and Sir Tristram were both hit. Sir Tristram was fighting fires and had a UXB onboard.

Harriers and GR3s attacked the airfield and got a Pucara on the runway.

Also splashed today were:

Three Argie planes, by Rapier missiles ashore

Three   "   "   Hermes CAP

Three   "   "   Fearless

The Argies were now quite annoyed by us and tried to hit our Carriers (gulp.) We should be out of range, but a Kamikaze could reach us, and we expect them to try.

After a count, it is estimated we splashed around fifty per cent of their Air Force. Antelope finally sank in San Carlos Bay.

Glasgow, as reported earlier, managed to pull out.

25 May Tue

The morning weather is quite bad, which means there will be no flying yet. 800 sqdn is due to bomb Port Stanley if the weather improves.

1400hrs. Report of intense air activity over the Falklands, and that Coventry's Seadart had splashed an A4 Skyhawk. Broadsword Seawolf splashed a Pucara.

1540hrs. Yarmouth, not to be outdone by the more modern ships, decided to get in on the act and splashed an A4 with her Seacat.

To complete the A4s misery, the Rapier batteries ashore also got one.

1800hrs. Coventry and Broadsword both hit, and a feeling of sadness and intense anger welled up.

At the time, a lot of us would have liked the Vulcans to bomb the Argentine mainland air bases.

After calming down and looking at the situation objectively, I realised that bombing the mainland would only allow Galtieri to glean sympathy from the world, as happened when we sank the Belgrano.

1908hrs. Broadsword reported a bomb bounced off the sea and went into her side, then due to the ship's roll, it had left via the flight deck without exploding and with no casualties, the lucky sods.

1925hrs. Coventry sank, and Broadsword picked up survivors. We later discovered at least twenty had died.

We were further shocked by the news of the Atlantic Conveyor being hit by an Exocet missile. It was launched at the Hermes, from thirty-three miles away. We deflected it, so it chose another target. Unfortunately, the Atlantic Conveyor had no defences.

2030hrs. Atlantic Conveyor abandoned. Our helos picked up survivors from life rafts and the sea.

The survivors seemed cheerful enough when they arrived onboard, but many broke down later with delayed shock. A guard was mounted on them overnight.

We were told that about nine of the crew were dead. I went up to 3F pocket to watch the rescue operation, she was burning fiercely, and smoke was billowing out of her.

I stood watching the swarms of helos picking up survivors. I was stunned when I heard a bang and she disappeared. I assumed she had sunk, but later discovered that the explosion killed the lights and that she was still afloat.

26 May Wed

The Commander confirmed that nine died on the Atlantic Conveyor and that there were twenty dead, and twenty injured, on the Coventry. The casualties were remarkably few considering the devastation caused, but a sad loss, nonetheless.

We were told the troops ashore had extended the beachhead from ten to sixty miles, which was great news.

1715hrs. Air raid warning Red over the islands. Our Harriers are launched to assist.

Two GR3s were attacked by a Puma helicopter, the cheeky bugger, not surprising they returned the compliment and vandalised it.

Mail arrived onboard (Yipee)

27 May Thur

Both Sir Tristram and Sir Lancelot, and also the Argonaut, still have UXBs. All are being dealt with by bomb disposal experts.

It was extremely foggy so there was no activity that morning, but the troops were still advancing ashore.

1225hrs. Air raid warning Red on the Hermes group. A4s, their electronic emissions picked up by Ambuscade. Two of the A4s landed on Hermes, looking astonishingly like our Harriers.

1721hrs. One of our G3s was shot down whilst on a bombing mission over the Falklands. The pilot was seen bailing out over an Argie-occupied area of Goose Green.

2000hrs. Troops came under heavy attack.

QE2 arrived at South Georgia, carrying three thousand troops.

The Commando advanced towards Gouglas settlement. The Para's to Darwin, Goose Green, and Teal Inlet.

Two A4s were splashed by Rapiers and one of the Fearless's Seacat (Two strikes for Seacat... bloody hell.)

28 May Fri

Another foggy day that restricted air activity.

Antrim collected the General of War to go ashore after visiting Hermes for a sitrep.

Argonaut UXB was removed at last. That must be a relief for them.

Word reached us of a bombing run on our troop's position yesterday, which resulted in slight damage to our field hospital and other installations.

1225hrs. Our troops are attacked by Pucara's, one of which was splashed.

The Commander of the Paras and ten of his men were killed during the advance.

29 May Sat

Douglas and Teal Inlet have been taken.

There is still heavy fighting at Darwin and Goose Green. Our Harriers are sent to help, and there are hopes of taking it today.

1430hrs. Goose Green won back, and 1400 prisoners were taken. Our casualties were light. One A4 and one Mirage splashed.

Another cock up by Invincible.

A Harrier fell over the side, the pilot ejected safely. The prat must have thought it was an angled flight deck.

Atlantic Causeway arrived. She landed Seakings to us for fuelling before they went ashore.

The Trawlers, which had been converted to Minesweepers, arrived in South Georgia.

1545hrs. We went to action stations in case the day's events had further annoyed Argie.

30 May Sun

British Wye was bombed by a Hercules, but all missed except one that bounced off the Forecastle without exploding. The Commander made the understatement of the year when he said, "They had been fairly lucky."

The Harrier pilot who bailed out over Goose Green on the 27th had been hiding out at a farmhouse. He approached our troops when they took the position. The pilot is Lt Cdr Iveson.

A GR3 was damaged by anti-aircraft fire. The pilot ejected when he ran out of fuel, but he was rescued.

1640hrs. Action stations due to build-up of air activity.

1905hrs. Stood down.

1920hrs. Quarters stand to, a missile launched at Hermes (A distinct sign of sweat on my brow.) Chaffe fired, and a Lynx launched our 'goalkeeper' is up threat, so hopefully the sod will miss us.

Our CAP is engaging two A4s and two Super Entendardes. The missile was launched from 30 miles south but was successfully decoyed and splashed into the sea.

One of the A4s bombed the Avenger, it missed, however. Avenger didn't miss when she returned fire and splashed it.

An A4 was also splashed by a Rapier battery ashore.

It was revealed that during the taking of Goose Green, the Para's captured some Howitzers and anti-aircraft guns intact. Over two hundred and fifty Argies were killed.

Forgive me if I don't shed a tear.

The Argies claim the Invincible was hit and seen to burst into flames, obviously, the pilot was pissed.

31 May Mon

1015hrs Action stations. Intelligence reports suggest a Super Entendarde attack is on the cards. Nothing happened. Our group moved further east to confuse the enemy.

2005hrs. Action stations again, but no action. Now I'm confused as well.

For the last two days, our troops were consolidating their positions, and moving prisoners to San Carlos.

Blue Rover, Atlantic Causeway, and Baltic Ferry, escorted by Brilliant, are going in to offload Rapier weapon systems, runway gear, and three thousand troops. Our 'Blue Berry' platoon will guard the prisoners.

The prisoners will be repatriated, probably to show the Argies they are getting thrapped.

Argonaut is trying to head for home, with limited power and in very rough seas, she is having a hard time of it.

A new CO for the Para's is dropping in from a high-level aircraft today.

1 Jun Tue

0745hrs. Action stations due to a possible Entendarde attack.

0820hrs. All ships in the operating zone are on red alert. A Canberra flew over and dropped three bombs, all of which missed their target.

Mount Kent, which is only twelve miles from Stanley, has been taken by the Paras.

The Ghurkas, and Scots Guards, plus 40, 42 and 45 Commando, are due to land today.

Two GR3s arrived onboard from Ascension, after a three-thousand-mile trip, which involved refuelling in mid-air several times. It took them seven hours nonstop. They must be knackered.

1350hrs. 801 sqdn shot down a Hercules transport plane which had been landing stores. Invincible did something right at last, yippee.

We were informed the Ghurkas landed last night, and the Scots and Welsh Guards landed today.

Invincible lost a Harrier, which splashed just outside Port Stanley. The pilot was seen to land in the sea. a Seaking was sent to rescue him.

It has been revealed the Argies used two Napalm bombs against our troops in the battle for Goose Green. A large stockpile of these weapons has been found.

My immediate reaction is to use the stuff against them, but we won't of course, we fight fair.

2 June Wed

The is a buzz going around that we sank a sub last, night although nothing has been said officially.

1455hrs. Went to state 2 condition Yankee for the first time in four and a half weeks, and five deck mess decks may now be used, which seems to back up the sub's report.

The official reason given is we are now one hundred and forty miles east of the islands, and the air/sea and sub threats were low.

All troops are now ashore and moving up heavy artillery for the final assault on Port Stanley.

1620hrs. Action stations due to electronic emissions thought to be enemy aircraft to the southwest, were picked up by a Lynx and Cardiff. CAP launched from Invincible, and Broadsword is up threat, bless her.

1700hrs. Stood down

1725hrs. Quarters stand to, due to electronic emissions from the north-west picked up by Cardiff, then Lynx. (A right bloody double act we've got here) Chaffe fired, and our little Exocet deflector and CAP launched.

1732hrs. Fell out, suspecting the EMF was from Uganda's radar. Due to these two incidents, and due to taking twenty minutes to get to 1Z, we have now reverted to 2Z and banned the use of five deck messdecks.

Oh well, for one hour and twenty minutes, it was luxury.

3 June Thu

A very foggy day which stopped our bombing runs to back up the troops. It also means that Argie can't bother us, which is nice.

Our troops have advanced to Beagle Ridge, which is only seven miles from Port Stanley. The Guards have taken Port Louis and Johnsone Harbour. The Para's have advanced along the coast to Bluff Cove, which has an important bridge, which still seems to be intact.

Port Stanley is now surrounded on three sides. It has the sea on the other. The Argies are being shelled from Mount Kent, so they can't be happy. The only other positions held by Argies are Mount Moody, and Mount Foxbury, on the West Falklands.

One of our Vulcans had to land in Brazil for straying into their airspace after a bombing run, maybe short of fuel.

4 June Fri

Flight Lt Glover, who was shot down on 21st May, and presumed dead, is in a hospital in Argentina.

The Brazilian Government allowed our Vulcan to leave after first removing the single Sidewinder it still had onboard.

We dropped leaflets on the Argies, urging them to surrender. The leaflets contained a safe conduct pass.

Four high-flying enemy planes were spotted. They did not attack. We suspect they were Mirages escorting a supply run.

Invincible and Brilliant are going to the southwest of the islands to put up air cover to deter further attempts to supply the islands.

Monsoonman, an island ferry commandeered by the Argies, but later beached after being attacked by one of our frigates, is now being used to ferry Ghurkas, and stores, from San Carlos to Bluff Cove.

Heavy artillery has been brought to Mount Kent. We now have about twenty-four Howitzers up there, which should give them a headache. Our artillery outranges most of theirs, except for three large artillery guns. They will no doubt become an SAS target.

The new CO of the Para regiment made a spectacular entrance by paratrooping from a Vulcan flying at 25,000 feet. He carried a signal transmitter and wore oxygen-breathing gear. He free-fell for 21,000 feet before opening his black chute for the final four thousand feet. He touched down yards from his HQ on Mount Kent, with the aid of radar.

This was probably the most romantic story of the war and was genuinely thought to be true at the time, but alas it was not true but is still a good story.

One Argie plane tried a bombing run on our troops but didn't hit a thing.

5 Jun Sat

Invincible and Brilliant returned to our position. No incidents were reported.

1835hrs. Action stations due to intelligence reports of a possible air strike. Five CAP launched, two Harriers and two GR3s for a reconnaissance run to the west Falkland, where Argies may be trying to para drop.

Lynx with deflector on deck burning and turning

A fuel depot to refuel our planes has been set up in San Carlos. It is to be used as a forward operating base to save them from returning if they are fully armed.

Three of the trawlers converted to Minesweepers left South Georgia for the Falklands. They are ready to sweep.

6 Jun Sun

Avenger is shelling Fox Bay, while Cardiff and Yarmouth are shelling Port Stanley. Cardiff has splashed one aircraft, but it was unidentified.

The Welsh Guards left San Carlos to go to Lively Island, before hopping across to Bluff Cove.

Invincible again going southwest to give total air cover. The Special Forces have deployed to West Falklands to mop up the odd outposts.

7 Jun Mon

Five CAP were launched from Hermes, due to an air raid warning over the Falklands.

Exeter's Seadart splashed one aircraft.

Cardiff and Arrow bombarded Port Stanley overnight and five hundred rounds of artillery shells per gun (thirty guns), have been brought to the forward position.

8 Jun Tue

Today goes down as the second bloodiest day so far, surpassed only by D-Day.

1650hrs. Action stations due to build-up of air threat to the Southwest, air raid warning red ashore.

We launched three Harriers as CAP and had the lynx burning and turning on deck. Our goalkeeper, Broadsword, is in position up threat. There are reports of fierce action in the Falklands area, Argie aircraft are attacking our ships with some force.

Plymouth was hit by a possible bomb, but reports suggest it may be only splinter holes.

The 4.5" gun and Mortars are damaged, but the Seacat system is ok. Fires are being fought aft.

Two troop landing ships, Sir Tristram, and Sir Galahad, have been hit by bombs in Fitzroy Cove, Galahad has been abandoned, and Tristram is fighting fires. Both were unloading ammo at the time of the attack.

An American-owned Liberian-registered tanker was bombed by the Argies, four hundred miles from the Falklands. She is the 22,000-ton Hercules and is listing to port, trying to make for the nearest port whilst fighting fires.

Plymouth has splashed one aircraft with her Seacat, obviously, the Argies have upset her.

Invincible CAP splashed one aircraft and badly damaged two. They are not expected to make it back.

We lost a GR3 when Wing Cdr Squires crashed whilst refuelling at San Carlos. The second wave of Mirages were all splashed, one by Invincibles CAP, and the other three by our CAP. Flt Lt Morgan got two and Lt Smith got one. His second kill of the conflict.

Two more GR3s arrived after a flight from Ascension Island, lasting over seven and a half hours.

The converted trawlers Junella, Farnella, and Northella, are going into Stanley area tonight minesweeping.

Avenger was hiding in Albermarle Harbour. She was waiting to pounce on anything that tried to break the blockade.

Hermes is going in close to give total air cover. The assault must be close.

Plymouth update: A bomb went through the mortar handling room. It didn't explode but a stray bullet set off a mortar bomb which did most of the damage. Five were injured but none fatally.

Sir Galahad. Now burnt out with over fifty dead and one hundred and twenty injured, mostly Welsh Guards. The rest had to swim ashore without their arms and equipment, a tragic blow to the final assault.

Hercules was attacked by four planes. The first one bombed it, and the rest attacked with rockets. Hercules is a super tanker of 220,117 tons. The thirty officers and men onboard are all Italians, but the tanker is American owned. She is listing and heading for a southern Brazilian port.

9 Jun Thu

1900hrs. Action stations due to a build-up of the air threat over the TA. Six CAP are airborne over TA and two over our group.

1910hrs. ECM Lynx launched and our goalkeeper up threat.

1930hrs. Two more CAP launched to assist over TA.

Norland, containing Prisoners and our 'Blue Berry Platoon', is on her way to Montevideo.

The flight deck party have, to date, used 1,25000 tons of Avcat.

10 Jun Thur

We are prewarned of action stations due to 'something happening ashore'.

1050hrs. Action stations, six CAP airborne over TA and GR3s are supporting the army.

1145hrs. Air raid warning red over TA but only because the sun is breaking over the horizon causing early morning haze that would be ideal for attacking aircraft.

1150hrs Nothing happened, so fell out. Four Mirages attempted a run but turned back when met by a sky full of Harriers.

11 Jun Fri

Sorties carried out by units of the SAS, SBS, and Para's. There have been several clashes resulting in nine dead Argies and nil of our boys.

We had a very quiet day.

Phase one of the final assault begins at midnight, the plan being for a Vulcan bombing run, followed by a series of Harrier attacks on key positions.

Vulcan Run was successful.

Four warships are carrying out shore bombardment of key positions, using 1500 rounds of 4.5.

Harriers attacked the racecourse and airstrip, to knock out Argie HQ and Pucaras. The shelling is very successful, resulting in several gun positions being knocked out and judging by the explosions after the Harrier runs, several aircraft on the ground were destroyed.

2300hrs. World news announced the surrender of Port Stanley. Some relief spread through the ship, and a few tinnies were cracked.

The Commander warned against exuberance. The Argentines had not admitted defeat and we were still liable to attack from the Argentina mainland. However, I believe that they are well and truly beaten. Their navy is trapped in the harbour, their Air Force is almost wiped out, and we have several thousand prisoners.

The surrender was at 2200hrs. It included an unconditional surrender of all troops on east and west Falklands. The surrender was accepted by Major General Moore, Commanding Officer of the troops ashore.

Arrangements were being made to return some 12000 Argies home, although officers and other key personnel may be held until the formal cessation of hostilities is announced by the Junta. The prisoners are suffering from everything from scabies to malnutrition.

Admiral Woodward sent a signal to the UK, urging an end to all hostilities by Argentina to enable us to feed, cloth, and shelter the prisoners. He warned the defence of the task force would remain his top priority and that if attacks were carried out many hundreds of prisoners could die of exposure.

Nothing has been announced on an end to hostilities.

It seems there have been disagreements amongst the Junta, and the demonstrations in Buenos Aries, which had to be smashed by police.

President Galtieri has resigned... Yippie.

We are still carrying on as normal, just in case.

19 Jun Sat

The troops ashore are busy clearing up the battle area, and Argie prisoners are being used to clear up their own shit.

Apparently, the whole island is in a mess that will take some months to put right. The Stanley area, from the town to the racecourse, has been covered in turves.

Two men have been injured, one in a minefield, due to plastic mines being difficult to detect, and one who was investigating a machine gun post.

20 Jun Sun

Glamorgan, Plymouth, and British Wye are leaving tonight for home. Geatsport arrives.

1224hrs. The South Sandwich Island of Thula today surrendered to British warships.

Around fifty Argie military, and a group of scientists, have been there for several years.

21 Jun Mon

The EEC have lifted sanctions with Argentine, on the condition they would re-impose them if hostilities resumed. They are continuing an arms embargo. The UK and USA will continue with trade sanctions until an assurance that hostilities have ceased.

The Argies have condemned our actions in 'booting out' what they term as Civilian Scientists from Thula.

Still, no new President was elected as their three services could not agree on who should get the job.

The army ashore is having difficulty in clearing the minefields. Each Argie unit planted mines but neglected to tell the other units where they put them. Many Argies have been killed as a result.

22 Jun Tue

Resource, Fort Grange, and Geatsport are going into Stanley, to feed the troops. Brilliant is recovering her helo, before going home later today.

Onyx has been patrolling shallow waters around the islands and is coming out for a break to enable our 826 pilots to carry out detection exercises, as the Argies didn't show up for them to practice on.

SPLICE THE MAINBRACE FOR THE BIRTH OF PRINCE CHARLES AND PRINCESS DIANA'S BABY.

24 June Thu

Action stations at sunset. Seemingly pointless and very boring, however, the captain made a broadcast. (I suspect the action stations were called to ensure everyone was awake on this momentous occasion). He tried to cool down the buzz that was flying around but only succeeded in confirming them. He said Hermes would be released after Invincible had returned to the TEZ, and FOF3 had taken over, which happen by 2nd July, and we could sail after that.

25 Jun Fri

Resource, Fearless, Elk, Norland, Europic Ferry, and Canberra are leaving for home, full of troops. The Commander said, in case we are feeling lonely, there are still seventy-eight ships south of Ascension.

Taff left for duty as Falklands postie. He, and the five ratings helping, were described by the Ops Officer as a 'Team of Experts' going ashore to carry out daily mail delivery from Stanley.

Admiral Woodward is going ashore to welcome Governor Rex Hunt back.

1 Jul Thu

FOF3 coming aboard for handover. He takes over from FOF1 at midnight.

Abelone Star joined our group, she has mail and stores. Carrying out a vast vertrep of stores that should have been done yesterday but couldn't be due to very bad weather.

2 Jul Fri

Continuing with vertrep.

Taff, the intrepid explorer, returned onboard.

The Commander informed us that, due to the bad weather causing damage ashore, we cannot now land our GR3s for at least another twenty-four hours, maybe longer, so our departure will be delayed. (Gloom)

3 Jul Sat

0800hrs. Anchored at Port William, Falkland Islands. I was quite impressed with the view of the mountains and rugged terrain, now covered with a thin layer of snow. At last, I saw a real live wild penguin, it swam up to about twenty feet from the ship. It was small and greyish, with an orange-yellow head.

0830hrs. Sir Lancelot sailed past, under her own steam, despite having been hit twice. She looked in better nick than us.

About nineteen ships were in the harbour, including Uganda.

1230hrs. Flypast of Harrier, Wessex, Seaking, and Lynx. Very impressive.

1300hrs. FOF1 and staff left.

1600hrs. Sailed.

4 Jul Sun

Ship ordered back to port.

Captain going to dine with the Admiral. The rumour is that the Admiral wants to keep us down here. (Instant gloom and despondency).

On his return, the captain informs us there is a communications problem ashore and we cannot be released until it has been sorted. However, we have been allowed to steam 400 miles north, to await release in company with Broadsword.

5 Jul Mon

We were informed by the captain that we had been released and were now on our way home (Yahoo).

Come down from breakfast. We were making about twenty-two knots, it was a lovely day, and noticeably warmer, although still bloody cold.

The Ops Officer informed us we were fast steaming to catch up with RFA for RAS.

6 Jul Tue

Nine hundred miles north of the Falklands. Still doing twenty-plus knots. We should reach Ascension on the eleventh of July.

A happy birthday to me.

7 Jul Wed

0800hrs. We are now two-thousand miles from the Ascension, and one thousand miles from the nearest point of Argentina.

1630hrs. Fell out of defence stations, hooray, fresh air and a bit of time off at last.

8 Jul Thu

Sunday routine today, followed by two Saturdays and another Sunday to unwind.

9 Jul Fri

Two Russian Bears were sighted eight to five miles east.

11 Jul Sun

Two Russian Bears sighted eighty-five miles east. Our Harriers intercepted one, and a Nimrod from Ascension the other. The Russians completely ignored them and flew several very low passes over us. The Harrier was sitting on his wing and looked like a gnat alongside the enormous Bear. He could have landed on his tailplane with comfort.

15 Jul Thu

We were visited by a Russian Hormone helicopter which came right alongside, I thought it was going to land, it was so close, they sat there merrily taking pictures they were seeing if we had sustained any damage, sorry to disappoint them.

16 Jul Fri

We were visited by a Russian Kresta 11 Cruiser, who came close enough to RAS with us. This ship is obviously where the Hormone came from, and they are making sure we are not damaged.

21 Jul Wed

We are visited, this time by one of our ships, who steamed alongside and 'cheered ship'. It was a training frigate, onboard were WRNS, the first females we had seen for almost four months.

It was a nice gesture, followed a couple of hours later by the Illustrious doing the same and showing her paces. She was better looking than Invincible. Her Vulcan Phalanx guns looked mean. We anchored at Spithead at 1930hrs to await high tide at 1200hrs tomorrow.

It must have been the longest night on record.

22 Jul Thu

Well, we were at last, and what an incredible welcome it was.

There were hundreds of small boats escorting us in and jostling for positions. One gorgeous bird on a sailing yacht took her bikini top off and waved it.

I seriously thought of jumping over the side there and then.

After what seemed like hours, we got alongside, and I managed to be first off. Waiting were Mary, Mom, Lynn, Annette, Emma, Mick, and Madge from the pub, which was a pleasant surprise.

After a couple of pints, I decided that the war was over.

***

I am not saying that Rocky's diary is one hundred per cent accurate, (*or even fifty per cent, it may only be thirty per cent accuracy, or even thirty per cent inaccuracy, and forty per cent fantasy*) but it was written in good faith, based on what he was told and what he found out.

Some entries are written retrospectively.

Although we were there, we were told little about what was happening. It's difficult to remember the exact sequence of events without undertaking research.

But this diary was written with emotion, and I thank Rocky for allowing me to take a copy.

I was due to leave the ship.

The Boss said he would get me a foreign draft. See, it pays to keep the boss's fridge filled with beer.

I fancied S.H.A.P.E in Belgium, (Supreme HQ Allied Powers in Europe), a multinational Police Force that protected the NATO HQ in Belgium. I heard lots of good stories about SHAPE, everything cheap, new cars, good social life.

"Nah," said the boss, you go there, and you will do Police work for two years and be behind the times for promotion when you get back.

Good point I suppose, so he got me a draft to Gibraltar.

I wasn't sure about it, as I said before, it was just a watering hole for the visiting ships, cut off from the rest of the world, including Spain, which it was physically attached to.

But I wasn't going to turn it down, so, the wife and our two kids packed our crates and got ready to go.

Much of our stuff was sent in advance, so we stayed with Mum and Dad for a few days. They took us to Luton Airport, where we stayed overnight before flying into the unknown.

It was a bit of an experience for Mum and Dad too because, when they dropped us off at Luton, they got lost and it took them hours to find the M4 to get home.

The atmosphere in that car must have been steaming.

MICHAEL J HENNESSY

HMS Hermes

Returning home

GIBRALTAR

1982-84 - Aged 25-27

We were picked up from Gibraltar Airport by the Duty Provost, who took us to our Married Quarter flat. It was three bedrooms, very clean, and nice.

We unpacked, and I went across to the RNPHQ to meet the night watch. There were a couple of lads I knew from Portsmouth. It is always good to see friendly faces when you arrive at a new place.

In the RNPHQ there was also a bar, so I got to meet many of the other guys too.

The provost HQ was not situated within the dockyard or military facility but next door to a cinema on a public road. It gave quick access to Main Street and other parts of the town which could be considered 'problem areas', for instance, a couple of the popular nightclubs where visiting sailors would congregate in the early hours.

I was to work in the RNPHQ.

There was a day and night watch system and a total of ten staff. There was HMS Rooke, the naval Establishment in Gibraltar, where there were a further six staff, and two more at the Mail Office in the dockyard.

So, there was a chance for a job change because two years working as Provost would have put me in the same situation, I would have found myself in if I had been drafted to Belgium.

The main role of the staff at the provost was the same as any other RNPHQ, but we did tend to get more of the drunks due to the visiting ships, and there were a lot of domestic disputes.

Because of the amount of drink on the Rock, we had a unique system whereby, if a person was drunk but no trouble and conscious, we would just get a signature off the ship's OOD, and it would be left for the ship to decide what action to take.

They were called Indulged to Capacity (ITC) and saved a lot of report writing. If the ship were to receive a Patrol Report, they would be obliged to charge the individual and report to outcome of the trial to us.

If we were writing too many ITC chits the boss would have a word for not getting enough drunks and using the ITC as a means of avoiding extra work.

Of course, we bloody were. If it's a signature or a four-page report for every drunk. No competition, so we used to give him a damn good ignoring.

Things were beginning to look like what I expected them to look like; a watering hole for sailors who wanted a good drink.

But it turned out to be a great place to live. Although only three square miles, there was lots to do.

There was the Rock itself, always nice to go up and see the Rock Apes and the views. The beaches were second to none, there were the historic caves, carved from the Rock during the long siege when Spain was trying to get their bit of land back, and there were the lower caves used during the war, when they housed everything from offices to a hospital.

St Michael's cave is a huge natural space in the rock. It is used for all sorts of public events, such as the Miss Gibraltar competition, and music concerts. Of course, there was the mess, where there was always something going on for the family, especially at weekends.

All I saw on previous visits to the Rock was Main Street and the pubs, so this was a great surprise, and a lovely place for the family.

We had a good relationship with the Army RMPs, who were available to help us, and us them, should there be any problems.

One, who I remember, was 'China' Roberts.

He had spent a lot of time in Northern Ireland and, although he never confirmed it, the story goes he was injured in an explosion and was pinned under a twisted vehicle. The medics who were in attendance decided the best course of action was to amputate China's leg. Unfortunately, they told him this whilst he still had a sidearm. He persuaded them to try harder at getting his legs free. They did and he made a full recovery.

The RMPs had a great mess in the middle of town, though anywhere on the Rock is near to the middle of town, it was an open invitation for us to go, and for them to use our mess.

The RAF police were also there but they were hardly ever seen.

They kept to their base and airfield, if by chance, we came across a drunken 'Crab Fat' we would take him to the RAF Police office and spoil their quiet evening of knitting and dressmaking.

'Crab Fat' is the nickname given to the RAF. It is because their uniform is the same colour as raw crab meat.

I mentioned earlier that Gibraltarians consider themselves British because it suits them. I stand by this, but if you make a friend of a Gibraltarian then you have a friend for life.

Soon after arriving, the wife started working at one of the Bars in Irishtown, which is the street parallel to the Main Street. The wife of a friend already worked there, so it was a known pub.

The Landlord was a very generous man who, every Sunday, if we were off watch, would take me and George, the other girl's husband, to different places around the Rock. Places we would never have known existed, and where we met people, we would never have come across had we kept to only socialising with the military contingent, which a lot of people do.

Some of the Civil Police were sociable, mainly CID. They were renowned for their Christmas parties but, in the main, kept to themselves.

The Rock's equivalent of the MOD Police are the Gibraltar Services Police (GSP), they were glorified security guards who got paid a lot of money for doing nothing.

They were usually pissed with power and best left to themselves.

The other Service, which turned out to be a good crowd, was the Prison Staff.

The prison is not an obvious structure, it is part of the old Moorish Castle overlooking the town. There were never many prisoners, so it was a nice quiet number.

They have a lovely little club, one with unique 'old world' exposed beams across the ceiling. Unique because they used to be the gallows.

At that time, the border to Spain was closed, or only open to pedestrians, so crime was practically non-existent, but after we left Gib, the border opened, and the Prison Officers job became a far busier one.

I was on duty on the first Christmas Day I was there along with Phil who I knew from Pompey. There was no need for two of us but the RPO in charge wanted two vans out and about.

Phil wasn't having it, so he 'doctored' one of the vans and told the RPO I was going home because there was only one vehicle. Legs, the RPO didn't believe him for one minute, but I was sent home anyway.

He kept asking me, after that, if Phil had done something to the van, I denied any knowledge until Phil had been home for some time and Legs was about to go.

It was too late for him to do anything but I'm sure he would have been a vindictive bastard if he had stayed.

It was pretty much a holiday, with the odd blast of hard work when there was more than one ship in.

But once a year there was a NATO exercise, called 'Spring Train', when we had up to twenty ships of various nationalities in port at the same time. When that happened, the locals were never to be seen, and the landlords wrung their hands with the thought of all the extra money they were going to make.

They hired extra staff but usually kept a low profile themselves.

The Navy drafted in about twenty-five extra Regulators to help. It was nonstop, scraping drunks off the street, breaking up fights, returning sailors onboard ITC, and report writing.

Then you had the poor buggers who dared to lean onto a car. They were in court, fined, compensation for the car owner was awarded, and the sailor returned to their ship, not to be let ashore again.

There were a lot of them. This went on for about five days. And the Reggies who volunteered for a week in Gib, thinking they would be on the beach, never volunteered again.

If I experienced 'Spring Train' before being posted to Gibraltar I would have never gone. When the ships left, it was back to normal for another year, we still got busy at times, but never to that extent.

Sometimes we would offer to take some visiting ship's crew around the Rock in the Provost van. It was a nice break and a laugh to show off your driving skills around all the narrow streets and winding roads.

This once, I was showing a van full of Officers around; we went up to the top of the Rock, via the Apes, and St Michael's cave.

On my way down the zig-zagging road, I was going a bit too fast, mainly to put the shits up the Officers. On the second sharp bend of the zig zags I found, to my horror, the brakes weren't responding the way they should, like, not at all.

I resisted the urge to scream and jump out of the van. It wouldn't have looked good, especially as the Officers in the back were locked in. The doors could only be opened from the outside.

The stretch of road was only about three hundred yards long before the next sharp bend. I was sweating and pulled on the steering wheel as I pushed down on the brakes, still with little response. I started to slowly pull up the hand brake at the same time and, just as we reached the bend, the van slowed enough to take the corner, still a little too fast but I managed to stay on the road.

I slowed down, and the brakes started working normally again.

There were a couple of comments as we went around the bend, and the Officers were thrown around a bit, but I could handle that better than a crumpled mass of metal and blood at the bottom of the Rock.

I was probably the most sensible driver in Gibraltar after that.

I had been on the Rock for three months when I heard my grandmother had died, she was 77.

I was allowed home for the funeral and, to kill two birds with one stone, (forgive the pun), I was to go on a short course at Mill Hill, which was where the Fleet Mail Office was, it was run by the Army.

I didn't mind because it would mean I was in line for a job change to the Gibraltar Mail Office, further down the line.

After the funeral, I went to the London RNPHQ, where I was accommodated during the course. London RNPHQ is a much sought-after job, mainly because of the extra money you get for living there. But when you have been once, they tend to send you back, because of the difficulty learning the traffic systems as much as anything. There is a good mess, and it is well supported.

After the short course, I was at the RNPHQ for two more nights before my flight back to Gib.

The first night in the mess I was introduced to a drink called 'Jellybean'. This was put in a pint glass and consisted of all the white spirits and some orange juice topped with lemonade. It tasted gorgeous. I managed two before I retired hurt. Strong shit!

The second night we had a few in the mess until closing time but we fancied another drink. It was Sunday and the drinking times were strict, so one of the local lads told us to go to a certain Italian Restaurant and ask for a 'Pot of Tea', nudge, nudge, wink, wink, and we would get a pot of wine.

He told us he was a frequent customer. So, we went. Ordered a meal and a 'Pot of Tea'. Twenty minutes later the Spaghetti

Bolognaise arrived and then the Tea Pot and cups. Inside the Tea Pot was… Bloody Tea!

Another early night. Bollocks.

Back in Gibraltar, things ground on. The work was mundane and nothing of any interest.

The social life was pretty good. The Navy had a two-lane Bowling Alley, and we ran a league. The only thing was, that you needed to put the pins into the rack yourself for them to be reset. There was no machinery. So, there was always someone behind the pins setting them back up.

You couldn't see who was there except for a two-inch break in the panelling above the pins. Chris Mansfield, a larger-than-life character was setting up the pins. A funny guy who would always do something surprising for a laugh. He and his wife were always at each other's throats, usually in a joking kind of way, but sometimes serious. He didn't seem to care.

Once, Chris had a few drinks and he became mischievous. To everyone's amusement, after each strike, he would throw an item of clothing out from behind the pins. This culminated in the climax of his skivvies being lobbed out.

He thought he couldn't be seen, but that break in the panelling was waist high and you could see Chris's winkle, or as he put it, "A quarter inch of steaming, hot throbbing, winky."

His Missus was livid and gave him hell. He didn't care.

Half an hour later it was Chris's turn to bowl, he got a strike and to his surprise, a piece of clothing came flying out from behind the pins. Another strike and another piece of clothing.

He recognized the dress that came flying out, it was his wife's. He legged it towards the pins, picking up the clothes as he went. They had a right old argument, which made great entertainment for everyone and made our night.

They were good mates again by the end of the night.

I had news from home that doctors had found a cancerous lump on one of my father's kidneys, which they removed. He was having a bad time because, after the surgery, he got a blood clot in his lung, which was painful and life-threatening. Thank God he pulled through. He came to visit after, with my mum in tow.

They stayed a week.

My brother and his family also visited for a week; he never turns down a cheap holiday!

One of the traditions in the Navy is that visiting ships would have a 'Rock Race'.

That's exactly what it is, a race to the top of the Rock. It is probably the toughest race anyone can take part in, at least on the Rock.

Sometimes we would join them. We took ourselves up the winding road, past onlookers who clapped as we passed. We took a little time to glance at the magnificent views as we went higher and higher. It was hot, and very steep in parts but to get to the finishing line was a huge sense of accomplishment and satisfaction.

We sat in a daze at getting to the top without stopping and then, when we opened the van door the heat hit us like a sledgehammer.

What?

You didn't think I ran to the top, did you?

One afternoon, I took the kids to the pub, the Royal Oak, where the Missus worked. I left the eldest, Daniel playing pool in the bar while I took Deanne to the Video shop to choose a couple of films for the evening.

It took about twenty minutes to choose the movies, then I went back to the pub. I was there for ten minutes, showing the wife the films when she asked, "Where's Deanne?"

I looked around and said, "No idea."

I looked a bit more, then shouted "OH SHIT."

I'd left her in the shop. When I got back, it was only three hundred yards away, she was still looking at the films on the rack, oblivious that I had left her, so, I nonchalantly walked over to her, held her hand and walked out. Phew.

That was a good thing about Gibraltar, it was safe, at least when the border with Spain was closed.

There was no crime and no worries.

There were a lot of parties at people's homes.

One day, we held a BBQ on our balcony, with a punch to drink on top of the normal beer and spirits. I know it was a flat, but we had two balconies which was ideal.

Unfortunately, I didn't invite the people who lived below, which I should of, because late in the evening when I was on the kitchen balcony, I felt the uncontrollable urge to throw up, which I did. Over the edge of the balcony.

Wow. That was some good punch.

We all used to use the balconies for drying clothes, our neighbours below had clothing out when my bodily fluids spilt out of me, heading downwards, and of course, splashing their nice clean clothes.

They didn't say much about it thankfully; they never said anything. After that, I should have apologised at the earliest opportunity, but I was such a coward and they were a miserable, unsociable couple anyway, which is why they weren't invited in the first place.

The provost vans were Leyland Sherpa vans, and our yard, where they were parked was off a narrow one-way street with fishbone parking to one side.

We had to approach, pull to the left and then reverse along the narrow alley into our car park. There were always kids speeding around the road on their motorbikes, or souped-up sewing machines as we liked to call them.

On this occasion, I was parking up for the day. I indicated right because that is where I was going to reverse, but as I indicated I pulled to the left to get in position. As I did, one of these 'Boy Racers' overtook me on my left and I, well, I drove into him. He hit my wing, came off his bike, and went sliding down the road.

Thankfully, I had the presence of mind to change the indicator from right to left, so by the time he looked up, and a couple of witnesses looked to find out what the noise was, I was indicating in the right direction I was travelling.

He was in the wrong. Ask my witnesses.

He was unhurt, but his pride was dented. Although the paperwork involved after an accident with a MOD vehicle is horrendous, I was judged 'not to blame'.

I became one of two Social Secretaries for the mess, which meant we needed to provide entertainment for the members and their families. We did a pretty good job, arranging quiz nights, theme nights, more mess dinners, ladies' nights, BBQs and more, but one of my failures was my cocktail cards.

I thought it was a good idea to have a selection of cocktails and make a pile of cards with the cocktails we created printed on them. Things like 'Hennessy Ball Wanger', and 'Bucket of Vomit', to name but two. I made up the names and the contents as I went along.

But we started playing a game with the cards.

You may have played 'Jacks', where the cards are dealt face up to each of the people playing. Whoever gets the first Jack nominates a drink, or in this instance, picks a card, the second Jack buys, it and the third drinks it.

Now, as most of these cocktails had at least three spirits in them people got drunk quickly, and the drunker you got the more you wanted to play, which resulted in people being rat-arsed during a quiet afternoon drink. So, for the sake of our health, sanity, and reputation, the cards were disposed of.

Another social event in Gib was, 'It's A Knockout'. It was quite cold, so we arranged to be followed around the course with an urn of coffee and a bottle of rum. It was a lot of fun playing silly games. There was a trophy for the winner, but nobody cared who won, it was simply a good day of fun for the whole family.

As you get older, I was only twenty-six, you tend to get more sensible, especially when you have kids. Your priorities change from having a damn good time with your mates, whatever the consequences, to advancing yourself, getting yourself promoted, and providing for your family.

I'm not saying I didn't still have a laugh or a good time, as you will see, it is that there were fewer disregards for the consequences of my actions, and more concern for setting the right example, being a role model, and trying not to drop myself in the shit.

This is one reason the Regulators have their individual mess, and you tend to socialise with them more than anyone else.

The mess in Gib was well supported. We held many functions, including formal dinners. Gone were the days when I served the meal, now I was the one sitting down to eat it. These functions generally ended with everyone pleasantly drunk and, on more than one occasion after the mess dinner, we would move to the local bar at opening time of six am (06.00hrs) and carry on drinking until no more could be drunk.

It wasn't all drinks for the boys, the wives had their functions, and there were many nights we both attended. But things were very grown up. The sole aim of a night out wasn't to get rat-arsed as quickly as possible but to have a good time. If getting rat-arsed was a consequence of this, then so be it.

As my time on the Rock progressed, I was given a job change. I was moved to the administration side of things. It was great to get off watchkeeping and have no more duties.

My job was to manage the joining and drafting of senior ratings, (PO and above), and to book hotel accommodation for visitors who could not be accommodated in HMS Rooke, and for crews of visiting Submarines. Submariners stayed at hotels whenever they were in port. I suppose, after three months below the waves in a cigar tube, they deserved a little bit of comfort.

It was a nice office job, and a good crowd to work with.

Whilst working there, I got my arse into gear and took my PPE for RPO. I found out sometime later I passed, which meant a nice pay rise. Now I had to wait for a promotion... and more courses. Also, something happened that made the RN system look bad in my opinion.

I was asked to go to the Captain's Office, which was the General Admin Office run by the writers.

When I got there, the PO Writer said, "Hi Taff, catch."

He threw a small box at me. I said thanks and left, opening the box as I went. It was the South Atlantic Medal, which I earned on the Hermes in the Falklands.

No ceremony, no well done or congratulations, just a, "Hi Taff, catch."

I don't think any of the staff there were in the Falkland conflict.

I was in admin for six months, until I had the opportunity to go to the Mail Office. This was a nice break. It was just RPO, Dave, and I working in N08s (working clothes) and driving to and from the airport to pick up the mail bags, sort the mail, and then deliver them to Rooke, where it was collected by the families. We also handled ship's mail. We were on the jetty to meet any ship with their mail. This was a good cushy number and a nice way to finish my tour of Gibraltar.

My good friend, Jeff, who was in the habit of turning up wherever I lived, came knocking on the door, asking if I fancied a pint. It was as if he had just popped in from next door, not all the way from Wales. He had come out before, but this time I didn't know he was coming. His marriage had collapsed, and he needed a break. We were more than happy to give him one. We had a great week, and hopefully, it took his mind off things at home.

Towards the end of my tour, there were a couple of Regulators visiting from the Royal Navy Special Investigation Squad (RNSIS). They mentioned, in the bar one night, that they were looking for a dog handler to take over from the guy who was leaving. The deal was, that on completion of the dog handling course, you were sent to Diego Garcia for a year, followed by two years in Portsmouth, working as a member of the RNSIS.

The RNSIS was later to be brought in line with the other two services and called the RNSIB (B=Branch) or SIB. This appealed to me, so I applied, and whilst I was on leave, after leaving Gib, I was offered the job, which I eagerly accepted.

The 'ROCK'
Gibraltar

RNSIB – PART 1

1985 - Aged 27

In February of 1985, I joined the RNSIB based at HMS Nelson, Portsmouth spending three months working alongside the existing dog handler, Brian.

Brian had done the job twice, so he was experienced. A good man for me to follow around before I started my course. He had two dogs at the time, Penny, a German Shepherd, and Storm, a Flat Coated Retriever, a beautiful dog full of character. Both dogs were trained to sniff out Cannabis, Cocaine, and Heroin. I helped with the training and went on operational jobs with him.

His job was to respond when the dogs were needed, at any time. There was also an agreement that he could be called on by the Police, or Customs if their dogs were not available.

It was a great job. One which I couldn't wait to start.

The SIB Office was attached to the RNPHQ, so I was familiar with the setup. Some of the characters from my previous time were still there. We worked in civvies and were often given extra money to go ashore for a pint and keep our eyes and ears open, so we could nip anything untoward in the bud.

RAF NEWTON

1985 - Aged 27

I joined RAF Newton in May.

I was put on a course with three Customs Officers. The RAF has a huge training school in Nottingham, where they train many organisations from home and abroad.

They trained Attack and Patrol Dogs, Arms and Explosive Sniffers, and Drug dogs. Firstly, we were introduced to the dogs, which were trained at the same time we were.

I was given a Weimeraner to start with, but he turned out to be a bit temperamental. He had such a temper he wasn't suitable for a new handler, so I was given Robbie, a black Labrador who was a nice dog but tended to go off on his own sometimes. Before we got to the nitty gritty, we were taught how to look after the dogs, feed, groom, keep their kennels clean, and all things to do with animal welfare.

The other three on the course were Sue, whose daddy was a senior officer with Customs. We took the piss out of her about only getting the job because of who her dad was.

As it happens, we were right, because she was crap at the job and very spoilt. Then there was Andy, the comedian of the litter, and Harry whom we called 'Harry the Bastard' because he was a bastard and was what you envisage a Customs Officer to be. But having said that, we all got on well and had a good time in each other's company.

There was an old airfield a couple of miles from Newton called Syerston. It was full of derelict buildings which were used for training, a big airfield for exercising, the kennels for the dogs' accommodation, and classrooms for us.

We started learning and teaching the dogs the basics at Syerston. Starting with cannabis and giving rewards, and then progressing to the harder-to-find drugs. Once we proved ourselves to be competent, we were taken to places outside the airfield. It could have been anywhere, post offices, rail yards, anywhere which was different, and where we could get permission to use for training.

This gave the dogs experiences in all areas, surroundings, scents, and flooring, all things that can affect the way the dog worked if he wasn't used to it or didn't like something. Then they could just 'switch off', so it was good to get the dogs into as many situations as possible.

We would be out all day, then back late afternoon to walk the dogs and feed them. When at the kennels, we had to keep alert and check all door handles, tools, and car doors before we opened them, because there was always someone who would put some dog shit on it for a laugh.

How childish.

I told Andy I would race him back to Newton for a fiver. He was game for it. We ran to our vans to start, and when he opened his door, it was covered in dog shit. He wasn't getting in the car with shit on his hands. He needed to wash.

I was five quid better off. Live and learn Andy.

After about five weeks, we began going around the country to give the dogs the widest range of situations. We would work all day and B&B at night. The dogs slept in the vans. We would be out for a few pints in the evening, and sometimes working with a hangover the following day. What a life.

We went to Ipswich for the week. I remember Frank, from the Tiger, telling me he lived on a council estate there called Whitton. Well, I passed the estate, so went back in the evening to see if I could find him.

A bit of a long shot.

After work, I went to the paper shop on the estate and asked if they knew of a Frank Flemming. I was surprised when she said did. She gave me his mum's address, and his mum told me where he was.

I knocked on his door and he couldn't believe it when he saw me standing there in uniform. He was married with twins. Sadly, one of the twins was severely disabled. This was a side of Frank I couldn't have imagined. But down the pub that night, and for the rest of the week, he was the same old Frank I remember. We made all the promises to keep in touch but, we never did.

It was the last time I saw him.

In 2013, I decided to look for Frank again. I have often thought of him and the great times we had. I 'Googled' his name and a list of people with the same name came up. I kept clicking on the names hoping he would show up. I had already found him on directory enquiries on the net, but his number was not shown. I went on this one website, a newspaper in Ipswich, which is where he was from, so I became a little excited, he may have been in the paper for some reason or other. There was a photograph of him, just as I remember him. An old photograph. My excitement then turned to a feeling of sickness as I realised this was a memorial for Frank.

He had died in 2008.

I hadn't seen the man for twenty-eight years, but I felt as though a member of the family had passed away. I don't know how he died but I left a message on the memorial page, hopefully, someone will read it and get in touch someday.

Sue had her fair share of hassle from us, but I'll never forget the colour she turned after me and Andy played a good one on her.

We were in Dover, which is where Andy grew up, and I told Sue we were all going to the local theatre to watch Andy's sister, who is a dancer, in a show that night.

She was surprised and very excited. I already primed Andy on what to say because I knew Sue would mention it to him.

And she did. "I can't wait to see your sister in her show tonight," she said.

"What show?" asked Andy.

"The one she is dancing in, of course."

Andy replied, "My sister is in a wheelchair." His face was like concrete, very serious, and looking annoyed.

That's when Sue went that lovely shade of crimson. At the same time, she wished a big hole would open and swallow her. But we couldn't hold it any longer and burst out laughing. Her expression went from shock to confusion, to rage when she realised, we had just wound her up.

Andy doesn't have a sister, by the way.

Another day, when we were bored, we were having a pint at a local pub and started talking about things which scared us. I told a 'true story' about the time my wife and I picked up a hitchhiker one night, on the way to Wales.

The hiker was a bit weird and carried a large holdall (grip). He got in and sat on the back seat with the grip on his lap and was constantly staring into it. I could see him through the rearview mirror.

I introduced us, and asked, "What's in the bag mate?"

He didn't look up but said "Mind your own f*cki%* business."

That was a bit of a shock. My wife and I looked at each other. I told him that was not very sociable, as I only asked what was in the bag.

He said again, "Mind your own f*cki&g business."

I was getting annoyed and worried, no, scared at the same time. I told him I would not have anything illegal or dangerous in the car, so he had best tell me what was in the bag.

For the third time the weirdo, still looking in the bag, said, "Mind your own f*c%i*g business." We were both crapping ourselves, so I brought the car to a screeching halt and told him to get out.

He threw the door open, jumped out and legged it into the darkness, leaving the bag on the back seat. I told them that was the scariest night of my life.

Sue looked shocked and said, "What was in the bag?"

"Mind your own f*cki*g business," I said.

There were groans and laughter.

What was funnier, was Sue said, after a short pause, "No, serious, what was in the bag?"

The course was hard work and long hours but very enjoyable.

We travelled the length and breadth of England. It was the best course I have done. It was peppered with tests, both practical and theory. For the final big exam, their method seemed strange.

They gave us the complete question bank - over three hundred questions. We would be getting a selection of any forty of them. But there was a method in their madness because we learned the answers to every one of the questions. None of us got the 100%, but it was a good way of learning everything.

It was a high pass mark. We all passed.

Back to SIB for a couple of weeks, before flying to Diego Garcia.

DIEGO DARCIA

1985-**1986 - Aged 27-28**

Diego Garcia (DG) is a small British Island in the middle of the Indian Ocean, part of the British Indian Ocean Territories (B.I.O.T.). It is shaped like the outline of a foot. At its widest point, it's only one mile but it is seventeen miles long.

There is an American Air Force base, and many US merchant ships are permanently at anchor in the Island's natural bay. These ships hold everything the US needs should a war start. Everything is there, from washing machines, to tanks.

The airfield was used during conflicts in the Middle East. Besides the US servicemen, there is a labour force of Philippine, and Mauritian nationals, who are accommodated in basic shanty camps. As the Island is British, there is a 'British Representative' (Brit Rep), an RN Commander, and his RM Captain assistant. The Police, Customs, and

Immigration were made up of Regulators, RM Police, and other ranks in the RN and RM.

We were all seconded to the Foreign Office and got our authority from a Royal Ordnance, which is why we were called Royal Ordnance Police Officers (ROPO). I was ROPO 5. ROPO 1 was the boss, a Master at Arms, the other seven were a combination of corporals in the Royal Marine Police, RPOs, and a WRN Reggie.

Diego Garcia holds a very controversial space in British history.

In the sixties, the then Prime Minister, Harold Wilson, leased the island to the USA for fifty years. Controversial, because the island was inhabited. To the shame of us British, the natives were 'relocated' with no compensation, and in complete disregard to their wishes. The final act of arrogance, 'we' tied up any loose ends by destroying the pets of the natives, by gassing them. How can you criticise the rest of the world when you have a history like ours?

Before I left the UK, I was to collect a fresh supply of drugs for the training of the dogs. Which was 100g of Cannabis Resin and 20g each of Heroin, Cocaine, and Amphetamine.

I was to take them to DG via Singapore.

All the authorities were informed and approved the transit of the drugs, especially Singapore, as there was still a death penalty for trafficking drugs. Wouldn't you believe it, when I declared the drugs in Singapore, nobody seemed to know anything about them.

This caused a mild panic with their customs... and a major panic with me.

Eventually, well, after a couple of hours, they found someone who knew about the drugs and with the help of the RN liaison officer in Singapore, the panic was over. I was allowed to continue my journey.

I transferred to the military airport where I was flown to DG on a C5 USAF aircraft.

When I got off the plane at DG the heat hit me like a sledgehammer. I was met by Dave, the handler I was relieving. He took me to my quarters, a big bedroom connected to a lounge which was shared with three of the RM ROPOs.

It was customary to meet everyone, first at work, and then in the 'Brit Club' in the evening. The 'Brit Club' was just that, a club for the British contingent. It was very popular. The Yanks thought it a privilege to be invited.

That night I got to meet everyone, as well as the few other new joiners. Besides me and the MAA, the other Reggies were two RPOs and a Leading WRN Regulator.

The following day, I was shown around the Island. It is a beautiful place, with white sandy beaches. There's an old coconut plantation on the half of the Island which isn't used. Donkeys roam free, and there is an overabundance of chickens and cats, which are culled every so often. Coconut crabs are also plentiful. They are armed with one huge claw, so get given a wide berth. The other creatures given a wide berth were the Red Ants.

I once stood in the wrong place, very close to a nest, and felt pinpricks on my feet and ankles, the ants were crawling over them, and each bite left a little blister. Nasty bleeders.

We also needed to be careful of the coral, it's a coral island so it is everywhere. I slipped in the car park and grazed my calf; the medic used a nail brush to clean it. Ensuring all the coral was removed. I was informed that it will grow inside of you if it is not cleaned out.

Never did that again.

I got issued with my new uniform, which was a beige short-sleeved shirt and shorts. The material could have been more lightweight for my liking, but it was OK. I was lucky I didn't have to wear it all the time and was in a T-shirt and shorts when walking the dogs.

I did that more than I worked them.

Chris, an RAF Sergeant Instructor, came out to do the 'Re-Team' training, which is carried out when there are new dogs with new handlers.

The dogs were gorgeous, a friendly Labrador called Ben who had been there for about four years, and a new dog, a German Short-Haired Pointer called Snuff. A pain in the arse.

The training consists of loads of searches to ensure the dogs are working for me, and of course, I am working for them. The kennels were shared with US Navy dogs and handlers, they were there just for the US forces. The handlers were OK but kept themselves to themselves. They had other duties, which kept them out of the kennels for long periods.

The training lasted two weeks, then we were on our own.

I was carrying out continuation training with the dogs so they wouldn't lose interest in the scent. Every so often I would get an operational job looking for 'stuff' for real, where I would meet and search any visiting aircraft.

One of the first searches I did was at the Air cargo shed close to the runway. Stores had been taken off a plane. I was to search for it in the shed. I decided to use Snuff, mistake. I let him go inside the shed to do a free search. Not on a lead or directed by me. There was a door open in the corner of the shed which I couldn't see, I was following Snuff around when he disappeared through the door.

By the time I went through it, he had gone. I was looking and calling for him but nothing. Then I noticed a black spot moving across the runway.

Oh shit.

I got in my truck, and it took another half hour before I saw him again. The ground controllers were not happy seeing a dog on their runway. Luckily there wasn't an aircraft landing or taking off at the time. I always worked Snuff on a lead from then on.

When I walked them, Ben was always by my side, but Snuff had to go trotting off in the jungle and would come back later with a coconut or a crab. No way was I trotting off into the jungle after him.

If he was getting his exercise and coming back in one piece, I stopped minding. It wasn't so bad on the beaches; if he wasn't in the jungle he was in the sea where I could see him. I was worried when I saw the odd shark prowling around in the shallow water, but they never bothered the dogs thankfully, and they were not the nasty unpredictable sharks you expect them to be.

It was always very hot and humid, especially working in uniform, so it was a great relief to walk on the beach wearing just shorts, and when it rained it was even better. It was quite an easy job; I would work or exercise in the mornings and long walks in the afternoon. Unless they needed to work, there was a lot of grooming, and the kennels needed to be kept clean. That was my routine unless one of the ROPOs went on leave. Then I would stand in for him doing shifts in the Police Office.

There was a lot to do on a small island, there were a few bars, a cinema, ten-pin bowling alleys, a swimming pool, fishing, and sailing. We even got part-time jobs in Cable and Wireless, which provided the telephone network. We just sold the phone cards. It was a bit of extra pocket money.

Booze was cheap. We got our food from the stores if we wanted a BBQ or caught fish. Fishing wasn't my thing but was a huge thing for the enthusiasts and was a dream for them to fish in these tropical waters. A couple of marines were fishing in the bay and took ages pulling a catch in, only to be left with a 30lb Tuna Head. Sharks ate the rest as they were pulling it in, not my idea of fun, especially as they were in an inflatable boat at the time.

US Marines used to visit the Island for training purposes.

It was a bit of entertainment for the Brits because we had only seen these 'Sir, Yes Sir' people on the TV. They were just like the TV too. Absolutely brainwashed.

The highlight of their visit was their platoon ten-mile run, not far for fit Marines I hear you say, but this run was at mid-day, 100+ degrees of heat, and wearing a complete chemical suit and gas mask.

It was an unbelievable sight. Two ambulances followed them to pick up the dropouts. We used to have $5.00 each on who could guess how many were left at the end.

I began jogging myself. I got talked into it by a couple of our Marines. At first, I was holding them back, and they were more or less walking those couple of miles, but then I got used to the heat and began to enjoy it. I saw the weight fall off me, so much so that the Missus didn't recognise me when she picked me up from the airport when I got home. We never jogged in a chemical suite though and didn't keep going until we needed medical assistance.

The odd prank was played now and then. One regular prank was when three of us used to break into Tony's (RPO) room when he was on watch, have a few of his beers, and shots, and leave the place as we found it, but with a lot less beer. He commented a few times on his beer disappearing but never accused anyone. To put him out of his misery we stayed there until he came in one night, and after much shouting, joined us in finishing off his booze. The following watch, he returned to his room to find it empty. I mean no furniture. We had put it all on his flat roof.

One day, we were informed there was a lot of drug use in one of the US Navy rooms. We arranged to do a 'raid' with the dogs and a search party. We carried out the raid at about six am. It seemed they were expecting us, everyone was awake and gave us no problems. I used Ben for the search, he indicated there were drugs in the room but couldn't pinpoint them, which is normally a sign that drugs were there at one time, or maybe smoked in there.

It became obvious they knew we were coming, so anything which may have been there would have been moved. So, just to piss them off, we carried on with the search taking every bit of furniture to pieces and laying it in neat piles outside. Then we left it lying there. It took the smirk off their faces.

The Filipinos weren't lucky enough to have inside information, so when Snuff found a nice little stash of hashish, several of them were prosecuted and sent home. The British Representative is the Magistrate and deals with this kind of offence. Serious crimes are dealt with by Scotland Yard, as in the case of a murdered Filippino just before I arrived. Detectives and a Judge would be flown out to deal with it. In this case, the murderer was sent to the UK to carry out his 'time'.

We had a new ROPO1, who happened to be Irish. He made the mistake of trying to make his mark by making changes and upsetting people. We were pissed off, and two of the RMPs, and ROPOs 4 and 6, had a great idea to piss him off. ROPO1 had a Land Rover and used it to go everywhere.

When he went to lunch, Clive, or Dave (ROPO 4 and 6), would get the spare key out of the boss's locked cabinet. They would then move the Land Rover from the dining hall, about a half mile away, back to the office and act as if nothing had happened.

The Boss came back to the office, saw the vehicle, and scratched his head, but said nothing. This happened about six times over the next few weeks. He still said nothing.

It wasn't until he had been on the Island a few months and 'chilled out', the lads admitted what they had been doing. He thought he was going mad, and he even had a good laugh about it. He turned out not to be such a tosser after all.

However, before he arrived, I would stand in for ROPOs who were taking an extra week's leave on top of the two weeks which was usual at the halfway point of the tour. By the time it was my turn to go on leave, he had stopped the extra week, so I only had two.

So, thinking back, yes, he was a tosser.

I had a week's break in the sick bay after going down with a mystery headache. I never get headaches, but this was the mother of all. At first, they thought I was suffering from a hangover and needed to go back a couple of times before they took me seriously. I was in bed for a week, couldn't have the lights on, and didn't eat a thing. The doctors didn't know what it was. When I asked what they thought it may have been, one said, "You don't want to know."

I didn't push it, and I still don't know what it was.

One of the most worrying moments was carrying out a training session with the dogs.

I was using the Brit Club and asked one of the guys, Tony, to hide a 10g bag of heroin. I gave him something for it to be put in, to protect it from the dog, but he decided to just put the bag in a crack in the wall in one of the rooms, thinking the dog wouldn't come into contact with it.

It wasn't hidden well enough, the panic started when I saw a 'Puff' of the powder leave Snuff's mouth. I was close enough to get it out of his mouth without much loss, but he did get some in his mouth. I dragged him into the sea, which was just yards away, and forced a cup of seawater down him to make him sick.

He showed no signs of being sick or 'high'. I rested him for a few days anyway so I could monitor him, just in case.

This was a pain. I needed to send a report to the UK to explain where a gram of Heroin went and why. Luckily, I had Tony as a witness and to blame, poor Tony. No action was taken against us for the loss of a gram of Heroin. And Snuff was fine.

I also lost a gram or two of cannabis.

I was issued with a large lump of cannabis resin, but one big lump is no good, you need small quantities to make it difficult for the dogs. I was carefully using a small hammer and chisel to break the lump into smaller pieces when the dam thing shattered into a thousand bits. It went all over the office and took me ages to collect as much of it as I could. I had a couple of grams of dust and dirt mixed in with it, but if the weight was right, I was OK.

I haven't been having much luck with these drugs, have I?

My boss called me in and told me I needed to see the British rep. He didn't say what for, so I was a bit worried. I thought it may have been the Heroin or Tony's furniture.

It was neither.

I went into his office, and he shook my hand, promoting me to RPO. Excellent. Pay rise, some perks, and a bigger room, and of course, the obligatory promotion party. I was soon to go home, so it would be nice to start a new job as an RPO.

Diago Garcia was an experience, and it turned out to be one I enjoyed. It was sometimes hard work, always hot, but compensated by a great social life.

I was now to spend the next two years in Portsmouth and the RNSIB, doing the same job, but with a different area of responsibility.

Snuff and Ben stayed in Diego Garcia, as all the dogs do. When they retire, they become the British Representative's pets, so it's quite a nice retirement for them.

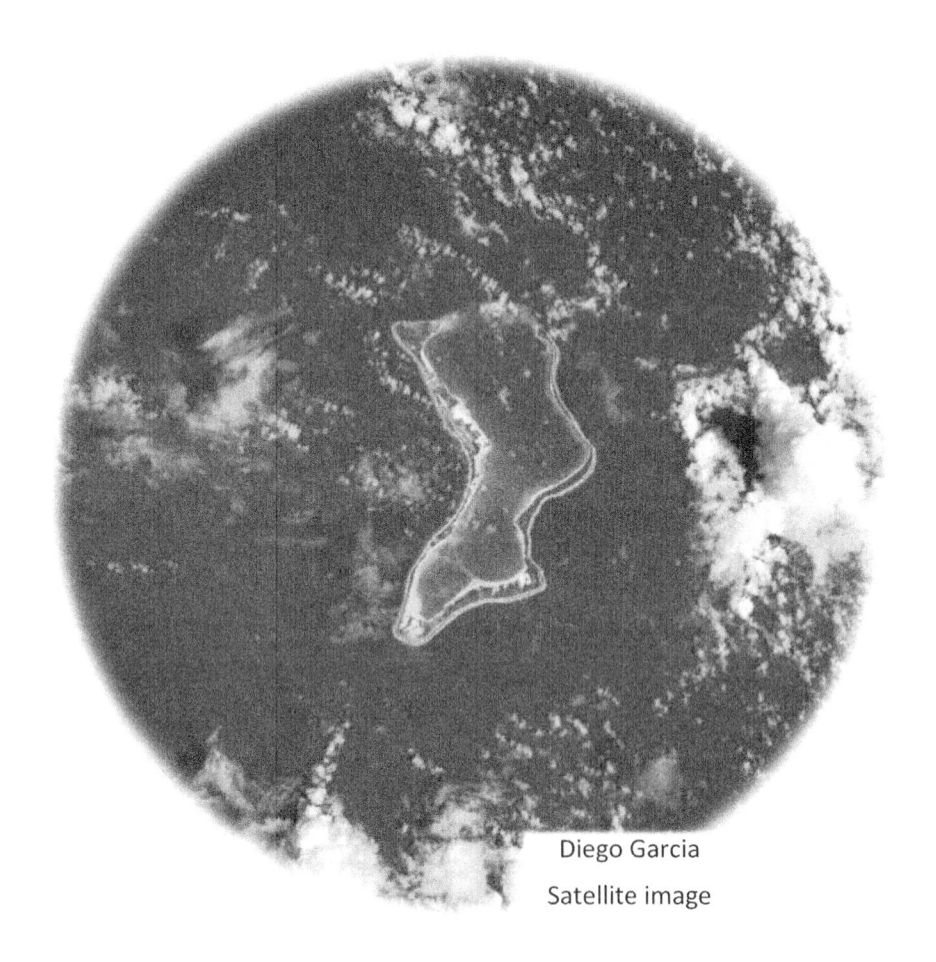

Diego Garcia
Satellite image

RNSIB – PART 2

1987-1989 - Aged 30-32

After about a month's leave, I returned to RAF Newton to take a 'reteam course' with two different dogs. One was Bizmark, or Bizzy, a black Lab Bitch. The other was my old friend Storm. I was so glad he was still there. The course took two weeks, then we became 'operational'. That doesn't mean I just got on with it for two years. It meant that me and the dogs were working well together, and we could get on with any work which came our way.

Every six months I would get an RAF dog inspector visit. They came to see if we were still working well. This would be a Flight Sergeant who put us through various tests and situations, making sure we were fit, well, and working satisfactorily. I would take the dogs back to RAF Newton to be looked after when I took my leave, so I wasn't tied down for the complete two years. I moved into a dedicated

Married Quarter in Hilsea, Portsmouth, where there were two kennels and a shed in the garden.

The food stores in HMS Nelson would supply the dog food, and the dogs would get a six-month check-up at the local vets. If I wasn't busy, between exercising and training the dogs, I would assist in any investigations which were happening.

Every six months I would get around to all the RN establishments in England and Scotland and carry out random searches of offices and accommodation.

I was on call for any investigations where a dog was required and was called out regularly by customs, to search vehicles coming across the channel.

I did one or two jobs for the Police, but they have their dog teams in the area, and I would only work for them if their dogs were committed elsewhere. I was kept busy, and, as always, there was the mess, which I was familiar with, and which I looked forward to supporting, again.

When I went to Scotland, during a six-monthly check, I would take one of the investigators with me in case I was to find something, and secondly to keep me company.

Once, when we got to Helensborough RNPHQ, there was a message waiting for us. I was instructed to search, of all things, a Nuclear Submarine.

I used Storm because he didn't mind where he worked and nothing put him off, but he was massive, and getting him down the hatch was an evolution. It was a hell of a job getting Storm around the sub. It took a good couple of hours, and nothing was found, but it was a good exercise.

We carried out two days of searches at HMS Neptune and the Submarine base, then travelled over to the west coast to HMS Cochrane and the Rosyth Dockyard for another couple of days.

On one occasion, Kev, the investigator and I were having a drink in a bar in Inverkeithing when two lads walked in and stood next to us. They started talking about taking Heroin and Cocaine, we looked at each other as if to say "What the…"

We weren't sure if they were sailors, so when they left and jumped into a car, we followed them in the dog van. They went straight to HMS Cochrane, the local RN shore Establishment. That was our job for the morning then.

We had them in the interview room. They were surprised when we walked in. I think they knew straight away what it was about. They were questioned and we searched their accommodation and got nothing. The talk we overheard was just them showing off to each other, we couldn't prove it was anything else, so we handed them over to the Cochrane Reggies to do with them what they pleased.

On another occasion in Scotland, we were taking the dogs for a walk in a wooded area, they went about doing their thing, coming back now and then to make sure we were still there. Bizzy came back after a third wander when I noticed something hanging down between her front legs, thinking it was a twig or some foliage. I was shocked when I saw a hole in her chest and the skin hanging down.

No blood strangely.

The rest of the day was spent finding a suitable Vet and getting her stitched up. Bizzy had her feet up for the rest of the week, whilst Storm did all the work.

When I got back to Portsmouth my boss, Lt Beardall, insisted I write a statement, you can't make someone write a statement, but Beardall was vindictive and wanted to see if I was negligent in caring for the dogs. Nothing came of it, except the boss proving he was a bigger arsehole than I thought.

Kev and I became good mates, and when we weren't busy, we would go for a pint at lunchtime. It wasn't frowned upon so much then, as we were given a little money to use in local pubs to pick up any 'Intelligence'.

It was the best job I have had.

Things were going well, my first visit from the inspector was a very good one. He was happy with the way we were working. Nev, the Flight Sergeant Inspector, stayed at my place and we fed and watered him for a couple of days.

They preferred this rather than staying in barracks for the durations. Being quite friendly with the inspector has its merits, if he could see a problem, or wanted something done differently, we would discuss it and leave it out of the report. Less writing for him, good report for me.

I undertook a search of Royal Arthur as one of my random visits. It looked the same as when I was drafted there. It brought back some happy memories. There was no one there I knew, except a couple of civvie drivers. At this time, they were running the place down because it was to be closed down.

Very sad. It was a good place to serve.

Have you noticed that since I became a Regulator the things worth writing about are getting less and less? Well, I could write about any old thing, but it won't be the same as the events and situations I wrote about when I was not worrying about a career.

Like I said, things get, or you take things more seriously as you get older. Not saying we didn't laugh, just not as often.

Every year, RAF Newton holds an open day which consists of demonstrations by their display teams, stalls, games, and a procession by the working dog teams from around the country, and from different organisations they supply dogs to.

I had to attend with the dogs. I was asked by the Warrant Officer in charge of the dog school to provide a photograph for their program. I contacted the Navy Photographic section who said they would do some photographs for me. I turned up at their lab/studio with the dogs. The WRN photographer, who was to take the photos, was new. She had never taken photos of dogs before, so she had me in all these poses that were unsuitable for a military open-day program.

I didn't want to seem ungrateful, so I let her carry on. When I received the photos, I was right, they were unsuitable for the program.

I was in civilian clothing, posing in all sorts of positions, but as I needed to send one anyway, I did. It was too late to get more done, and I couldn't seem ungrateful for the photos.

I had all sorts of stick from the staff at RAF Newton, comments like, If I wasn't so short, or fat, or ugly, I would make a great model.

They were just jealous.

The pictures were cool.

One of the more interesting things, which happened during my time with the SIB, was an exercise with the Serious Crime Squad based in London. They came down to Portsmouth to familiarise themselves, as they do with many parts of the country. The RNSIB were assisting them in the exercise.

The scenario was that we had kidnapped someone and were trying to get the ransom without being caught. We were to give our instructions and try to recognise any Police who may be following us.

It covered the whole of Portsmouth, Gosport, Lee on Solent, Havant, and Hayling Island. Keith (RPO) and I were to go to Havant, to give them the runaround. We split up at Havant Station when getting on a train to Portsmouth. Keith got on the front of the train; I got in the rear compartment. Two coppers must have thought Keith was one of the bad guys because they gave him a wide berth so they could keep their eyes on him. But they got in the same carriage as me, and I overheard them talking about Keith giving the game away as to who they were.

At the end of the day-long exercise, there was a de-briefing at Havant Police Station. We thought we had done well. We thought that between us, we must have picked out most of the coppers. But at the de-brief - there were over two hundred Police - they had been using over one hundred and twenty vehicles of all descriptions. We thought we had done well picking out eight of them. We did do well as far as they were concerned, and when I told them I heard the two talking, it was like a major disaster.

The looks I got from those two coppers were frightening.

It was later explained no one should have been picked out, especially by talking about the situation in public. Usually, a group in our position are just lucky to pick a few because they know that they, the Police, are all over the place and it's just guesswork.

Thinking about it later, we agreed most of our sightings were just guesses as we had no real reason to pinpoint any of them, other than we knew they were there somewhere. They were a highly professional team.

Looking back, it was funny because we were loaned a 'Mobile' phone for the exercise. It was long before they were on sale to the public. This one was the size of a briefcase. You had to stand on someone's shoulders to get a signal for a dial tone and even that didn't guarantee you would get to talk to anyone.

See, I was at the cutting edge of technology.

Every three months the Regulating School organised a security seminar for Senior Officers from all three services and VIPs from civilian organisations.

I gave a twenty-minute talk and a demonstration with Storm. It was always Storm because he was such a clumsy lovable dog.

We put a sample of Cannabis under one of the seats before we went in. I would then let Storm search amongst the audience. I used to put the drugs in tins, or pipes, or wrap them so the dogs don't come into direct contact with them.

During these seminars, I took two in with me. An eight-inch plastic tube, and an old telephone handset.

To finish off, when Storm found the drugs, I would tell the audience Storm also did impressions of Prime Ministers. I'd put the phone in his mouth, and it looked like a pipe, I would hold him up on his hind legs facing the audience and tell them it was Harold Wilson.

I would then put the eight-inch pipe in his mouth and hold him up. This would look like a cigar so that one would be Winston Churchill. I then held him up with nothing in his mouth and told them it was Maggie Thatcher. (A dog, get it?)

It always got a laugh... You had to be there.

I went to carry out a training session with the dogs at HMS Mercury, the RN Communications School, which is not far outside of Portsmouth. I used anywhere to do the training if it was OK with the local command.

I had one of the local Reggies put out a couple of training aids (containers containing drugs) and worked the dogs one at a time. Bizzy worked well and found her drug. I rewarded her with a game and then started with Storm. He also worked well finding his drug without a problem. As I was playing with him, he became uninterested in me and the game and began working again, sniffing around the room. I let him get on with it until he pinpointed a locker in the mess. His indication was strong, and it was obvious to me there was something in there.

The owner of the locker was brought into the mess, along with his Divisional Officer as a witness. I did the formalities asking if it was his locker and if everything in his locker was his etc. I then opened the locker door and let Storm put his nose in to confirm. He went straight to the bottom of the locker. The lad began to look very worried at this stage.

I got someone to take Storm outside and got on with the search. At the bottom of the locker were a pile of dirty clothes. At the bottom of the pile was a pair of jeans, and inside a front pocket was about an eighth of an ounce of Cannabis Resin.

By this time the lad was sweating profusely, he was taken away for questioning and I heard later he had denied any knowledge of the drug but was found guilty and sentenced to forty-two days of detention, and demoted.

When a rating commits a serious offence, as I said earlier, he could get a Warrant Punishment, what I didn't mention is the rating gets the choice as to whether he wants the Commanding Officer (Captain) to deal with his trial, or he could choose to be tried by Court Martial.

The Summary trial (CO) is limited on the amount of punishment that can be awarded, but I must say there wasn't always the sense of a fair trial. Then you have the humiliation of the punishment warrant reading, which is witnessed by the ship's company.

A Court Martial is different, whereby it is open to the public, which means the Press. You are allowed to be represented by a real-life lawyer, which isn't always a benefit as some solicitors are not familiar with Naval Law and procedures, and the Navy has its qualified Barristers who are more than capable of carrying out successful prosecutions.

Most importantly, there are no limits to what punishments can be awarded by the Court. If a rating is guilty, he should go with the CO, not try to blag a not guilty verdict. But if he is innocent, then go the whole hog, lawyer the lot. This is an option for ratings because officers and Warrant Officers will automatically be sent to trial by Court Martial.

The Navy's Detention Quarters are in Portsmouth dockyard (RNDQs). Sentences were normally up to forty-two days. It is manned by ex-RN senior ratings. Time is spent on the parade ground, preparing kit for regular kit musters, and many other mundane time-wasting things designed to keep inmates occupied.

On completion of their sentence, the rating would rejoin the fleet with nothing more said, unless he screwed up again. The sentence would impact the man's career by delaying promotion but was usually unnoticeable.

More serious offences, and longer sentences, were served at Colchester Army garrison and Military Prison. Used by all three services. The man would be expected to be kicked out of the service after his sentence. This was a very hard time, compared with RNDQ's, and dreaded by sailors who would be put through the same gruelling routines as their army counterparts, but inevitably were nowhere near as fit, or militarily 'conditioned'.

For extremely serious offences, men could be sentenced to 'real' prison and kicked out of the navy. I knew of a couple of men who were sent to prison, one of whom was a Regulating Petty Office who I knew quite well and who, for some insane reason, married a woman in Australia.

I don't have anything against women from Australia, they are very nice ladies, it's just that Jim, (we'll call him Jim) was married to an English woman at the time and had been for about twenty-six years.

He got sentenced to about six years and lost his pension, gratuities, everything. The most insane thing about it was his wife, who I also knew, stuck by him and insisted he was tricked into the marriage. I'm sorry, but if I was stood in front of a vicar with a woman and he started reading marriage rites to us, I'm not sure but, I think I would suss out what was going on. When the vicar asked, "Do you take this woman to be your lawful wedded wife," it would have been the clincher for me.

These points, and fifty or sixty others, would have set the alarm bells off surely?

Homosexuality was illegal in the armed forces up until the two thousands, and looking back, it was shameful the way homosexuals, and even those who experimented with the opposite sex, were persecuted. If someone was suspected of being homosexual or carrying out a homosexual act, then all the stops would be pulled to get a conviction.

I was never involved in this type of investigation. I am glad I wasn't, because it was degrading, humiliating, and something people should look back and feel ashamed about.

I was often called by customs at Portsmouth, who asked me to search suspect vehicles when their dogs were busy elsewhere. I never found anything, but the dogs indicated on several occasions, which told me drugs were either used or stored there at some time.

The same happened when called by the local police to search a suspected drug dealer's house. The dog indicated behind the toilet in the bathroom. There was some ripped lino, but we didn't find anything. It is suspected that 'stuff' had been previously stored under the floorboards.

I enjoyed working with the Police and Customs, but it was usually in the middle of the night and at a moment's notice, my boss got some nice letters of appreciation, which only did well for me. I was getting to the stage where every little helps. I was hoping to become a Master at Arms soon.

The two years with the SIB were brilliant, but it was time to get back to the mainstream Regulating work if I wanted to progress further in my career. So, when I left the SIB, I was off to the Regulating school to do the six-week Senior Regulators course. This course was a make-or-break.

If I failed, I would be reverted to Leading Regulator. If I passed it would be the last promotional course I would need to do. I would be safe up to Master at Arms.

No pressure then.

RB & RNPA

NE CEDE MALIS

HMS EXCELLENT – PART2

1989 - Aged 32

After being out of mainstream Regulating work for over four years, being back in uniform and on a strict course was a culture shock. I had been working with Naval Discipline but not with the administration I would be expected to know much more than I did, so I had a lot of bookwork to do before the course.

I did well in the Naval Law, framing charges, the mail, and oral exam, and was in line for an overall average of over the seventy-five per cent required for further promotion to Officer, but I couldn't get to grips with the administration, which is a huge part of the course and the longest exam. I did pass, but my average dived.

To be honest, all I wanted was a pass, but if I had ambitions to become an officer, I needed the big average. As I said, it was a pass, so all I needed to do now was my best and hope to get recommended for promotion to Master at Arms.

It was a huge relief to get the course over without incident and in a better atmosphere than the original Regulators course.

Everyone passed.

One was suspected of cheating, and one, Banjo West got his seventy-five per cent (plus) average which he needed to become an Officer, and soon after he did. Banjo become a Commander, and the Provost Martial (RN). The most senior regulator in the navy. He was a good bloke and deserved everything he achieved.

I was quite happy to be sent to HMS Daedalus for my next draft.

HMS DAEDALUS – PART 1

1989- 1990 - Aged 32-33

Daedalus is a Fleet Air Arm airfield and Air Engineering School at Lee on Solent, Gosport.

At first, I was assigned to the Administration Office, but my new boss, Ken Davies was chuffed I came from the SIB, so decided I was the best man for the Discipline Office. Ken was the Warrant Officer Master at Arms (Warrant Officer replaced the Fleet Chief or Fleet Master at Arms) of the very old school.

Not liked by many in the branch, never mind within Daedalus, but his thing was discipline and he normally liked anyone working in the Discipline Office. I got on well with him, and he gave my career a big boost. I ended up standing in for him when he was on resettlement courses (he was leaving the RN shortly.)

I was reporting to the Executive Officer every morning and briefing him on anything he needed to know. I ran the various Defaulters and Request men 'Tables'. It was quite funny when you brief those waiting to appear before the captain, it goes.

"Payattention... Whenyournameiscalledshout'Sir'. Marchinsmartlyandcometoahaltapacefromthetablewhenlgivetheor der'OffCap'takeyourcapoffinthetraditionalmanneroncompletion.Iwil lorderyoutooncaprightturnrightwheelquickmarchreporttomyoffice. Do you understand." (Breath)

He also advised me to make a complaint, or representation as it was called, because whilst I was working with the dogs, I was given an offer I could not refuse, and that was to buy a house at a very big discount.

Before going to Gibraltar, I rented a house from a housing society which only rented to Naval personnel. This made me eligible for the big discount. I couldn't move until I had finished my dog-handling duties because the married quarters went with the job. But I had to buy the house, or I would never get on the housing ladder.

So, for the last nine months of my dog duties, I was paying married quarter rent and a new mortgage. Ken thought my Divisional Officer at the time should have done something to help. I was a bit naïve and didn't think to ask, but it was common knowledge I found it difficult.

It is everyone's right in the RN to make a complaint if they feel they were unfairly treated, and I suppose I was. The regulations say anyone making a complaint should not be penalised, victimised, intimidated, or threatened if they choose to do so.

When my old Divisional Officer, (Beardall), heard I was making a complaint he sent for me. So back I went to HMS Nelson in Portsmouth, to have him give me a right earful because I had suggested he didn't take his Divisional Officer's responsibilities seriously.

It made me carry on with my complaint to the highest level, even though I knew I wouldn't get anywhere. I am glad he was pissed off and needed to explain his actions to the Admiralty Board. That was enough satisfaction for me. If he wasn't such an arrogant vindictive bastard, I would have let it drop.

Most of the discipline work was the mundane naval offences like, late for work, failing to attend a duty, being late back from leave, etc. But two jobs earned me the needed recommendation from Ken Davies to become a master at Arms.

The first one was a Petty Officer Medical Assistant, who was due for retirement and set to collect his lump sum and pension.

Everyone is entitled to claim mileage allowance instead of having a rail warrant, as long as it is your car, and you actually do the trip. This PO was being a bit cocky and brazen about his claims. It saddens me a man's pension would be at risk from my investigation, but this bloke didn't help himself, he claimed for a lot of trips he did not undertake, and he had to admit to many charges of fraud.

He lost everything and was demoted.

The next was more satisfying.

One of the trainees was assaulted when he returned to a darkened mess in the early hours of the morning. His attacker was waiting for him after an earlier argument. He kicked the lad between the legs as he walked into his mess. The attacker wore his boots for maximum effect.

The lad was taken to hospital and lost a testicle.

The attacker had a solicitor present during my interviews, denied most things, and generally made it awkward and protracted for me.

It eventually went to Court Martial. He was kicked out of the RN and spent time in prison. That was a good result. Ken, by this time, had every confidence in me and consistently gave me good reports.

During the quiet times, we used to chat about old jobs and spin a few dits (tell a few stories).

One day we were comparing the best excuses for being late for work. Kev, my office partner, said one bloke explained to the captain he was late because he used to let his budgie out of the cage at night, and on this occasion, the bird had perched on the top of his alarm clock pushing the button down and turning the alarm off, so it didn't go off, and because of that and he was late.

Mine was: This man was late because he sleeps with his widow open, there were workmen outside working on the road and the noise was so bad he didn't hear his alarm go off.

Daedalus was also the home of the Fleet Air Arm Field Gun Crew.

This was an annual competition between Portsmouth, Plymouth, and the FAA.

It is based on the heroic efforts of sailors during the Crimean War when they had to transport the field guns over the rugged countryside to a position where they could fire on the enemy. Volunteers are put through a gruelling selection process, with the final men spending months training for the competition and becoming, probably, the fittest and strongest sportsmen in the country at that time.

The competition sees a full-sized field gun, taken through a course representing a chasm where the gun is dismantled and assembled in a super-fast time. The strength and timing required are unbelievable. It must be seen to be fully appreciated.

Once they have entertained us and the local public at HMS Daedalus, they head off to London, Earls Court, where they would fight it out with Portsmouth and Devonport to decide the Champions. This competition was followed, with great enthusiasm, throughout the Fleet and was great for morale.

Unfortunately, this all stopped with the defence cuts in the Nineties. A sad end to a historical event.

The biggest event of the year was the Daedalus Open Day.

Air displays, and various forms of entertainment. This was an extra duty for us on weekends and long days. Fortunately for me, Emily, my youngest daughter, was due to give birth, she was taken to hospital on Friday, accompanied by my wife, so I was given the weekend off.

Perfect timing.

Ken Davies recommended me for promotion to Acting Local Master at Arms.

This means I would go to sea as a Master at Arms (MAA) if there were a shortage of substantive MAA, but it would mean reverting to RPO on completion of the appointment unless I was on the annual promotional signal.

This was a signal, or telegram, which was issued naming all those who are to be promoted, and in what order, during that year.

I decided to take a gamble and accept any LAMAA job which may come my way, hoping I wouldn't need to revert to RPO after gaining the valuable experience it would give me.

Soon after, I was informed I would be joining a brand-new Type 23 frigate in Glasgow, one which was still being built.

This would mean living in digs for three months, working out of an office in the shipbuilder's dockyard, and getting my areas of responsibility ready for operational duties.

This would be my last promotion.

To progress to Warrant Officer I would need 3 GCSEs. I attended classes for English at Daedalus, but the teacher wasn't one to keep me interested, and rather than embarrass us both by falling asleep in class I gave it a miss. Another reason why you should get your education before you leave school.

So, back to sea.

HMS ARGYLL

1990- 1992-Aged 33-35

Before joining the ship in Glasgow, as a Master at Arms, I first needed to complete several courses related to the jobs I would be doing.

First, I attended the Regulating School at Whale Island, for a Post Promotion Course with four other newly promoted MAAs.

This prepared us for the tasks ahead, including new responsibilities we had not done before, like Whole Ship Coordinator, Flight Deck Officer, Prisoner Handler, Tactical Questioner, and Security Officer, on top of the usual Police and Admin duties.

As the Whole Ship Co-ordinator (WSC), I would be responsible for reviewing the ship's programme with the Departmental Coordinators (Senior CPOs) at a weekly meeting, which I would 'Chair'.

We would ensure there were no conflicts with each department's programmes, like training, maintenance, etc. and if there were, to resolve the issues before I took the ship's programme, with the suggested changes to the Executive meeting, which I and the Heads of Departments attended.

I was also responsible for the Emergency watch and station bill, which gave details of everyone's responsibilities during emergencies. As a newly promoted MAA on a brand-new ship, surrounded by Senior CPOs, the WSC job proved to be the most daunting job I have ever undertaken. But whatever my seniority, I was the 'Senior Rating' onboard as I was the 'Ships Policeman'. If I didn't act like 'The Policeman', I was going to be fine after all.

I needed them more than they needed me.

I then attended the Flight Deck Officer's (FDO) course at Portland Naval Air Station, HMS Osprey. Yes, the same HMS Osprey from my early days.

This was a lot of classroom work, and a lot of practical work on a floating Flight Deck in the harbour, in ALL weathers. We learnt the arm waving signals, emergency responses, weapon handling, night flying, and when it is unsafe for a helicopter to land.

There is a standard chart of wind speed and direction for each helicopter type, and we had to compare the reading from the Anemometer to decide whether to go through with landing, or not.

A tough job. The MAA was responsible for the Flight Deck when at flying stations.

Then it was onto the Security Officer's course at an Army Camp in Ashford, Kent, which took us through documentary and physical security within the ship, which included the record of all one hundred and fifty safes, their combinations, when the combinations must be changed, and their safekeeping.

It was an interesting, easy, laid-back course.

Then it was onto the Prisoner Handler and Tactical Questioning Course. This was also carried out at Ashford, but the final exercise was held at HMS Sultan, in Gosport.

The theory was, that if the ship was attacked, or we were at war and prisoners were captured, then I would be initially in charge of their handling and questioning.

The classroom work consisted of a lot of role-play within the class; record keeping of the information given by the prisoner, and what their mental and physical state was like, which would dictate how any future questioning would be conducted. I must emphasise, that we were not trained to torture anyone, but some things we were told to do might come within some people's definition of torture.

The final exercise held at HMS Sultan was part of a bigger exercise.

The first part involved Aircrew - pilots, navigators, etc, possibly Special Services, being set free in Brecon, or the Black Mountains. They were first hunted down by the army, who then transported them, blindfolded, to the old fort at Sultan where they were kept in one of the old damp rooms within the fort.

They were placed on their knees or leaned against a wall. This is a stressful position and very uncomfortable after a short while. They were kept blindfolded while 'white sound' was played constantly. This could be a loud crackling or buzzing. See what I mean about 'could be torture'. We were in pairs, usually assisting a qualified questioner who does this regularly.

To cut a long story short, the idea was to get any piece of information from the prisoner besides name, rank, and serial number. The theory is, that once they give something mundane, like an address or their wife's name (so we can let them know they are OK), then the floodgates would open. The questioning was based on humiliation, stripping them naked for instance, and threats.

An interesting course, but I wouldn't call it enjoyable.

We were asked if we wanted to be placed on the list for attending future exercises, at first, I agreed, but later retracted it after giving it a bit of thought.

So, that was it, courses done. I was now ready to join the ship, which I did in November 1990. I drove up to Scotstoun in Glasgow, to Yarrows, where I was met by Phil Keen, an experienced MAA. His job was to prepare the many ships being built for the MAAs joining them, and vice-versa.

I learnt a lot from Phil. He became a good friend, along with his partner, July.

It was good to have my ship as an MAA, and it felt good to be in a position which has historically been respected, and sometimes feared, by crews throughout the ages. The old saying again sprang to mind:

The Bosun sits at the right hand of the First Lieutenant

The First Lieutenant sits at the right hand of the captain.

The captain sits at the right hand of God.

The Master at Arms IS GOD.

No one was working on the ship at this time, except to familiarise themselves with the systems, Engineering, Weapons etc. We had offices in a nearby building. The Regulating Staff on a ship this size is an MAA and a Leading Regulator (LREG). The LREG, Chico, was already working with Phil, an MAA who was permanent staff at the shipbuilders. Chico was good, but he left after a few weeks, leaving the RN to become a Policeman in Manchester.

Clem was his replacement, and his job was to do all the admin work, under my supervision and assist me in other areas of responsibility. My boss was the second in command Lieutenant Commander (Lt Cdr) Simon Hail, also known as the First Lieutenant or 'The Jimmy' (don't ask, don't know).

We, along with three Seamen Specialists, a PTI, and a Leading Medical Assistant (Doc), formed the Executive Department. The smallest department onboard. The boss showed me around the ship on the first day. It was a brand-new design with no right angles on the superstructure, which gave the image of a much smaller ship on an enemy's radar screen. It could easily be mistaken for a fishing boat.

The weapons were a 4.5-inch gun on the bow, twenty vertically launched Sea Wolf missiles, which can take out other missiles, ships, or aircraft, and the Harpoon sea-skimming missile like the Exocet, which can pinpoint targets at sea or on land, anti-submarine weapons, and special sonar. As I was the MAA, I was the only NCO with a cabin, everyone else needed to share, but it wasn't as good as it sounds. It had a bunk with cupboards underneath, a sink, and a wardrobe. Which left just enough room for a collapsible chair.

It was tiny, but it was mine.

My job, whilst at the shipbuilders, is to prepare my department for sea and generally do what I would do anywhere else as an MAA.

As we were not fully operational, there was a lot of socialising. When I didn't go home for the weekend I would go out with Phil and his partner July, sometimes have Sunday dinner with them and generally have a laugh.

I remember one Sunday going to the local Workmen's Club, where we had a few drinks with July's family, who I got to know and like very much.

Her brother's first words to me were, "What is your name?"

"Michael Hennessy," I said.

"Great," he replied, asking, "You are a Celtic supporter."

I didn't like football much, but didn't argue with him, it's a religion there, as was the reason for telling me which team I supported, with a name like mine I was clearly a Catholic, and if you are a Catholic you support Celtic, not Rangers. I don't know why they refer to religion so much because I have never heard anyone swear so much as the Glaswegians.

Anyway, after the workman's club closed, I followed the crowd which was Phil, July, and her family. I don't know how it happened, but we ended up in a nightclub at three o'clock on a Sunday afternoon, listening to Karaoke.

This turned out to be the first time I sang Karaoke, not by choice, I was handed the mike and told that all Welshmen can sing, and then Tom Jones's Delilah started, and I proceeded to prove them wrong.

I stayed in digs on the twelfth floor of a high-rise block of council flats, with two CPOs who I hardly ever saw.

The rent included laundry, breakfast, and an evening meal. Which was usually nice but lacking in gravy. It's a Scottish thing I hear.

The culture was to go to the nearest pub, The Dry Dock, after work. It often turned into a 'session', which usually resulted in me missing my evening meal. In turn, this resulted in my landlady being a tad pissed off, so I had to remember to call her and cancel dinner when I could remember. I don't know why because I was paying for it, so it was my decision whether I ate it or not.

The ship spent a lot of time out of the water having work done on the ship's bottom. One lunchtime the Engineering Officer (EO) was looking for one of his CPOs, John.

"He's in the dry dock," said one of the lads when asked.

"In the bloody Dry Dock, he should be bloody working... etc etc. Tell him I want to see him as soon as he gets back."

An hour later John walked into the office and was told the boss was looking for him, and he was not in a good mood. John went to see his boss who laid into him straight away about going to the pub for a lunchtime drink when there was so much work to do. For five minutes he ranted and threatened him with all sorts of promises. John just stood there, taking it and waiting to speak. When John managed to get a word in, he told the boss that he WAS in THE dry dock, working on the ship. He was not in the Dry Dock pub having a drink.

I don't think John could put a foot wrong after that.

Of course, the story went around quicker than a roulette wheel, and the EO got stick off everyone, including the captain.

I returned from home one weekend, I found some good news waiting for me.

The annual promotions signal was issued. I was on it, so there was no reverting to RPO when my time on the Argyll was over. I would be appointed to an MAA job at a shore establishment.

Happy days.

The Captain of the Argyll was a Submariner. He was taking his first command of a surface ship or as submariners like to call them... Targets.

He seemed OK. He told me if I needed to talk to him or discuss anything I had a direct line to him. This was unusual and, I thought, undermining my boss the 'Jimmy'. Going directly to the captain could ruin a good relationship with my boss, so I never went directly to the Skipper for anything.

The ship's company were invited by the Royal British Legion (RBL) in Glasgow, to provide a platoon for the 11th of November Remembrance Day Memorial celebrations.

At about 0930hrs on the Sunday closest to that date, we went to the RBL club to get ready for the memorial. They showed us a room set aside for us, and as the gent leading us opened the door, he said, "Help yourselves, lads, it's for you."

There were crates of beer, lager, Guinness, and a few bottles of whisky. It put us in the mood for marching in the freezing cold. It was a very good day for 'local liaison'.

I was in Glasgow for three months and had a great period stint. By the time the ship was ready, and we had moved onboard, we felt it was time to go.

So now the work starts. It would be around two years hence before the ship completed its trials and was fully operational. In the meantime, we spent a lot of time around the UK, especially the Western Isles of Scotland, short trips out to the Med and Gibraltar, and down to the west coast of Africa. Specifically, Dakar in Senegal, and Ascension Island.

Our home base was Plymouth, and a couple of months after leaving Glasgow, we had the Commissioning ceremony in Plymouth Dockyard. All the crews' families were invited, and the ceremony included a dedication by Lady Lavene (wife of an Admiral) who had launched the ship.

There was a full ceremonial Divisions. That's where the whole Ships Company are fell into platoons and inspected. As the MAA it is customary for me to lead the leading dignitary and the captain around inspecting the platoons. The MAA is the only 'Rating,' or non-commissioned officer, entitled to carry a sword, and I did on this occasion.

It's a tradition which goes back to when ships were made of wood and the men were made of steel, (now it's the other way around) and the MAA was the armed ship's policeman.

The ceremony was followed by a day at sea with helicopters, weapon displays, and other entertainment to keep the families occupied and amused. Being the Flight Deck Officer (FDO), I was involved in the Flight Deck activities, including the launch and recovery of our helicopter. I had a great time. A good day was had by all. Daniel and Deanne, (my kids) had a whale of a time working behind the mess bar, unpaid.

It took me back to HMS Juno all those years ago.

The Argyll was the second Type 23 Frigates to be built and commissioned, the first being HMS Norfolk, and, as they were being built at around the same time, there was always a rivalry between the two ships.

Each ship had small, round stickers printed with the ship's crest. These were the main weapons for us. For instance, if someone got a 'call around' to the other ship, before leaving, a sticker or two would be left at prominent places on their ship, on the captain's door, or the ship's mast. Somewhere where you had to be impressed if you found one.

This was being 'Zapped'.

This was not confined to the ships. I remember being in London, tied up alongside the Second World War ship, HMS Belfast, close to Tower Bridge a week after the Norfolk had been to the same place. The Belfast had been 'Zapped', forward, midships, and aft… all for our benefit.

We found a pub in the city called The Duke of Argyll. That must be worth a couple of pints we thought. We introduced ourselves to the landlord as being off the Argyll.

He said, "Aahh, yes, I've been expecting you."

"Uh?"

"'Yes," he said, "HMS Norfolk were here last week, they left something for you." and with that, he showed us 'The Finger'.

Good one Norfolk.

A new Sub Lieutenant joined the ship. 'Subbies' were usually young officers under training, as this one was. What was unusual about this Subbie was his name was Sub Lieutenant Lord Huw Montgomery.

Yes, he was an actual Lord. A hereditary title handed down from his father.

Monty, as we named him, was a bit dim and a bit stereotypical. He had the piss taken out of him by officers and Senior Rates alike, but he was a good sport and took it in his stride.

Now, Monty wasn't very good at his job. He was happiest at cocktail parties and social functions. Unfortunately for him, the captain did not suffer fools gladly, and as Monty was a fool, the captain did not like him at all.

Monty didn't help when he was the second officer of the watch on the bridge. We were off the Western Isles of Scotland when the captain mentioned the name of an Island we were passing.

Monty corrected him, telling him the correct pronunciation.

Ooo, not good.

The captain mentioned the island once more, and again Monty corrected him.

Not happy with being corrected by Monty, not once but twice, the captain laid into him with a couple of minutes of verbal bashing.

"And how would you know the correct pronunciation anyway, Montgomery?" the captain asked.

"My family owns it," said a smug Monty.

It was downhill from then on for our own little Lord Fauntleroy.

Monty used to pop into my office for a cup of tea and to get out of the way of the Senior Officers. He used to come ashore with us when he could. He was tickled by the fact the 'Lord and Master' (me and him) went ashore together.

What sealed his fate was, one evening in Portland, we held an afternoon social function attended by Officers and Senior Rates. We all had a few too many. The plan was to have a nap and go ashore in the evening. Monty asked me to get him up if he sleeps too late. I was up and ready to go, so I thought I'd see if he was awake.

I knocked on his cabin door, no answer, opened the door, in complete darkness, as I stepped over the threshold to go in and turn the light on, when I smelt this stench. It was as if someone had had a dump in the cabin. I realised that is exactly what had happened... when I put my foot in it.

Yep, Monty had curled one down on the carpet.

I was out of there like a shot. Unfortunately, Monty was called for by the Duty CPO, who saw everything and told the 'Jimmy'. He put everything in the Daily Occurrence Logbook, so it was all in writing. That was it for Monty.

I heard sometime later he had resigned from his commission and was working in London somewhere.

As there is such a small ship's company on this class of frigate, the CPOs were expected to attend cocktail parties, which would only be privy to officers on another class of ship. It was nice to get to know local celebrities and invite them to our mess for a few drinks after the cocktail party, which would usually lead to them reciprocating. So, the cocktail party became a social event which was well looked forward to.

Between social events, we were working hard in preparation for the Final Trials at Portland. For four weeks we were tested, daily, by senior officers and Warrant officers, whose job it was to catch us out, to ensure we all knew what we were doing.

Everyone hated these trials, and the Flag officer in charge of Flag Officer Sea Training or FOST, as he is unaffectionately known, took no prisoners.

From the Captain down, everyone was scrutinised.

The training, system trials and maintenance kept us all busy and stressed out. I spent a lot of hours on the Flight Deck, landing and launching helicopters under supervision, until I gained the hours required, and passed a competence test. There were only two FDOs at this time, the other was a CPO Electrical Engineer who was under training, so I had to supervise him until he qualified.

When not on the Flight Deck, I carried out my other duties. As the Whole ship Coordinator (WSC) I was kept busy. As it was a new class of ship with less crew, it meant most people had at least two jobs, and we needed to ensure everyone knew their respective responsibilities.

With such a small crew the huge and important job of cleaning was difficult. This was recognised by the powers that be, so in the case of the type 23 Frigates a new system of contract cleaning was introduced. This meant, that wherever we were in the world, we could arrange for a team of civilians to come on board and deep clean the areas of the ship which needed cleaning.

As this was a new system, it took many months to get the cleaners to do the job properly, but the worst thing was educating the Captain and Senior Officer, who still expected the crew to do the same amount of cleaning as they would on other ships.

We would have the contractors in, have the captain's rounds and the crew would be expected to clean again for the rounds. This is what happens on a new design ship. You need to forget how it was done on your old ship and start from scratch.

We worked hard but also played hard.

Some of the lads took it upon themselves to rabbit some souvenirs from a pub on a secluded Island in West Scotland, where they had been having a drink. They weren't the sharpest tools in the box, because it could only have been someone from Argyll who could have taken the items. So, we had a complaint from the pub. Some of us were not happy so, after an unsuccessful search of the messes, I gathered the Leading Hands of the Messes (LHOMs) together.

I told them they had been given an amnesty. If the items stolen from the pub were not left outside my office by midday they would have major problems. They knew what I meant.

All Regulators have been in their position and understand that, although it is illegal to have more than the regulation three cans of beer per day, we know everyone does, and that they save their ration to hold a 'bit of a party' now and then.

Been there, done that, got the T-shirt.

The threat of me spoiling their party and confiscating their stash of beer did the trick. This is where the 'Poacher turned Gamekeeper' system works.

By midday, I had a nice little collection of artefacts and ornaments from the pub. There were also ten to fifteen items which the landlord did not list or even knew were missing.

I nominated a Senior Rating and two LHOMs to return the goods and apologise for their colleague's behaviour.

They returned to the pub in a hire car as we were miles away from the port by this time. They humbly apologised and returned the items, restoring a little respect for the RN in that little community.

Another incident worth mentioning was 'The Captain's Mug incident of Ascension Island'. (Sounds like a book title!)

We were anchored off Ascension Island for a social visit. The captain invited a couple of RAF officers on board for lunch.

As they boarded their barge to return ashore, the captain noticed his mug was missing from the bridge, and of course, he instantly called me, the ship's policeman, to solve the heinous crime.

The mug, he said, was a gift from his son and had 'Cap'n' written on it.

Whilst I was inquiring about the mug's whereabouts, the captain was recalling the RAF Officers, accusing them of nicking it.

Whilst we were both making our enquiries, the PO Steward approached me and said he had the mug. They, the stewards, intended to hold the mug to ransom for charity, but the captain went ballistic very quickly, so their plans were scuppered before they could get the ransom note in the post.

To save the POs blushes, I told the Captain I had spread the word for the mug to be left in my cabin. Nothing else would be said as it has been recovered. It was like 'Pubgate', in Scotland.

The Skipper was happy with that outcome.

Soon after the captain was reunited with his mug the following was posted on the main noticeboard.

"What do a double-glazing salesman and the MAA have in common? They both spend all day looking for mugs."

The hard work continued. This was like no other period in my career, there was no one to carry the can if anything went wrong, no one to look to for advice. I was the one giving it. Any fun came a distant second to work, especially during training and trials. I had far too many people looking over my shoulder making sure my work was up to scratch.

Our foreign visits were limited but we had some morale boosters, mainly because HMS Argyll was sponsored by Safeway the supermarket chain.

"So what?" I hear you say, who needs groceries for morale boosting?

Well, supermarkets also have booze. In the UK and Gibraltar, where there are British supermarkets, they would sponsor football and rugby matches with local teams and provide after-match refreshments.

As you can imagine, the matches were very well-supported. The 'Hard Rock Café' in London is also part of their group of companies, and The Argyll ships company were invited to visit at any time, go to the front of the queue and enjoy a free meal.

Many of us did.

The ship went to Bremen (Germany) for a weekend visit. This was a great weekend.

Some of us took a boat trip around the harbour, which was absolutely SHIT, but every so often a bottle of freezing cold Schnapps was passed around, and as Bremen is home to Beck's beer, a few bottles of that went around too.

As usual, the bad events were not always the bad social events.

From contacts made at the cocktail party in Bremen, we were invited to the British Army Barracks, which was about two hours away by road, to attend their annual Regimental party.

The Army were great, they provided transport for the ten volunteers from the mess, of which I was one. It was a formal event, so we were dressed in Number1s, or Mess Dress (Monkey Suit).

I had my Mess Dress onboard, never expecting to use it and at the cost of using up valuable space in my tiny cabin. It's always good to get dressed up now and then, this made my sacrifice worthwhile.

Anyway, the party was held in a huge hangar, there was great entertainment from the Regimental Band, who also did a turn as a pop group, and there were imported singers and comedians.

The food was excellent, and the beer flowed. THEN, one of the funniest things I had seen for a long time. Tim, who was our Mess

President, was approached by the Regimental Sergeant Major (RSM), who was holding a huge brightly decorated goblet. He began telling Tim that the goblet had been in the Regiment for a hundred years, and it contained the Regimental cocktail, and what you must do is...

Tim was way ahead of him, and he held his hand up to stop the RSM, "I know exactly what I have to do," Tim said.

He took the goblet, downing the entire contents in one go, and handed it back to the RSM empty, wiping his mouth with the back of his hand and burping.

"Well done, Tim," said the RSM. "But what you have to do is take a sip and pass the goblet onto the next person."

A visit to Lisbon in Portugal gave us another laugh.

Four of us had a few beers before leaving the ship, so we were in a happy mood when we went ashore. Later, in a bar, we stood together behind two women, one of whom was fancied by our mess ladies' man, Des.

Suddenly and without warning, Des thought he was Tom Cruise from that bar room scene in Top Gun. He started singing 'You've Lost That Loving Feeling' to the two women.

Without being prompted, and in unison, all of us became his backing singers. Pathetic, crap, but funny. We got a round of applause; the two women left the bar suitably embarrassed.

Des was gutted.

One Saturday at sea, we had a mess dinner.

It was a traditional dinner to celebrate the Battle of Trafalgar, but it was also a celebration of our Chief Stoker, Phil Morrisons's, forty-year career, which was coming to an end when we arrived back in Plymouth.

Two or three of the mess member's names were drawn out of a hat, so they could say a few words. One (of (the lucky ones) was me.

I can't remember much of the speech, but it started with. "When Phil left school, he went to the careers office and said, "I want to join the navy."

The careers officer replied, "That's a good idea, let's start one."

It was five minutes of taking the piss out of the poor man, which carried on with the other speakers. It was a great night and one which Phil always remembered.

Even though there was much stress because of the extra work due to the small crew, and the continuous trials and training, we always managed to chill out and laugh when we could. There was always some entertainment, or sporting event, in the ports of call for the crew.

After several cancellations, the date was set for our visit to Portland, FOST, and the dreaded final sea trials. They were delayed for such a long time I was to leave the ship before the big one began.

I had mixed emotions about this.

I had spent the best part of two years preparing my part of the ship for this big event, and half of me wanted the credit for it. The other half was relieved that I wasn't to be on board for all the hassle, early mornings, late nights, long exercises and inspections.

After careful consideration I thought, sod the credit, I'm off.

Before leaving, I spoke to an old friend, Scouse, at HMS Centurion. (Centurion is the pay and appointments for the RN and RM). I was with Scouse at Daedalus before joining the Argyll, to whom I mentioned I would love to go back to Daedalus, however many beers it would cost me. Scouse was obliging. He arranged for me to become the Security Master at Arms (SECMAA) at Daedalus.

I couldn't have asked for a better place to work.

HMS ARGYLL

HMS DAEDALUS – PART 2

1992-1996 – Aged 35-39

I was now to become the Security Master at Arms (SecMAA,) which was a new job for the Regulating Branch.

During my time at sea, we lost the administration duties, and gave up the responsibility of physical security duties on shore establishments; so, it was another course at HMS Excellent.

I was also to become a Divisional Officer (DO), another extra duty needed another course at the same place.

As a DO, I would have up to thirty Junior Ratings in my Division and be responsible for their career, welfare, and writing their appraisals, which is a serious and important job as this would affect their career, promotion and pay.

In short, if they needed anything they came to me and would decide how it would be dealt with.

At Daedalus, I was responsible for the armed guards who were placed on the external gates, which may be open, and who carried out rounds around the three-mile perimeter fence. They had certain tests and training to undertake regularly. This was to ensure they were competent to carry and fire weapons.

I also had unarmed men at the gates. They included the contracted civilian security and the Ministry of Defence Guard Service (MGS), a new organisation designed to take some of the weight off the RN and the MOD Police. Each element had its areas of responsibilities, and if they carried them out effectively everyone was happy.

My boss, the Security Officer, who had very little to do with security but was our figurehead, was an Officer called Lieutenant (Lt) David Andrews.

He was a legend for all the wrong reasons.

He joined the RN as an Able Seaman, working his way through the ranks to Lt. Sounds good, but he should have been promoted to, at least a Lieutenant Commander, long ago. He was primarily a Gunnery Officer, the type who would be screaming at people on the Parade Ground.

He had been in the Navy forever, that is what Gunnery Officers did that long ago. Nowadays they are more of a technical officer responsible for the weapons on ships and the complicated protocols of warfare.

This new technology was too much for the old fossil, so he was appointed 'safe' jobs ashore. He ate, slept, and breathed the RN. He was divorced and had one son, who he spoke about now and then. He once told me he was having problems talking and relating to his son, he said to me "I don't know what the problem is Master, I treat him like any other Junior Rating."

He sincerely couldn't see anything wrong with that statement, sad really, or maybe sad because I didn't see it as a joke.

I'm unsure.

You could hate or feel sorry for Lt Andrews, but you couldn't love him, he didn't want to be loved, he wanted to be respected but he always did something to make that impossible.

Sometime earlier, when he was the Security Officer at HMS Drake in Plymouth, it was announced that WRNS were to be allowed to serve on ships at sea. This caused an uproar amongst naval wives, and a group of them protested outside the gates of HMS Drake, the main barracks in Plymouth.

A group of about fifty, some pushing their prams, some holding placards, were congregating on the pavement on the main road outside the barracks.

Lt Andrews decided the protest needed serious countermeasures, so in his infinite wisdom, he positioned two armed guards at the top of the church tower overlooking the gate.

What was happening at the gate was not what was going on inside his head. The captain of the barracks was not happy when he found out, and it is suspected this is the reason he was now in Portsmouth, not Plymouth.

He was nicknamed 'Shovel Face' because he had no cartilage in his nose, so no bridge, and it looked like he had been smacked in the face with a shovel. This meant he always had problems with his nose, and one day I was running the Captain's Request men and defaulters, that's the people who get promoted or patted on the back, and those on a charge.

This was usually done by Roy, the Warrant Officer MAA who oversaw all the Regulating duties, but he was away so it was down to me.

Anyway, Lt Andrews was there as a DO. He wrote something on paper, to read out when his man was in front of the captain. I saw Andrews with his handkerchief earlier, so he must have had the sniffles or a cold. As he started reading from his paper with his head bent, everyone present was looking at him. Then his nose started running, it slowly left his nose and crept toward his piece of paper, he was oblivious until he saw it land on the paper he was reading, everyone looked away, acting as if they had never seen it.

That was the feeling sorry for him part.

Most establishments held open days, or events for the public to attend.

Our job was to control the public when inside the establishment and make sure they all left when required. The big annual event was the public open day, with lots of things going on, field gun runs, stalls, etc. It was a huge occasion.

Well, I thought it was until the D-Day celebrations in 1994. The whole of Portsmouth had something going on during the week of 6th June.

Daedalus held many events, culminating in a large concert in one of the big hangers, starring Anne Sheldon, a forces sweetheart and singer from the war years, along with bands from the Royal Marines. There were a couple of thousand attending, most using their cars. Arriving wasn't the problem but leaving was, and we needed to open and man gates.

They hadn't been in use for years.

All of Daedalus's security staff were involved, with the local police directing traffic in and out of the establishment. Everything went smoothly on the day. I don't mention this for any other reason than to give an example of what the security job was all about. This was the biggest event, but smaller ones were happening almost constantly.

It wasn't just me either, I had three Leading Regulators who did the hands-on supervising and planning in the first instance, and once it was scrutinised, we put the plan into operation.

I would send the signals informing national security organisations and asking them for approval. I responded accordingly to any conditions or requirements they may demand.

I would attend meetings with local and MOD police, keep them updated on any changes or requirements, and ask for assistance when needed. The Security Officer would poke his nose in now and then, and sometimes he caused us problems, but he was usually ignored.

On top of the Security, I had my Divisional Officer responsibilities, which consisted of a lot of appraisal writing, because security billets were filled by ratings of any branch on a short-term basis, the turnover was huge and regular.

That was my job.

There was a very good Warrant Officers and CPOs mess at Daedalus. It held regular functions and formal dinners. Many would pop in for a lunchtime pint, most on a Friday for the meat draw.

There was a Portsmouth area RN Establishment Senior Rates Darts League. I was a keen darts player, so that was a highlight of the week for me.

One lunchtime, one of the shortest CPOs had seriously fallen out with one of the biggest, and by biggest, I mean he was the Field Gun trainer. He was 6'2" of muscle. The short one, Tom, was at the bar when the big one, Joe, came through the swing door at the other end of the room. When Joe walked towards the bar Tom started walking towards him.

"Oh my god, phone an ambulance." someone said, as they met in the middle of the room. Tom laid Joe out with the quickest widest swinging punch you have ever seen. Talk about David and Goliath, he was a hero after that, Joe was a bully anyway, so it was a good example of poetic justice.

Daedalus was a good place to be for my final years in the RN. I was due to retire on my fortieth birthday, which was in February 1997.

I should have been drafted to sea, on one last ship, but it was decided I may not get time for any resettlement course I needed before starting my career as a civilian. Resettlement courses are exactly what they say. We are given money to attend courses, which would help us settle into 'Civvie Street'

The grounds of Daedalus were being inspected by contractors, including a gent who looked after the plant life, flowers etc. It was a pleasant surprise when I was introduced to him. It was Pete Shackloth, my old MAA from Sultan. We chatted about old times and people we knew; Pete was a big golfer. He invited me and a partner to play a two-ball game with his pal at his golf club in Southampton. Chris, the Chief Gunnery Instructor and friend was volunteered. We had a great day, won the golf, and had our lunch paid for by Pete and his mate.

I became a bit of a sporting freak. Every lunchtime I would play five-a-side football in one of the hangers, which was fitted out as a gym. The sessions lasted an hour. Sometimes I would play two sessions if a team was short. This was the fittest I had been since HMS Royal

Arthur and the Tiger in the 70s. But it was brought to an abrupt end in 1995 when I was playing against the Gunnery Staff.

I was pushed from behind and went down like a bag of spanners. I knew there was something wrong immediately.

A bit of a giveaway was I couldn't feel, nor move anything, from the neck down.

This was the scariest moment of my life; I had a vision of myself in a wheelchair moving it by blowing into something in my mouth. No idea what it was but had seen it on the telly. It may have only been a minute or two but seemed like ages before I began to get any feeling back.

I could feel Chris, the Chief GI, pinching my legs continually, seeing if I had any feeling. When I could feel it hurt so I told him to piss off and started kicking him away. Besides that, I had the worst pain you could imagine in both index fingers.

How weird is that?

Anyway, the establishment ambulance came, they strapped me on a stretcher and took me to the sick bay where they promptly unstrapped me and sat me down where I waited for a doctor who never came.

When they decided I was in pain, they sent me over to another part of the establishment to see another Doctor, one who was not part of the sick bay staff.

When I told him what happened and he saw I was in pain, which became even worse when he touched my finger with a cotton wool bud, he called the medical staff again and told them to put a collar on me and take me to Royal Navy Hospital Haslar, which was about three miles away.

It gets better…

When they showed me to the A&E waiting room and sat me down, they took the collar off, because they didn't want to lose it, and left me there. Good practice, eh?

When the A&E doctors realised the situation, they strapped me up again, arranged a CAT scan, and then told me I had broken my neck. I was getting this excruciating pain throughout this process until they gave me a shot of morphine, which was brilliant stuff.

Not sure if it got rid of the pain or I just didn't give a shit about it. Either way, it was good stuff. After a month or so, I was back at work but without the lunchtime sporting activities.

Unfortunately, it was decided HMS Daedalus was too close. This was to happen in the summer of 1996.

It was a sad period leading up to that day as we got rid of all equipment and stores, until by the time the final day had arrived. Daedalus was then more or less empty.

We had a small 'marching out' for the last time parade, which was one of the saddest times of my career.

HMS DAEDALUS

HMS SULTAN – PART 2

Aged 39

At this time, I had about seven months of my career left.

I was told I was going to HMS Sultan in Gosport, which was the Marine Engineering School and where the schools from Daedalus were moved.

I was supernumerary at Sultan, meaning I didn't have a real job. For six weeks, I assisted a Commander in organising an event. One during which civilian contractors would rent an area of our main hall and sell their products to the RN.

As I was doing this, I got a call from HMS Centurion (pay and drafting) telling me that, unfortunately, I would be drafted to HMS Nelson's Discipline Office for my last five months.

This was probably the worst job you can have in Portsmouth.

Nelson is the main barracks, support for visiting ships and ships in refit. Nelson gets all the dregs from the naval society, men landed for disciplinary action, and men who have been released from, or sentenced to detention.

On top of this, I received a letter from my new boss, Commander Wills, who said, sorry, but he needed me to hit the ground running as it was a busy establishment, so, he would not release me for any resettlement courses.

Twenty-four years in the RN, and this is how I was treated when it was time for the RN to compensate me through resettlement.

I was disgusted.

I showed the letter to everyone, they were all on my side, senior officers and all, but there was nothing I could do. I could complain, but it would drag on far too long.

I was not happy.

Anyway, I had a few months of doing very little, which gave me time to organise the Carpet Cleaning business I was planning to start when I left the RN.

HMS NELSON – PART 2

Aged 39-40

I met my new boss, he knew how I felt, and I didn't try to hide it.

The good thing was, the Regulating Petty Officer, Scouse, who worked for me, was dead keen, so there was someone who gave a shit in my office.

To compensate me for being unable to take any courses, the boss took a short step back and arranged for me to sign on for an extra month. This meant I didn't have to work, but I would get one month's extra pay. It was better than nothing, but it didn't alter the fact the man was happy to deny me any resettlement help.

The last year of my career was a 'run-down period' (RDP).

As your time gets shorter the more enthusiasm you lose. Let's be fair, you have the rest of your life to organise, and it is a daunting prospect to leave the security of an organisation like the Royal Navy and go it alone.

I could have volunteered for a further ten years but felt it would be easier to find work when I was forty than when I am fifty.

Anyway, things change over the years and the real good times never return, as you can tell from reading this.

You eventually grow up. Things get more serious, and the laughs and fun times are fewer and far between.

So, it was now time for me to leave.

HOME

Aged 40 +

I don't regret one thing about the Navy.

Not even joining up as a steward. I hated the job, but the friends I made and the laughs we had were never bettered.

If I were honest, I never expected to go to war when I joined, but the Falklands conflict was something to be proud of.

The biggest letdown was the treatment I received in my last few months.

It was a bit unreal when I walked through HMS Nelson's main gate for the last time, with just a, "See ya," to a few people I knew but didn't consider friends.

If I were to summarise the twenty-four years, it would be:

The worst thing:

Spending the first five years doing a job I hated and found degrading. I thought it was a complete waste of manpower.

The best thing:

Ironically, having such a great first five years. Seeing and doing some wonderful but stupid things with some of the best friends I could wish for.

Proudest moments:

Sailing to the Falklands from Portsmouth onboard HMS Hermes, only surpassed on completion of the conflict when we returned to Portsmouth.

Disappointing moment:

After twenty-four years of loyal and unblemished service to the Queen and country, being told by a senior officer that it doesn't matter.

"We are busy, and I cannot let you have your resettlement entitlement," weeks before I was to become unemployed and needed to prepare for my future.

Shame on you Commander Wills RN

Regrets:

None.

Would I do it all again:

ABSOLUTELY

What next?

After having my carpets cleaned a year before leaving, I decided that I could do that.

And I did, for a year, but the money was either great or not so good, so I became a Prison Officer in a brand-new privatised prison in Bridgend.

So, it was back to Wales after all that time in the mob.

But.

Privatised prisons are crap, with most people feathering their nests and kissing arse for promotion. There was a huge turnover of staff. Securicor didn't mind because they were not "Investors in People."

I found a job, closer to home, and for a lot more money, looking after cheese rather than prisoners. It was as a reception and security officer, which turned out to be the worst job I have ever had.

My boss was an ex-Army RMP Sergeant Major. He recruited ex-Army staff and treated the office like his own little Guardroom.

We didn't get on.

I was saved by the factory closing and being made redundant.

In Wales at the time there was a 'redundancy fund' for retraining people like me, so I took advantage of that, completing the maritime courses I would need to return to sea. This time on cruise ships.

After working for an agency, I was taken on permanently by Princess Cruise Line.

First, as the officer responsible for security.

For a change of scenery, I applied for, and got a job, as the Environmental and Occupational Safety Officer, which was a little pay rise, and promotion to a position of a 'Senior Officer'.

There I stayed until the broken neck (Daedalus) got progressively worse and I retired early.

Now I am the full-time family taxi service.

Which I love.

TAFF'S TALES – THE TRUE STORY

HMS Raleigh—Aged 15

HMS Pembroke
Class Photo

Fun in Bermuda

HMS Argyll

Me & Chas Cooper

London Wedding

HMS Tiger

Me posing in the mess

Run ashore
Far East

Another run Somewhere

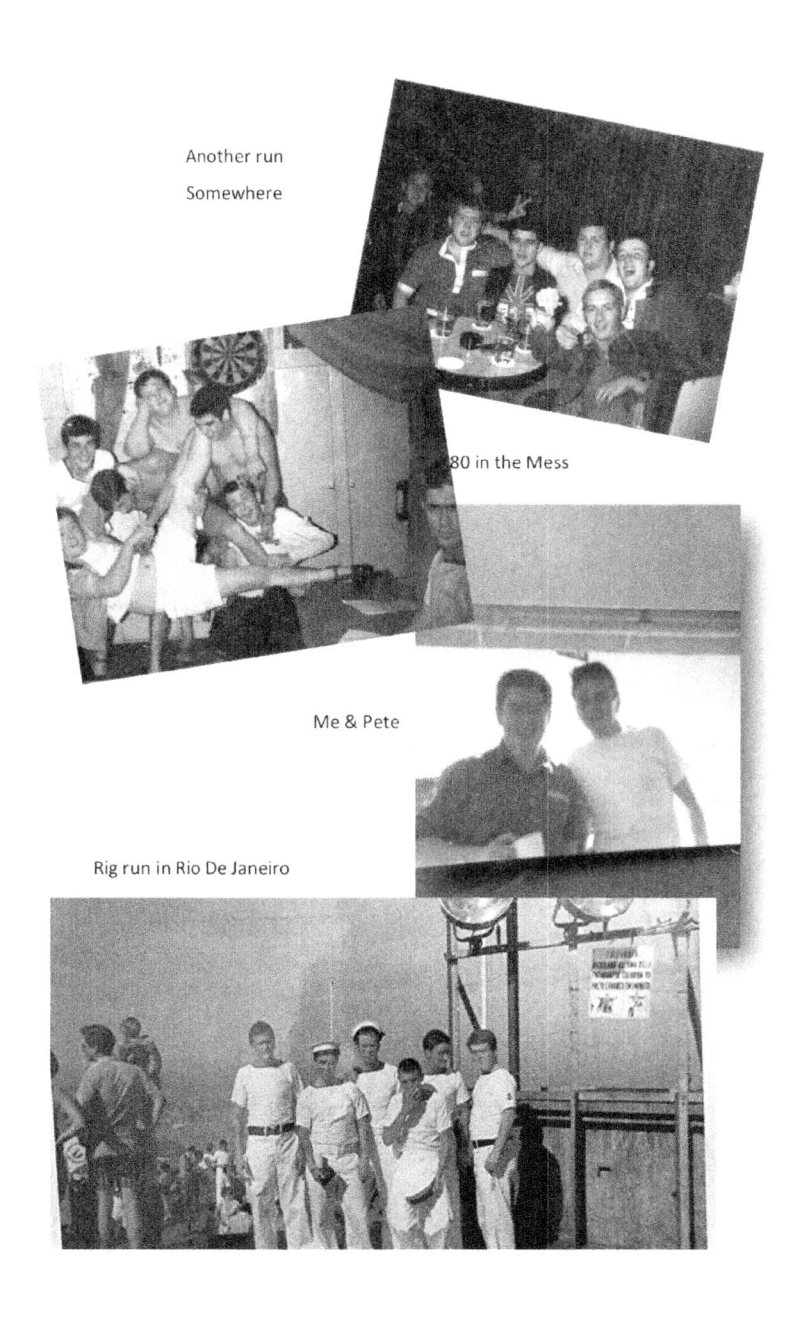

80 in the Mess

Me & Pete

Rig run in Rio De Janeiro

HMS Hermes return

Hermes staff & guests

Atlantic Conveyer

Me & Bill sorting mail

Chefs wall diary

TAFF'S TALES – THE TRUE STORY

Splice the mainbrace

Home at last

Dog handling course
with customs officers

Me, Ben & Snuff

Me in new uniform

Hard at work

HMS Argyll commissioning ceremony

My final Royal Navy photograph

Life after the Royal Navy

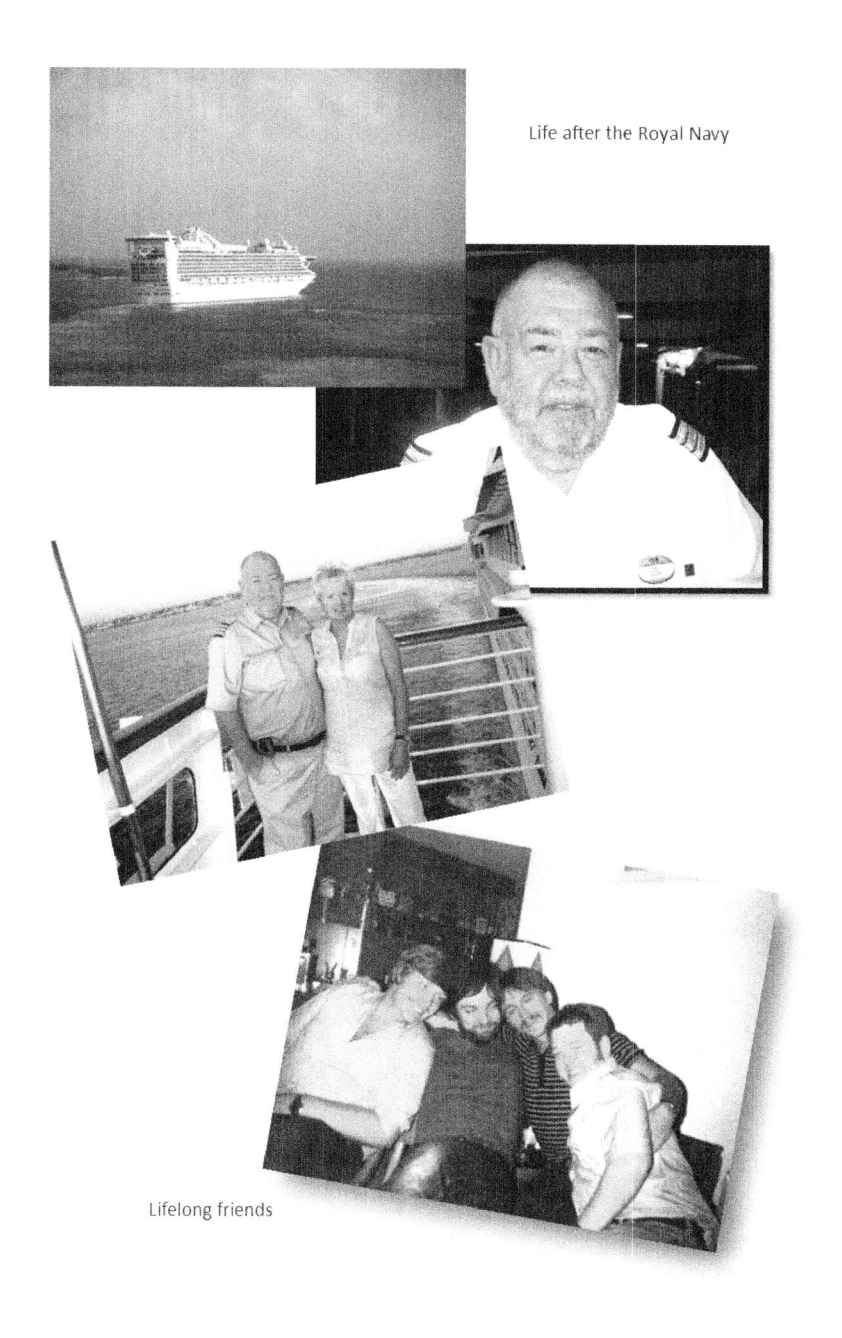

Lifelong friends

Printed in Great Britain
by Amazon